INVESTMENT ANALYSIS WITH YOUR MICROCOMPUTER

BY LESLIE E. SPARKS

TAB BOOKS Inc.
BLUE RIDGE SUMMIT, PA. 17214

FIRST EDITION

SECOND PRINTING

Library of Congress Cataloging in Publication Data

Sparks, L.E.
Investment analysis with your microcomputer.

Includes index.
1. Investments—Data processing. 2. Investment analysis—Data processing. 3. Microcomputers. I. Title.
HG4515.5.S65 1983 332.6'028'5404' 82-5995
ISBN 0-8306-2479-1 AACR2
ISBN 0-8306-1479-6 (pbk.)

Cover photo courtesy of the New York Stock Exchange Staff Photographer, Edward Topple.

Contents

Introduction

This book is about investment analysis and investment decision making with the help of a microcomputer. The key word is "help." The microcomputer can be a great tool and can help you make better decisions, but, as I will repeatedly point out, the computer is only a tool that can help. You must make the decisions; the computer cannot.

The purpose of this book is to translate the results of investment analysis and financial decision-making theory into practical computer programs that will run on a personal computer. The programs in the book are written in Microsoft BASIC. With only minimal changes—mainly dealing with crt formatting and printer control commands—the programs should run on almost all personal computers that use Microsoft BASIC. Some additional changes may be necessary to adapt the programs to other versions of BASIC.

The programs have been tested on the TRS-80 Model I and Model III. Changes necessary to allow the programs to run on other versions of BASIC are discussed in the Appendix.

The book begins with a discussion of the important concepts of investment analysis and then presents a discussion of three larger computer programs that make use of these concepts. The main purpose of the discussion is to provide a framework for using the computer programs. It is not intended to be a complete discussion of the concepts of investment analysis. There are many good books on these topics; you should refer to one of them for more details.

Several short computer programs, mentioned in the general discussion, can be used alone or as modules for larger programs. The major programs discussed in Chapters 10, 11, and 12 use some of the earlier programs as modules.

For most cases the input module and the output modules are the main modules that must be changed if the programs are to be used on a computer other than the Model I or Model III—especially if Microsoft BASIC is not used by the other computer. The input and output modules for each of the programs should run in Microsoft BASIC 80 version 5.2. This means that the programs should run as written, with the possible exception of the CLS command, on any computer using CP/M v2.0 and BASIC 80 version 5.2.

All programs provide the option of hard copy output, which gives a complete copy of all input information, a summary of the calculated results, and detailed results for each year of the investment.

All programs use the present value method of investment evaluation. Three programs are supplied: program INVEST1, program INVEST2, and program INVEST3.

Each program requires considerable information about the investment. How well the programs serve you depends mostly on the quality of this information; you should spend time obtaining all necessary information.

An efficient way to use the programs is to run them with your best estimate of all required information. If the investment appears favorable after this step, review your estimates and refine them if possible. (If the investment looks bad, don't try to find data that makes it look good.) Now rerun the program with your new information. If the results still look good, run the sensitivity analysis if INVEST1 is being used, or INVEST3 if a real estate investment is being studied.

After all this, if the investment still looks good, play with the programs. Change various assumptions and see what happens. You will often find that you've overlooked something important.

Pay careful attention to the yearly details. They often contain important information that can help you make a decision and help you manage an investment better. Pay special attention to spendable cash flow, which usually shows you how much working capital you need to maintain an investment and keep the bank happy.

INVEST1 is used to analyze investments that are expected to pay for themselves from the income generated. This type of investment is not intended to be resold at a profit. An example is the purchase of new equipment or a new business.

INVEST2 is used to analyze investments where most, if not all, of the expected profit comes from resale of the investment for a capital gain. The specific example used in the program is an investment in rental real estate; however, the program can be easily modified to examine other investments where capital gains are expected.

INVEST3 is a modification of INVEST2 to permit risk analysis. The program is useful for getting an idea of the risk and return relationship in an investment.

You should read the general discussion of investment analysis before using the programs. In this way you will be able to understand the limits of the computer programs, and you will also have a solid framework for interpreting the results.

In the final analysis, how well the programs work for you depends on how you interpret the results. Interpretation of the computer calculations is your responsibility. The computer only provides information—how it is used is up to you.

One final general point: investment decisions should be made by comparing all possible investment options, and then selecting those that best meet your requirements. An investment should never be considered by itself. Remember that not investing at all is one of the options that should be considered.

Listings for all programs are provided. The large programs, INVEST1, INVEST2, and INVEST3, require 48K RAM. They will run in 32K RAM if most of the remarks are removed and multistatements are used on individual lines.

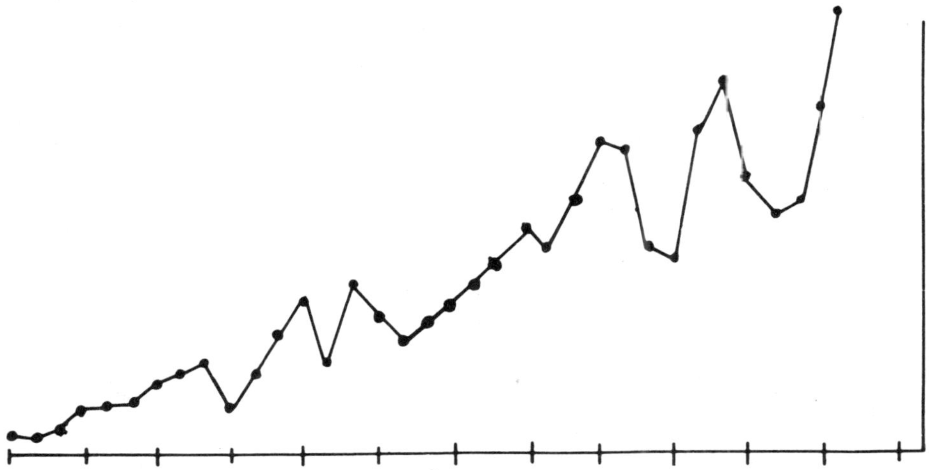

Chapter 1

Steps in Investment Analysis

Investment analysis is a multistep process that ends with the selection of the investment or investments that are best for you. The steps are:

- Define your investment objectives. Remember that your objectives are not the same as someone else's investment objectives.
- Determine the types of investments that meet your objectives. Because investment analysis is a time-consuming task, you want to limit the analysis to those investments that meet your objectives.
- Determine the cost and return for all investments that meet objectives. This is a crucial step.
- Analyze cost and return to find the best investments. This step is closely related to the preceding step. It may be efficient to loop between these two steps: first make optimistic assumptions about cost and income, then analyze cost and return; reject unsatisfactory investments, refine costs and returns, and repeat the analysis.
- Analyze risk, which always is present in investments. Analysis of risk must be one of the steps in investment analysis. Computer assistance in analyzing risk is discussed later.
- Select the investments you prefer based on the preceding quantitative analysis, together with qualitative analysis that determines if you are comfortable with the investments.
- Manage the investment to make sure costs and returns are as projected. This is not a step in the analysis procedure, but it is important if you are to meet investment objectives.

The emphasis of this book is on the analysis of projected costs and returns to determine whether the investment is a good one. The basic thrust of this analysis is based on the concepts of time value of money. Because the analysis is most objective and because it requires a considerable amount of computation, the computer is especially helpful in this step. Most of the other steps involve at least some subjective judgment, which is not susceptible to computer analysis. The analysis of projected costs and returns, on the other hand, is basically objective and involves some tedious mathematics; but this is what computers are good at.

The second area receiving emphasis is projection or forecasting of expected returns and expenses. A computer can be of assistance here; several programs for forecasting are provided. However, this area requires considerable subjective analysis. Thus it does not yield as gracefully to computer analysis.

Although these two areas are to receive the most emphasis, other steps are not totally neglected. Discussions are limited but do point out where the computer can help; in some cases computer programs are provided.

INVESTMENT OBJECTIVES

The first step in investment analysis is to define the objectives of the investment. Any investment that does not meet your personal investment objectives should be rejected. If you properly define your objectives, you will be able to eliminate several possible investments with little or no additional analysis.

Although you may have several objectives for investing (such as retirement or a vacation, you must realize that the first objective of any investment is to increase your future wealth. Unless the investment meets this objective, nothing else matters. You are better off spending the money now, not investing it for future gain.

Although it seems obvious that an investment must increase future wealth, people often make investments that aren't designed to do so. People forget the primary objective of investment and as a result make poor investment decisions.

In order to meet this primary objective you should choose investments that increase your future purchasing power, i.e., investments that keep ahead of inflation. The only way this can happen is if your investments make money.

Yet many investments don't meet this objective. Many so-called tax shelters, sold with the promise of reduced income tax, are good examples. At some levels of income the only way to reduce taxes is to increase expenses or losses. Since at best, a dollar lost only gives fifty cents in tax savings, you can cut your taxes and end up broke.

Again, the objective of investment is to increase future wealth. The only way this can happen is for the investment to earn money. Thus find the investments that earn the most money and pay the extra taxes. And enjoy the extra wealth you have earned.

If you cannot find investments that meet these objectives, spend your money now and enjoy it.

You may find it useful to make up a work sheet to help you define your investment objectives. Remember that you may have conflicting objectives—don't worry about that. You are the only person who can resolve the conflicts.

ELEMENTS OF INVESTMENT ANALYSIS

"Does this investment increase my future wealth?" is the question that must be answered by a rational investor. If more than one investment is being analyzed (as should be the situation), an additional question, "Which investment increases my future wealth the most?" is introduced.

The answers to these questions require analysis of three factors: money, time, and risk. All investments, whether in the stock market, gold, real estate, or comic books, involve consideration of these three factors.

The money factor is the easiest to analyze and is often the only factor considered. The essential questions are how much does the investment cost, and how much money does it return. The main thing to remember in analyzing the money factor is to be sure that all costs are included in the analysis.

The time factor is harder to analyze than the money factor—mainly because the mathematics involved is tedious. Yet careful consideration of the time factor is the heart of investment analysis. It is the factor that determines whether you will increase your future wealth. The essential questions are when must the investment be paid for, and when is the income from the investment paid.

Because all investments involve giving up present wealth or spending in exchange for future wealth, consideration of the time factor is essential to good investment decisions. A personal computer removes most of the hard work from time factor analysis.

You must understand the relationship between time and money to make good investment decisions. If you don't, you are very likely to find that your personal wealth has decreased.

Risk is the one factor that cannot be quantified. The essential question is, what is the chance that I will not get my money back? Risk is generally evaluated intuitively. You must make your own decisions about how much risk you are willing to accept and what the risk involved in a given investment is.

An important point to remember about risk is that risk and return are closely related. Low risk means low return and high risk means high return. There is basically no way to get high investment returns without accepting risk.

The amount of risk that you are willing to accept depends on the objective underlying a given investment. If you are investing for your retirement, you should accept less risk than if you are investing for a need which is not as important. You should only accept high risk if you can afford to lose all of the money invested. Be sure that you know how much risk you can accept before you proceed too far with an investment. But don't expect to find an investment with low risk and high returns.

OTHER FACTORS

Money, time, and risk are the three main factors that every investor should consider. These factors can be more or less quantified, and a computer can help in analyzing them. However, there are numerous other factors to consider. Most of them depend on the individual investor.

Most of the other factors are intangible, yet they are as important, if not more important, than the tangible factors of time, money, and risk. It is often the intangibles that determine whether a given investment will actually pay off for you. For example, if you don't want to be a landlord, then an investment in rental real estate will probably not work out—no matter what the quantitative analysis indicates.

If the thought of risk makes you stay awake at night, then you should stay away from risky investments, no matter how good they look.

In the final analysis you should select investments that you can live with. The computer, I'm afraid, won't be of much help.

THE RATIONAL INVESTOR

The rational investor must consider all three factors—time, money, and risk—in making an investment decision. In general, rational investors have the following preferences:

- For a given rate of return, they prefer the investment that returns money the earliest. Thus if the choice is $100 next year or $100 next month, the preferred investment is the one that returns $100 next month.
- For any given rate of return, they prefer the investment with the least risk.
- For any given degree of risk, they prefer high returns to low returns.

The last two preferences state that a high rate of return is required for risky investments.

The computer can help you sort all the factors involved in a given investment, and thus can help you make rational decisions.

HOW COMPUTERS HELP

First, remember that a computer is a tool. How it is used and how well it is used depend on you. The computer cannot make the decision for you. The final decision is yours and yours alone. (I realize that I have said this before, and I will say it again. However, I feel that we all tend to forget that the computer is a tool and begin to believe the calculated results too much. We must always be on guard against putting too much faith in the computer.)

Second, remember that no matter how impressive computer output looks—and it does look impressive—the analysis depends completely on the data and programs you provide for the computer. Often this is the hardest thing to remember. The computer printout tends to blind us to the fact that the computer is using the information we supplied, and the calculations are all based on our assumptions, some of which may be built into the program. The major danger of computer-aided investment analysis is that we all tend to read too much into the computer output.

Finally, remember that the computer cannot calculate subjective factors. It can only analyze factors that can be quantified in an objective manner. Don't expect the computer to help you with problems that concern subjective factors.

With all the warnings out of the way, let's look at what this powerful tool can do.

First, it can do a tremendous amount of calculation quickly. This fact alone has persuaded large companies to use their computers to help make investment decisions. Speed of computation is also the main justification for using a personal computer for investment analysis. The time factor is so important that we need all available tools to meet this issue adequately.

Second, the speed and ease of calculations means that several investments can be analyzed in a short time. Thus we can carefully analyze all pertinent investments. We are not limited to analyzing investments that are simple to analyze, nor are we limited to analyzing only a few factors affecting the investment. We can use the computer to make sure that all important factors are considered; that alone is worth the cost of the computer and the time we must spend working with it.

Finally, the speed of calculation allows us to estimate the risk involved. We can study the effects of various factors such as inflation rate, interest rates, higher expenses, etc.

After you have worked with a personal computer for awhile, I think you will find that it is more powerful than a main frame computer for investment analysis, because you work interactively with a personal computer. You can get an intuitive idea about the investment that is impossible with other methods of investment analysis.

Of course if the programs are not written to allow interactive use of the computer, you'll miss most of the benefits of using a personal computer. That's why all programs in this book are written to allow interactive use.

To make most effective use of a computer, whether it be main frame or micro, you have to build a computer model of the investment in which you're interested. A computer model allows you to simulate the performance of the investment for several years using different assumptions about income, expenses, inflation, and other important factors. Thus you will be able to see the effects of a 10 percent increase in expenses without actually having to make the investment.

Once the basic model is built, you can use the computer to help manage your investments. This is done by updating the information supplied to the computer and by changing the model if necessary. For example, if an investment is not working as well as you hoped, you can see what has to be done to make it work better, whether you should terminate the investment as soon as possible.

I think you will find that the personal or microcomputer is a useful tool for investment analysis. And you will soon wonder how you ever managed to get along without one.

Chapter 2

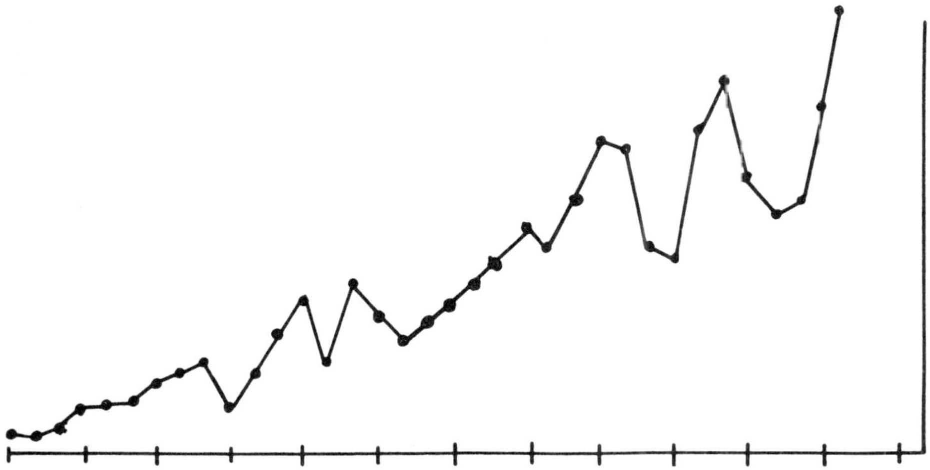

The Money Factor

The key questions about any investment are how much does it cost and how much does it return. These are the only questions that really matter. All other investment questions are primarily aimed at answering these questions.

The key questions have four parts:

1. How much does the investment cost?

2. How much does it cost to obtain the money necessary to purchase the investment?

3. What are the ongoing expenses and income from the investment?

4. Finally, and perhaps most important, what is the timing of future income and expenses?

In this chapter we will look at the first three of these questions. In Chapter 3 we will examine in more detail how much it costs to finance an investment. The question of timing is covered in Chapter 4.

HOW MUCH DOES IT COST?

You may think this an obvious or a trivial question. No one, you might say, would make an investment without knowing how much it costs. Yet we often do.

It is generally easy to determine what the selling price of something is. For example, if you purchase a stock you know what the selling price of the stock is. But the selling price is not the total cost of the investment. There are often other expenses that must be paid before you can purchase an investment. For example, there may be commissions, taxes, finder's fees, advertising costs, and numerous other costs that must be paid in order to purchase a given investment, and these costs are often hidden. Thus the first step in investment analysis is to determine the total cost of acquiring the investment. Using a worksheet is a good way to insure that all costs are considered.

THE COST OF MONEY

There are two sources of money for investment: yours and someone else's. In theory and in the absence of taxes, an investment decision is independent of the source of money. However, in the real world taxes exist, we cannot always borrow as much as we'd like, and so on; hence the source of funds does influence the investment decision.

Borrowed Money

The cost of borrowed money is easy to determine. It is simply the interest rate you must pay for money. The interest rate is specified in the loan agreement and can be calculated. If the interest rate is variable, you can still estimate it.

Because interest expense is an allowable business expense, the true cost of borrowed money is less than the interest rate on the loan. For example, if you are in the 50 percent tax bracket, the after tax cost of a 20 percent interest rate is 10 percent. Of course if you are in a lower tax bracket, your after tax cost of borrowing money is closer to the pretax interest rate.

Your Own Money

The cost of using your own money is somewhat more difficult to determine. You might think there is no cost in using your own money. After all it's your money; you don't have to pay interest if you want to spend it.

It is important to remember that if you use your money for one investment, it is not available for other investments, nor is it available to earn interest. For example, if you decide to purchase stocks, then your money is not available to purchase a term certificate of deposit. In other words, you have lost the chance to purchase a certificate of deposit and gain the interest it would pay.

Suppose that you have the choice of investing $1,000 in Sam's get-rich-quick scheme or putting your $1,000 into an all-savers' certificate that pays 12 percent interest tax free. If you invest in Sam's get-rich-quick, you pass up the all-savers' certificate and it costs you 12 percent (the amount you have forfeited by not collecting interest).

The loss of money for other investments is called *opportunity cost*. In our example, the numerical value of the opportunity cost is the return on the certificate of deposit or 12.0 percent of the cost of the certificate.

In general a good value for the opportunity cost is the return that can be expected from a risk-free investment. If you are considering a risky investment, you should add a slight amount to the opportunity cost to compensate for the risk.

Although the opportunity cost and the interest rate on a loan may be close, their true after-tax costs may be quite different. Tax laws that allow deduction of interest reduce the real cost of borrowing and thus favor the use of borrowed funds.

Equity and Borrowed Capital

Most investments are composed of a combination of borrowed money and equity (a fancy way of saying your money). The cost of using such a combination of funds is given by:

$$C = (BI + EV)/T$$

where C is the total cost of capital (given as a percentage), B is the amount that must be borrowed, I is the interest rate that the funds are borrowed at, E is the amount of equity, V is the opportunity cost, and T is the total amount of the investment.

For example; suppose you have an opportunity to buy real estate. Assume the cost of the property is $100,000 and includes all commissions, closing costs, etc., and assume you can borrow $80,000 at 20 percent (so you need $20,000 equity). You can invest in tax free government bonds that pay 8 percent interest. And your marginal tax rate is 40 percent. The after tax cost of borrowing is 12 percent. The average cost of capital for the investment is

$$C = (80{,}000 \times 12 + 20{,}000 \times 8.0)/100{,}000 = 11.2\%$$

This means that an investment must have an after tax return of 11.2 percent to recover the cost of making the investment.

As you will see later, it is important to know the cost of capital. The cost of capital combined with the concepts of time value of money tell us whether an investment has made a profit.

CASH FLOWS

The flow of money into and out of an investment is called the *cash flow*. Cash flow is made up of income, called cash *inflows*, and expenses, called cash *outflows*, and depreciation. The sum of the cash inflows, depreciation, and cash outflows determines the overall cash flow. If the cash inflows exceed the cash outflows, you have a positive cash flow and might have a good investment. If the cash flow is negative, you have a loss and a bad investment.

One major problem you face in investment analysis, and the one most books on investment analysis discuss is projecting cash flows for the life of the investment. Once you have made an investment, you have the problem of insuring that the cash flows actually occur. We will examine the problem of forecasting; however, the problem of how to make sure cash flows actually occur is outside the scope of this book.

Cash flow can vary from year to year. For many investments cash flow in the first years of the investment is negative, meaning expenses exceed income. (Of course this difference must be accounted for, which usually is done by borrowing additional funds.) After several years cash flow becomes positive. For the investment to be a good one, the final total of yearly cash flows must be positive. Otherwise, you will have lost money.

There are two important types of cash flow: spendable cash flow and taxable cash flow. It is possible for an investment to produce negative spendable cash flow and positive taxable cash flow, which is not a very good idea. The reverse is also possible and is more desirable.

These two types of cash flow are not the same. Spendable cash flow is the money that we actually have to spend. Taxable cash flow is the money that the IRS wants to tax.

The tax laws are the reason for the differences between spendable and taxable cash flow. The tax laws allow us to deduct certain expenses from income that are not out of pocket expenses, and prohibit us from deducting other out of pocket expenses from income. The worst possible situation is when the IRS says you made a profit (so you have to pay taxes) and yet you have lost out of pocket money.

Depreciation is the major tax law expense that is not an out of pocket expense. That is, you do not write a check for depreciation. Although depreciation can reduce our taxable income, it does not necessarily reduce our spendable income. (If we set aside funds for replacing depreciated equipment, then depreciation can also reduce our spendable cash. However, this is not often done.) This is why cash flow is usually defined as after tax profit plus depreciation. In this book we will call the taxable cash flow "cash flow." I will always use the term "spendable cash flow" when I'm talking about the spendable cash flow. This should avoid confusion.

Principal payments on a loan are the major spendable expense that is not an expense for tax purposes. An investment that is financed with borrowed money must produce enough income to make both the interest and principal payments. Otherwise, you would have to find additional funds to make the required loan payments. The programs in this book will flag all situations where the after tax income from an investment is insufficient to cover the interest plus principal payments on outstanding loans.

In mathematical terms the two cash flows can be described as:

Taxable cash flow = income − expenses + depreciation − taxes

Spendable cash flow = income − expenses − principal paid − taxes

Example: Spendable and Taxable Cash Flows.

Suppose you have an investment that produces $1,000 income per year. The allowable depreciation on the investment is $600, the interest payment is $200 and the principal payment is $400. Your tax rate is 50 percent. The tax paid on the investment is calculated by determining the net taxable income, which is $1,000 (gross income) − $200 (interest) − $600 (depreciation) = $200 taxable income. The tax paid is $100. The net after tax profit is $100. The after tax cash flow is $100 (net profit) + $600 (depreciation) = $700. The after tax spendable cash flow is given by $1,000 (gross income) − $200 (interest payment) − $400 (principal payment) − $100 (tax paid) = $300. Note that the investment yielded $300 for your pocket.

In general over the life of an investment, spendable cash flow and taxable cash flow from a profitable investment are both positive. However, it is important to realize that for individual years of the life of the investment, you may find that you did not earn enough to make the principal payments on your loan. In such situations, you should carefully examine the investment. Principal and interest payments must be made, so if you keep the investment you will have to find additional funds to make the necessary payments. Such funds will increase the cost of the investment.

Taxes and depreciation are discussed later in this book. The discussion is based on the 1981 tax laws.

Estimating Cash Flows

Estimating the future cash flows from an investment is a critical step in investment analysis. This step is discussed by most books on investment analysis. The methods used to make estimates vary with the type of investment. Only a general discussion will be given here.

The first cash flow that must be estimated is the initial cost of the investment, composed of the cost that the seller is asking and the cost that the investment is worth.

It is fairly easy to determine the price the seller is asking. It is somewhat more difficult to determine the price that you should pay for an investment. Techniques for estimating the value of an investment vary with the type of investment. For example, a technique that works for estimating the value of common stock or a business probably would not work for determining the value of rental property.

No matter what you're buying, the first step is to determine the price of similar investments. If the asking price for your investment is out of line with that of similar investments, be careful.

Once you've determined that the selling price is reasonable compared to similar investments, then you refine your estimate of the appropriate price. The steps you should go through depend mostly on the type of investment. The details of all the various techniques are outside the scope of this book. However, we will see later how to use the programs in this book to help with this step.

The next step is to estimate expenses and income for the life of the investment. Income can be of two types: income from the investment and income from the eventual sale of the investment. Many investments have income from only one source. For example, an investment in a new piece of equipment for a business would be expected to produce income from increased business. But it would not normally be resold for a profit. On the other hand, many common stocks do not produce income; they do not have dividends, but are expected to be resold at a profit.

There are two questions that must be answered in order to project the income and expenses from an investment. First, what are the expected first year income and expenses from the investment. These can best be determined by careful analysis of the income and expenses of similar investments. The basic idea is that income and expenses from similar investments should be about the same. Any investment that has projected income or expenses different from those of similar investments should be examined with great care, as something is probably wrong.

Once first year income and expenses have been estimated, the next step is to estimate the growth of income and expenses over the life of the investment. You should begin by looking at past trends in the particular investment you're considering. Also look at past trends for the type of investment you're interested in.

The techniques used to make cash flow estimates depend on the type of investment. You should carefully study the techniques available for a given type of investment and then use the techniques best suited for you. A brief discussion of estimating cash flows for rental property followed by a short discussion of common stock have been chosen because they are two of the most common forms of investment.

Estimating Cash Flow for Rental Property

First let's look at rental property investments. The first step is to examine the expense and income history of the particular property you're interested in purchasing. Analyze pertinent books for the past several years. Use some of the forecasting techniques discussed in Chapter 14 to determine data trends. Verify whether some expense, for example maintenance, is too low or too high. A low value for an important expense may overstate the profit from the property. A high value may indicate a problem with the property.

Next, evaluate the past income and expense history of rental properties near the units you're considering. Start with properties in the neighborhood of your units, then look at property throughout the rest of the city. If you see that your units are out of line with the competition, find out why. Otherwise, you may have a serious problem. You should use the forecasting techniques discussed in Chapter 14 to estimate the trends for these properties too. The trends should be similar to those of your property. If they are not, look at all the figures to determine the reasons for discrepancies.

Examine the age and condition of the various rental units. Compare with the age and condition of the property you're interested in. Remember that rental income can be expected to decrease as the age of the units increase, especially if the condition of the units falls below that of the competition. Also note that expenses for many properties can be expected to increase as a property ages.

Several techniques have been developed to help estimate income and expenses for real estate investments. You should be familiar with these if you are to take maximum advantage of the help you can get from a computer.

The final projection for real estate investment is the estimation of the future selling price. There are several techniques for making the projection; all give you an expected appreciation that can be used with the programs in this book.

The final step in estimating the future price of a property is to put yourself in the place of the buyer. Ask yourself if you would purchase the property. If you wouldn't, then why would someone else?

You should remember that the value of an investment is closely tied to the income and expenses produced by the investment.

Cash Flow from Common Stock

The cash flow from common stocks is the dividend paid by the stock and the capital gain from the eventual sale of the stock. Generally there are no expenses to estimate other than commission due when the stock is sold.

There are two basic techniques for estimating the future price of common stock, fundamental analysis and technical analysis. Fundamental analysis is based on the idea that careful study of the present and future prospects of a business can tell you the present and future value of the business's common stock. If the present price is less than the future value the stock is a good investment.

Technical analysis is based on the assumption that the present price and past price trends of a stock contains all the information necessary to determine the future price. If the future price is projected upwards, then the stock may be a good investment. If the future price is projected downwards, then the stock should be sold.

You should consult one of the many books on common stock evaluation to determine which method is best for you. Probably the best idea is to pick a method and stick with it.

SUMMARY

Estimating future cash flows can be a lot of work. Much information is needed and a considerable amount of study is required. The only way to reduce the effort required is to lower the number of investments that must be studied. An efficient way to do this is to make a best case study of all the investments you're considering. The information for this type of study is generally easy to obtain. Then use the programs discussed later in this book to analyze the investments. Reject all investments that the analysis shows are poor. If the investments are poor under best-case assumptions, there is little to be gained by making more realistic assumptions.

Go back and refine the projections for the investments that remain. Take considerable care in making the projections for these investments. Then rerun the analysis programs and select investments that meet your needs.

Chapter 3

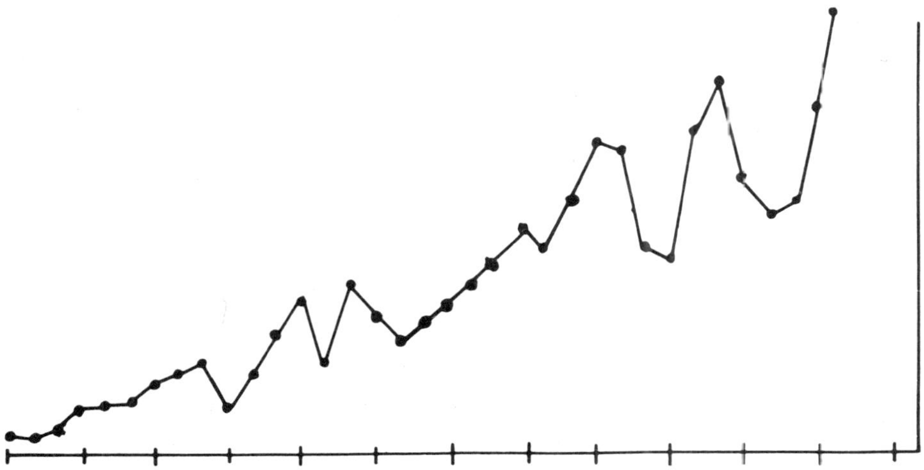

Interest Calculations

When you set money aside, you should expect to be compensated for the loss of the use of the money. When you borrow money from someone, you should expect to pay for the use of that money. If you were not compensated for the loss of the use of your money, there would not be any reason to invest. After all, why should someone else get the free use of your money? You would prefer to spend it on what you want now.

The cost of using someone else's money is called *interest.* This chapter looks at interest and provides several programs for calculating the interest you earn and the interest you must pay.

COMPOUND INTEREST

There are two types of interest, simple interest and compound interest. The amount we can earn or that we have to pay, strongly depends on whether we pay or are paid simple or compound interest. Simple interest means that only the initial amount of money earns interest. For example, if we set aside $1,000 at 10 percent simple interest for ten years, we earn $100 a year in interest. At the end of the ten years we have a total of $2,000. ($1,000 initial deposit and $1,000 from ten years of interest).

Compound interest means that you earn interest both on the amount originally set aside and on the interest the money earns. For example, using the figures of the previous example ($1,000 deposited at 10 percent interest per year for ten years), but with the interest compounded annually, you would earn $100 in interest the first year. The $100 in interest is added to the initial deposit, giving you $1,100 on which to earn interest in the second year. The third year we earn 10 percent on $1,210 ($121) which is added to our deposit to give $1321 at the end of the third year. The way our money grows is shown in Table 3-1.

With compound interest we earn a total of

Table 3-1. $1000 Earning 10 Percent Compound Interest.

End of Year	Amount on Deposit	Interest Earned
start	$1000	
1	$1000	$100
2	$1100	$110
3	$1210	$121
4	$1331	$133.10
5	$1664.10	$166.41
6	$1830.51	$183.05
7	$2013.56	$201.37
8	$2214.92	$221.49
9	$2436.41	$243.64
10	$2680.05	$268.00

$1,680.05 interest or $680.05 more than with simple interest. The lesson is that our money grows much faster with compound interest than it does with simple interest.

The compounding period may be any time—yearly, monthly, weekly, daily or continuously. The more often the compounding, the faster your money grows.

If the compounding period is yearly, quarterly, monthly, or daily or for any other unit of time, we say that the compounding is for discrete periods. The equation for calculating compound interest for discrete periods is

$$V = A \times (1 + r/n)^{mn}$$

where V is the final amount or the future value, A is the initial amount or the present value, r is the interest rate (a decimal fraction), n is the number of compounding periods per year, and m is the number of years.

If the compounding is done continuously, the appropriate equation is

$$V = A\ e^{-r/n}$$

where e is the number 2.71828. (In BASIC e^n is written as EXP(N)).

These equations can be rearranged to allow calculation of any variable if all the other variables are known.

COMPOUND/BAS PROGRAM

The BASIC program COMPOUND/BAS is based on these two equations. To use the program simply answer the questions it asks and provide the data requested. Each required piece of information is asked for by name. The program provides the option of hardcopy output. The hardcopy output consists of the input data followed by the desired answer. The program is written in TRS-80 disk BASIC. The remark statements show how to adapt the program to BASIC 80 version 5.2 for CP/M 2.0 and for other popular computers. To use COMPOUND/BAS, simply follow the instructions on the crt (see Fig. 3-1) and provide the information asked for. The crt displays for each step in the use of the program are shown below. The first step in using COMPOUND/BAS is to select the option. Then fill in the information asked for. The program does all the hard work for you. The program listing follows.

COMPOUND/BAS Listing

```
10 REM PROGRAM TO SOLVE COMPOUND INTEREST PROBLEMS
20 REM WRITTEN IN MICROSOFT BASIC BY LES
30 REM VERSION 1.8
40 REM CHECKED ON TRS-80 MODEL I AND MODEL III
50 REM ***************************************
60 CLS : REM REPLACE THIS WITH WHATEVER COMMAND CLEARS THE
SCREEN ON YOUR COMPUTER HOME FOR APPLE II
70 PRINT "COMPOUND INTEREST SOLVER"
```

```
80 PRINT "OPTIONS ARE TO CALCULATE:"
90 PRINT"1. FINAL AMOUNT KNOWING RATE AND NUMBER OF YEARS"
100 PRINT"2. INITIAL AMOUNT IF KNOW FINAL AMOUNT, RATE AND LIFE"
110 PRINT "3. RATE IF KNOW FINAL AND INITIAL AMOUNTS AND NUMBER
OF YEARS"
120 PRINT "4. NUMBER OF YEARS IF KNOW FINAL AND INITIAL AMOUNTS
AND RATE"
130 PRINT "***********************************************"
140 PRINT"ENTER THE NUMBER OF THE OPTION YOU WANT "
150 INPUT J$
160 IF INSTR("1234",J$)=0 THEN PRINT"TRY AGAIN ":GOTO140 :REM
ERROR TRAP FOR CORRECT RESPONSE
170 J=VAL(J$)
180 ON J GOSUB 230,370,490,640
190 PRINT"DO YOU WANT ANOTHER ONE Y OR N"
200 Y$=INKEY$:IF Y$="" THEN200 ELSE IF INSTR("YN",Y$)=0 THEN
PRINT"TRY AGAIN":GOTO190
210 IF Y$="N" THEN PRINT"END OF SESSION. REMOVE DISKS BEFORE
SHUTING DOWN":END
220 GOTO 60
230 REM HERE TO SOLVE FOR FINAL AMOUNT IF KNOW EVERYTHING ELSE
240 CLS
250 PRINT"SUBROUTINE TO SOLVE FOR FINAL AMOUNT"
260 INPUT"ENTER THE INITIAL AMOUNT ";PV
270 INPUT "ENTER THE YEARLY INTEREST RATE IN PERCENT ";IR
280 INPUT "ENTER THE NUMBER OF YEARS ";NY
290 GOSUB 1000
300 IF CP$<>"CONTINUOUSLY" THEN 340
310 FV = PV*EXP(IR/100*NY)
320 GOSUB 800
330 RETURN
340 FV=PV*(1+IR/(100*N))[(N*NY)
350 GOSUB 800
360 RETURN
370 REM CALCULATE INITIAL AMOUNT
380 CLS
390 INPUT"ENTER FINAL AMOUNT ";FV
400 INPUT"ENTER INTEREST RATE ";IR
410 INPUT "ENTER NUMBER OF YEARS ";NY
420 GOSUB 1000
430 IF LEFT$(CP$,1)<>"C" THEN 460
440 PV = FV*EXP(-IR/100*NY)
450 GOTO 470
460 PV = FV *(1+IR/(100*N))[-(NY*N)
```

```
COMPOUND INTEREST SOLVER
OPTIONS ARE TO CALCULATE:
1. FINAL AMOUNT KNOWING RATE AND NUMBER OF YEARS
2. INITIAL AMOUNT IF KNOW FINAL AMOUNT, RATE AND LIFE
3. RATE IF KNOW FINAL AND INITIAL AMOUNTS AND NUMBER OF YEARS
4. NUMBER OF YEARS IF KNOW FINAL AND INITIAL AMOUNTS AND RATE
*****************************************************
ENTER THE NUMBER OF THE OPTION YOU WANT
? _
SUBROUTINE TO SOLVE FOR FINAL AMOUNT
ENTER THE INITIAL AMOUNT ?
ENTER THE YEARLY INTEREST RATE IN PERCENT ?
ENTER THE NUMBER OF YEARS ?
YOU MAY SELECT ANY OF THE COMPOUNDING PERIODS
<D>AILY
<W>EEKLY
<M>ONTHLY
<Q>UARTERLY
<S>EMIANNUALLY (TWICE A YEAR)
<Y>EARLY
<C>ONTINUOUSLY
PRESS THE KEY FOR THE OPTION YOU WANT
    CALCULATE INITIAL AMOUNT

ENTER FINAL AMOUNT ?
ENTER INTEREST RATE ?
ENTER NUMBER OF YEARS ?
YOU MAY SELECT ANY OF THE COMPOUNDING PERIODS
<D>AILY
<W>EEKLY
<M>ONTHLY
<Q>UARTERLY
```

Fig. 3-1. Crt display for program COMPOUND/BAS.

```
470 GOSUB 800
480 RETURN
490 REM CALCULATE RATEK
500 CLS
510 PRINT "CALCULATE RATE "
520 INPUT"ENTER INITIAL AMOUNT ":PV
530 INPUT "ENTER FINAL AMOUNT ";FV
540 INPUT "ENTER NUMBER OF YEARS ";NY
```

```
<S>EMIANNUALLY (TWICE A YEAR)
<Y>EARLY
<C>ONTINUOUSLY
PRESS THE KEY FOR THE OPTION YOU WANT
WRONG INPUT
PRESS THE KEY FOR THE OPTION YOU WANT
CALCULATE RATE
ENTER INITIAL AMOUNT ?
ENTER FINAL AMOUNT ?
ENTER NUMBER OF YEARS ?
YOU MAY SELECT ANY OF THE COMPOUNDING PERIODS
<D>AILY
<W>EEKLY
<M>ONTHLY
<Q>UARTERLY
<S>EMIANNUALLY (TWICE A YEAR)
<Y>EARLY
<C>ONTINUOUSLY
PRESS THE KEY FOR THE OPTION YOU WANT
CALCULATE NUMBER OF YEARS
ENTER INITIAL AMOUNT ?
ENTER FINAL AMOUNT ?
ENTER INTEREST RATE ?
YOU MAY SELECT ANY OF THE COMPOUNDING PERIODS
<D>AILY
<W>EEKLY
<M>ONTHLY
<Q>UARTERLY
<S>EMIANNUALLY (TWICE A YEAR)
<Y>EARLY
<C>ONTINUOUSLY
PRESS THE KEY FOR THE OPTION YOU WANT
```

```
550 GOSUB 1000
560 IF LEFT$(CP$,1)<>"C" THEN 600
570 IR = LOG(FV/PV)/NY*100
580 GOTO 620
590 REM NOW CALCULATE RATE
600 R=(FV/PV)[(1/(N*NY))-1
610 IR = 100*R*N
620 GOSUB 800
```

```
630 RETURN
640 REM CALCULATE NUMBER OF YEARS
650 CLS
660 PRINT"CALCULATE NUMBER OF YEARS"
670 INPUT "ENTER INITIAL AMOUNT " PV
680 INPUT "ENTER FINAL AMOUNT ";FV
690 INPUT "ENTER INTEREST RATE ";IR
700 GOSUB1000
710 IF LEFT$(CP$,1)<>"C" THEN 740
720 NY=LOG(FV/PV)/IR*100
730 GOTO 760
740 MN=(LOG(FV/PV))/LOG(1+IR/(100*N))
750 NY = MN/N
760 GOSUB 800
770 RETURN
780 REM DISCRETE COMPOUNDING
790 FV = PV *(1 +IR/(100*N))[(N*NY)
800 CLS
810 PRINT USING "THE FUTURE VALUE OF $#,######.## INVESTED FOR
### YEARS";PV,NY
820 PRINT USING "AT ##.##% INTEREST COMPOUNDED %
%":IR,CP$
830 PRINT USING "IS $#,######.##";FV
840 PRINT
850 PRINT "PRESS <H> FOR HARD COPY "
860 Y$=INKEY$:IF Y$="" THEN 860
870 IF Y$="H" THEN GOSUB 900
880 PRINT "PRESS ANY KEY TO CONTINUE "
890 Y$=INKEY$:IF Y$="" THEN 890 ELSE RETURN
900 PRINT
910 PRINT "HARDCOPY ROUTINE. BE SURE THAT PRINTER IS ON"
920 LPRINT TAB(10);
930 LPRINT USING "AN INITIAL AMOUNT OF $#,######.## INVESTED FOR
##.## YEARS";PV,NY
940 LPRINT TAB(10);
950 LPRINT USING"AT AN INTEREST RATE OF ##.##% COMPOUNDED %
     %";IR,CP$
960 LPRINT TAB(10);
970 LPRINT USING "WILL GROW TO $#,######.##";FV
980 LPRINT " "
990 RETURN
1000 PRINT "YOU MAY SELECT ANY OF THE COMPOUNDING PERIODS "
1010 PRINT "<D>AILY"
1020 PRINT "<W>EEKLY"
```

```
1030 PRINT "<M>ONTHLY"
1040 PRINT "<Q>UARTERLY"
1050 PRINT "<S>EMIANNUALLY (TWICE A YEAR)"
1060 PRINT "<Y>EARLY"
1070 PRINT "<C>ONTINUOUSLY"
1080 PRINT"PRESS THE KEY FOR THE OPTION YOU WANT "
1090 Y$=INKEY$:IF Y$="" THEN 1090
1100 I = INSTR("DWMQSYC",Y$)
1110 IF I=0 THEN PRINT "WRONG INPUT ":GOTO 1080
1120 ON I GOTO 1130,1160,1190,1220,1250,1280,1310
1130 N=365
1140 CP$="DAILY"
1150 RETURN
1160 N=52
1170 CP$="WEEKLY"
1180 RETURN
1190 N=12
1200 CP$="MONTHLY"
1210 RETURN
1220 N=4
1230 CP$="OUARTERLY"
1240 RETURN
1250 N=2
1260 CP$="SEMIANNUAL"
1270 RETURN
1280 N=1
1290 CP$="YEARLY"
1300 RETURN
1310 REM
1320 CP$="CONTINUOUSLY"
1330 RETURN
```

Example 1: Find the Future Value of a Given Amount

Suppose that you have $2000 and you want to put it in a certificate of deposit. You check around and find that three banks offer different deals. Each bank claims that their deal is the best. The three deals are:

1. Pays 13.7 percent compounded yearly.
2. Pays 13.5 percent compounded monthly.
3. Pays 13.2 percent compounded continuously.

The question you must answer is which of the three choices will give you the most money in three years?

Run the COMPOUND/BAS program for each of the three cases. The output from the three runnings of the program is below. (Choice 2 above will give you the most money in three years.)

Choice 1. Output

AN INITIAL AMOUNT OF $2,000.00 INVESTED
FOR 3.00 YEARS
AT AN INTEREST OF 13.70% COMPOUNDED
YEARLY

WILL GROW TO $2,939.76

Choice 2 Output
AN INITIAL AMOUNT OF $2,000.00 INVESTED FOR 3.00 YEARS
AT AN INTEREST RATE OF 13.50% COMPOUNDED MONTHLY
WILL GROW TO $2,971.74

Choice 3 Output
AN INITIAL AMOUNT OF $2,000.00 INVESTED FOR 3.00 YEARS
AT AN INTEREST RATE OF 13.20% COMPOUNDED CONTINUOUSLY
WILL GROW TO $2,971.74.

Example 2: Compute the Present Value

Now let's look at another typical situation. You know that in five years you will need $10,000 for that trip around the world or that great new computer. You have found an investment that will pay an interest rate of 12 percent compounded daily. You want to know how much you must set aside now to have $10,000 in five years. To answer this question, merely select option 2 of COMPOUND/BAS and enter the required information. In just a few seconds the computer provides you with the information shown below:

Output:
AN INITIAL AMOUNT OF $5,488.78 INVESTED FOR 5.00 YEARS
AT AN INTEREST RATE OF 12.00% COMPOUNDED DAILY
WILL GROW TO $10,000.

So you need to deposit $5,488.78 today to have $10,000 in five years. Your money has almost doubled.

Example 3: Find the Appropriate Interest Rate

As a final example suppose you have $3,000 available today. You know that you will need $5,500 in 4 years. The problem is to select the interest rate, compounded daily, that you must earn to obtain the needed $5,500. This is option three of program COMPOUND/BAS. The output from the program for this case is given below.

Output:
AN INITIAL AMOUNT OF $3,000 INVESTED FOR 3.00 YEARS
AT AN INTEREST RATE OF 20.21% COMPOUNDED DAILY
WILL GROW TO $5,500.

Thus you must find an investment that pays 20.21 percent compounded daily. That's quite a high return and probably has a significant amount of risk.

We've seen how powerful compound interest is. If the interest rate is high enough and the time long enough, compound interest can turn a small amount of money into a fortune, provided inflation doesn't increase faster than our fortune grows.

ANNUITIES

Now that you know how compounding affects a single payment, you can look at the more interesting question of how compounding affects a series of payments (called a *stream of cash flows*). An example is a given monthly deposit for one year.

Once you have a program that can handle a stream of cash flows, you can answer such questions as how much will we have in 30 years if we set aside $2000 per year at 12 percent interest; or how much money, in one lump sum, must we set aside now to provide $1000 a year for five years if the interest rate is 12 percent?

These two questions concern the present and future value of an annuity. The equation for calculating an annuity is:

$$V = S\{[(1+r)^{mn} - 1]/R\}\ (1+R)$$

where V is the future value, S is the amount of the periodic payment, r is the interest rate (decimal

```
==============================================================
ANNUITY PROGRAM VERSION 1.0 BY LES
YOUR OPTIONS ARE:
     <F>UTURE VALUE OF THE ANNUITY.
     <P>RESENT VALUE OF THE ANNUITY.
==============================================================
MAKE YOUR SELECTION BY PRESSING <F> OR <P>.



==============================================================
FUTURE VALUE CALCULATION
YOU MAY CALCULATE THE <F>UTURE VALUE OR THE <A>MOUNT OF PAYMENT.

PLEASE MAKE YOUR SELECTION <A> OR <F>



==============================================================
FUTURE VALUE CALCULATION
YOU MAY CALCULATE THE <F>UTURE VALUE OR THE <A>MOUNT OF PAYMENT.

PLEASE MAKE YOUR SELECTION <A> OR <F>
ENTER  DATA ASKED FOR
CURRENT VALUE IS SHOWN IN ()
AMOUNT OF LUMP SUM ($       0.00)
?
INTEREST RATE ( 0.00%PER YEAR)?
```

Fig. 3-2. Crt display for program ANNUITY/BAS (continued on page 20).

fraction), n is the number of payments per year, and m is the number of years. (We are assuming the payment is made at the beginning of the period. This is called an *annuity due.*)

The present value of an annuity due is given by

$$A = S\,\{[1-(1+r)^{MN}]/R\}(1+R)$$

where A is the present value (or the amount that must be set aside now), and the other variables are the same as above. This equation means that if we set aside A dollars now and if they earn at an interest rate of r per period, then we can withdraw S dollars per period for M years.

ANNUITY/BAS PROGRAM

The short ANNUITY/BAS program solves these two equations. The program is self prompting and asks for all the information it needs by name. The crt displays for the program are shown in Fig. 3-2.

```
NUMBER OF YEAR (   0)?
NUMBER OF COMPOUNDING PERIODS PER YEAR (   0)
? _
===============================================================
YOU MAY CALCULATE EITHER THE <P>RESENT VALUE OR THE <A>MOUNT OF
THE PAYMENT.
PLEASE SELECT EITHER <P> OR <A>
ENTER  DATA ASKED FOR
CURRENT VALUE IS SHOWN IN ()
AMOUNT OF PERIODIC PAYMENT ($       0.00)?
INTEREST RATE ( 0.00%PER YEAR)?
NUMBER OF YEAR (   0)?
NUMBER OF COMPOUNDING PERIODS PER YEAR (   0)
? _
```

Fig. 3-2. Crt display for program ANNUITY/BAS. (Continued from page 19.)

ANNUITY/BAS Listing

```
10 REM PROGRAM ANNUITY/BAS
20 REM THIS IS FOR AN ANNUITY DUE
30 REM WRITTEN IN TRS-80 DISK BASIC
40 REM VERSION 1.0
50 REM JAN 1982 WRITTEN BY LES
60 REM **************************************
70 REM VARIABLES V FUTURE VALUE OF ANNUITY
80 REM S AMOUNT OF PERIODIC PAYMENTS
90 REM R INTEREST RATE IN %
100 REM M NUMBER OF YEARS PAYMENTS MADE
110 REM N NUMBER OF PAYMENTS PER YEAR
120 REM A PRESENT VALUE OF THE ANNUITY
130 CLS: REM CLEAR THE SCREEN USE HOME FOR APPLE II
140 CLEAR 100 : REM CLEAR SOME STRING SPACE DELETE FOR APPLE II
AND PET
150 B$ = STRING$(63,"=")
160 PRINT B$
170 PRINT "ANNUITY PROGRAM VERSION 1.0 BY LES"
180 PRINT"YOUR OPTIONS ARE:"
190 PRINT TAB(5); "<F>UTURE VALUE OF THE ANNUITY."
200 PRINT TAB(5); "<P>RESENT VALUE OF THE ANNUITY."
210 PRINT B$
220 PRINT "MAKE YOUR SELECTION BY PRESSING <F> OR <P>."
230 Y$ = INKEY$: IF Y$ = "" THEN 230
240 IF INSTR("FPFP",Y$)=0 THEN PRINT "WRONG INPUT. TRY
```

```
AGAIN.":GOTO 220 : REM CHECK TO BE SURE WE GOT WHAT WE WANTED.
250 IF Y$ = "F" OR Y$ = "F"  THEN 490
260 REM CALCUALTE PRESENT VALUE
270 CLS
280 PRINT B$
290 PRINT "PRESENT VALUE CALCULATION."
300 CLS
310 PRINT B$
320 PRINT"YOU MAY CALCULATE EITHER THE <P>RESENT VALUE OR THE
<A>MOUNT OF THE PAYMENT."
330 PRINT "PLEASE SELECT EITHER <P> OR <A>"
340 Y$ = INKEY$:IF Y$ = "" THEN 340 ELSE IF INSTR("PAPA",Y$)=0
THEN PRINT "TRY AGAIN.":GOTO 330
350 IF Y$ = "A" OR Y$ = "A" THEN FL=-1 ELSE FL=1
360 GOSUB 730
370 CLS
380 IF FL=-1 THEN 460
390 A = S*(1-(1+R1)[-(M*N))/R1*(1+R1)
400 PRINT USING "THE PRESENT VALUE OF THE ANNUITY IS
$######,#.##";A
410 PRINT USING"PERIODIC PAYMENT OF $######,#.## MADE ### TIMES
A  YEAR";S;N
420 PRINT USING "FOR ### YEARS WITH AN INTEREST RATE OF

##.##%";M;R
430 PRINT "DO YOU WANT TO RUN ANOTHER ONE Y OR N?"
440 GOSUB 1010
450 IF Y$ = "Y" THEN 30 ELSE END
460 K1 = (1-(1+R1)[-(M*N))/R1*(1+R1)
470 S = A/K1
480 GOTO 400
490 CLS
500 PRINT B$
510 PRINT "FUTURE VALUE CALCULATION "
520 PRINT "YOU MAY CALCULATE THE <F>UTURE VALUE OR THE <A>MOUNT
OF PAYMENT."
530 PRINT "PLEASE MAKE YOUR SELECTION <A> OR <F>"
540 Y$ = INKEY$: IF Y$ = "" THEN 540 ELSE IF INSTR("AFAF",Y$)=0
THEN PRINT "TRY AGAIN":GOTO530
550 IF Y$ = "A" THEN FL=-1 ELSE FL=+1
560 GOSUB 730
570 IF FL=-1 THEN 680
580 CLS
590 V = S*((1+R1)[(M*N)-1)/R1*(1+R1)
600 PRINT B$
```

```
610 PRINT USING"THE FUTURE VALUE OF THE ANNUITY IS
$######,#.##";V
620 PRINT USING"### PAYMENTS OF $######,#.## PER YEAR FOR ###
YEARS";N;S;M
630 PRINT USING "##.##% INTEREST PER YEAR";R
640 PRINT
650 PRINT"DO YOU WANT TO RUN ANOTHER ONE Y OR N?"
660 GOSUB 1010
670 IF Y$= "Y" THEN 30 ELSE END
680 K1 = ((1+R1)[(M*N)-1)/R1*(1+R1)
690 S = A/K1
700 V = A
710 CLS
720 GOTO 600
730 REM DATA INPUT ROUTINE
740 PRINT "ENTER  DATA ASKED FOR"
750 PRINT "CURRENT VALUE IS SHOWN IN ()"
760 IF FL = -1 THEN PRINT USING "AMOUNT OF LUMP SUM
($#####,##.##)";A ELSE 790
770  INPUT A
780 GOTO 810
790 PRINT USING "AMOUNT OF PERIODIC PAYMENT ($######,#.##)" ;S;
800 INPUT S
810 PRINT USING "INTEREST RATE (##.##%PER YEAR)";R;
820 INPUT R
830 PRINT USING "NUMBER OF YEAR (###)";M;
840 INPUT M
850 PRINT USING "NUMBER OF COMPOUNDING PERIODS PER YEAR (###)";N
860 INPUT N
870 CLS
880 PRINT B$
890 PRINT "CHECK DATA FOR ERRORS"
900 IF FL <> -1 THEN 920 ELSE PRINT USING "AMOUNT OF LUMP SUM
$######,#.##";A
910 GOTO 930
920 PRINT USING "AMOUNT OF PERIODIC PAYMENT $######,#.##";S
930 PRINT USING "INTEREST RATE                        ##.##%";R
940 PRINT USING "NUMBER OF YEARS ###";M
950 PRINT USING "NUMBER OF PERIODS/YEAR ###";N
960 PRINT "ARE THESE CORRECT Y OR N?"
970 Y$ = INKEY$ : IF Y$="" THEN 970 ELSE IF INSTR("YNYN",Y$)=0
THEN PRINT "WRONG INPUT. TRY AGAIN.":GOTO960
980 IF Y$ = "N" OR Y$ = "N" THEN CLS:PRINT B$:PRINT"PLEASE
REENTER DATA. PRESS <ENTER> IF CURRENT VALUE IS OK": GOTO 730
```

```
990 R1 = R/100/N
1000 RETURN
1010 Y$ = INKEY$: IF Y$ = "" THEN 1010
1020 IF INSTR("YNYN",Y$)=0 THEN PRINT "TRY AGAIN. ANSWER Y OR
N.":GOTO 1010
1030 IF Y$ = "Y" OR Y$ = "Y" THEN Y$ = "Y" ELSE Y$ = "N"
1040 RETURN
```

Example 1: Future Value

You know that in five years you must replace your car. The price of the new car is estimated to be $11,000. You would like to be able to pay cash for the car. You want to know how much you must set aside per year at 12 percent interest to be able to pay cash for the car.

This is a future value problem that can be answered by ANNUITY/BAS. Load the program and run it. The program asks what kind of problem (present value or future value) we want to solve. You press <F> because you have a future value problem. The program then asks if you want to calculate the amount of the payments or the lump sum amount. Press <A> because you want to know the amount to set aside per period. Enter the data on interest rate, number of compounding periods (1), and number of years as requested by the computer. Check the data for accuracy. When you are certain the data is correct, the program will perform the necessary calculations. The results are displayed on the crt.

THE FUTURE VALUE OF THE ANNUITY IS $11,000.00
1 PAYMENTS OF $1,545.99 PER YEAR FOR 5 YEARS
12.00% INTEREST PER YEAR.

You must set aside $1,545.99 per year at 12 percent interest compounded yearly to have $11,000 in five years.

Example 2: Yearly Savings

You are setting up a college education fund. You estimate that each of the four years of college will cost $7,000. You have 15 years before the money will be needed. How much must you save each year if the interest rate is 12 percent?

There are two parts to this question. First, you must determine how much money will be needed. You know that you need $7,000 for 4 years and that the interest rate is 12 percent. Second, you must determine how much you need to save per year to provide this amount.

The first part of this question is a present value problem. You want to know what lump sum you must deposit at 12 percent to be able to withdraw $7,000 per year for four years. The crt display for this part is:

THE PRESENT VALUE OF THE ANNUITY IS $23,812.80
PERIODIC PAYMENT OF $7,000.00 MADE 1 TIMES A YEAR
FOR 4 YEARS WITH AN INTEREST RATE OF 12.00%

So you know you must have $23,812.80 in the bank drawing 12.00 percent interest per year to pay for college.

Now that you know the lump sum that you must have, you can use the future value part of the program to find the amount you must save each year. This is a future value problem like Example 1. The computer display is

THE FUTURE VALUE OF THE ANNUITY IS $23,812.80

1 PAYMENTS OF $570.32 PER YEAR FOR 15 YEARS
12.00% INTEREST PER YEAR.

You have to put aside $570.32 per year to pay for college.

You can see how useful this little program can be. It provides you with the answers to many common financial problems with minimum effort on your part. A considerable amount of work with pencil, paper, and tables would be required to do the same job without the computer. It is worth adding this program to your program library.

BORROWED MONEY

The remaining question concerning interest is, how much does it cost to borrow money? Since most investments are financed, at least in part, by borrowed money, this question is very important.

The basic kinds of loans are:

- Loans where periodic interest payments are made and the principal is paid at the end of the loan term.
- Loans where the total amount, interest plus principal, is due at the end of the loan term.
- Loans where periodic payments are made to pay interest and principal. The loan is fully paid at the end of the period.
- Loans where periodic payments are made to pay both principal and interest but with a large payment (called the balloon) at the end of the loan.

Most of us are familiar with the third type of loan. Our homes, cars, and most other expensive items were purchased with this type of loan. Early payments are mostly interest; later payments are mostly principal.

The first type of loan is fairly common for short term borrowing. Many of us have used this type of loan for one reason or another.

LOAN/BAS PROGRAM

The fourth type of loan is typical of some second mortgages. The LOAN/BAS program handles all types of loans. The program results are displayed on the crt; there is a user option that provides for hard copy to be printed on a line printer. The program is constructed in modules. The first module initializes everything, the second gets information from the user. The third module calculates the loan payments. The important equation for this module is:

$$P = Ar/[1 - (1+r)^{-nm}]$$

where P is the periodic payment, A is the initial amount of the loan, r is the interest rate as a decimal fraction per period ($r = i/n$ where i is the annual interest rate), n is the number of payments per year, the m is the life of the loan in years.

The fourth module is the crt display module. The final module is the line printer output module. Note that the line printer output provides a copy of the complete input data and the complete details of the loan pay back. The program includes code to round the payment to the nearest cent.

The instructions for using the program are displayed on the crt. To use the program, select from the menu the type of loan in which you are interested. The menu is shown in Fig. 3-3. Press the key indicating your type of loan. You don't have to press <ENTER>.

After you have selected the type of loan, you are in the data entry portion of the program. The crt display after you first enter the data entry portion is shown in Fig. 3-4. You provide the required information as to amount of the loan, interest rate, number of payments per year, number of years, and balloon if any. After you have entered the data, it is displayed on the crt for verification (see Fig. 3-5). If you see an error press <N> and you will be transferred back to data entry. If the current value is correct press <ENTER>. If the value is incorrect, enter a new value.

Program execution does not start until you have verified your data. Then the program does all

```
LOAN PAYMENT CALCULATOR PROGRAM.

THIS PROGRAM WILL CALCULATE THE LOAN PAYMENT

SCHEDULE FOR THE FOLLOWING TYPES OF LOANS:

   1. PERIODIC INTEREST PAYMENTS THEN A LUMP SUM PRINCIPAL

   2  PERIODIC INTEREST AND PRINCIPAL PAYMENTS NO BALLOON

   3. PERIODIC INTEREST AND PRINCIPAL PAYMENTS WITH BALLOON

   4. TOTAL INTEREST AND PRINCIPAL DUE AT END OF LOAN.

PLEASE SELECT WHICH TYPE OF LOAN YOU WANT 1, 2  3  OR 4.

JUST PRESS THE NUMBER YOU WANT. YOU DO NOT NEED TO PRESS

<ENTER>
```

Fig. 3-3. Crt display of instructions for loan program.

```
INPUT DATA FOR LOAN PROGRAM. ENTER INFORMATION ASKED FOR.

PRESS <ENTER> AFTER EACH ITEM. IF YOU MAKE A MISTAKE

KEEP GOING  YOU WILL HAVE A CHANCE TO CORRECT THE ERROR

BEFORE CALCULATIONS BEGIN.

THE CURRENT VALUE IS SHOWN IN <>

AMOUNT TO BE BORROWED ($          0.00)?
```

Fig. 3-4. Initial crt display of input data.

```
PLEASE CHECK THE INFORMATION TO INSURE THAT IT IS CORRECT.

AMOUNT TO BE BORROWED           $    1,000.00

ANNUAL INTEREST RATE                   10.00%

NUMBER OF PERIODS/YEAR                  4

NUMBER OF YEARS                         3.00

ARE THESE CORRECT Y OR N?
```

Fig. 3-5. Crt display after all data is entered.

necessary calculations. Summary results are displayed on the crt. You are then asked if you want detailed results displayed on the crt. If you answer Y, a complete loan schedule is displayed on the crt. The schedule is shown a screen full at a time. When you want to move to the next screen, press any key.

Finally, you are asked if you want a hard copy of the calculated loan schedule. If so, all of the input data is printed. Then the loan summary data followed by the detailed loan schedule are printed.

After all data is printed, you are asked if you want to run another case. If so, you are returned to the input data section of the program. All information from your first loan is still available. Thus you can change one or two variables such as the interest rate to see how your loan schedule is affected.

Two sample runs for the normal loan with no balloon and a loan with a balloon follow.

LOAN/BAS Listing

```
10 REM PROGRAM LOAN
20 REM VERSION 1.0 JAN 1982
30 REM WRITTEN BY LES IN MICROSOFT BASIC
40 REM DEDUGGED AND TESTED ON TRS-80 MODEL I AND III
50 REM REF INVESTMENT ANALYSIS BY MICROCOMPUTER TAB BOOKS
60 REM ************************************************
70 REM VARIABLES  R INTEREST RATE % PER YEAR
80 REM A AMOUNT OF LOAN, B BALANCE LEFT ON LOAN
90 REM P PERIODIC PAYMENT, BX AMOUNT OF BALLOON PAYMENT
100 REM C1 AND C2 ARE CHECKS TO MAKE SURE THAT EVERYTHING IS
110 REM GOING OK
120 REM ************************************************
130 CLEAR 100
```

```
140 DEFINT J : REM REMOVE FOR APPLE II AND PET
150 D$ = "$####,##.##"
160 CLS : REM USE HOME FOR APPLE II
170 PRINT "LOAN PAYMENT CALCULATOR PROGRAM."
180 PRINT "THIS PROGRAM WILL CALCULATE THE LOAN PAYMENT"
190 PRINT "SCHEDULE FOR THE FOLLOWING TYPES OF LOANS :"
200 PRINT TAB(3);"1. PERIODIC INTEREST PAYMENTS THEN A LUMP
SUM PRINCIPAL."
210 PRINT TAB(3);"2. PERIODIC INTEREST AND PRINCIPAL PAYMENTS
WITH NO BALLOON"
220 PRINT TAB(3);"3. PERIODIC INTEREST & PRINCIPAL PAYMENTS
WITH BALLOON"
230 PRINT TAB(3);"4. TOTAL INTEREST AND PRINCIPAL DUE AT END
OF LOAN."
240 PRINT
250 PRINT "PLEASE SELECT WHICH TYPE OF LOAN YOU WANT 1,2,3,OR
4"
260 PRINT "JUST PRESS THE NUMBER YOU WANT. YOU DO NOT NEED TO
PRESS <ENTER>"
270 Y$ = INKEY$: IF Y$ = "" THEN 270  ELSE IF
INSTR("1234",Y$)=0 THEN PRINT "PLEASE PRESS 1,2,3 OR
4.":GOTO250
280 K1 = INSTR("1234",Y$)
290 ON INSTR("1234",Y$) GOSUB 340  ,670  ,670  ,890
300 CLS
310 PRINT "DO YOU WANT TO RUN ANOTHER ONE Y OR N?"
320 GOSUB 1160
330 IF Y$ = "Y" THEN  160  ELSE END
340 REM INTEREST ONLY THEN PAY PRINCIPAL SIMPLE INTEREST
350 CLS
360 K = 1
370 GOSUB 1190 : REM GET INPUT DATA
380 REM NOW HAVE ALL DATA
390 CLS
400 PRINT "CALCULATING "
410 R1 = R/100/N
420 P = R1*A
430 P = INT(R1*A*100)/100 : REM ROUND PAYMENT TO NEAREST CENT
440 REM NOW HAVE PAYMENT PER PERIOD
450 CLS
460 PRINT
470 PRINT USING "THE PAYMENT SCHEDULE FOR $#####,#.##
BORROWED FOR ##.## YRS";A;M
480 PRINT USING "WITH ### PAYMENTS PER YEAR IS $#####,#.## PER
PERIOD":N:P
```

```
490 PRINT USING "FOLLOWED BY A FINAL PAYMENT OF
$######,#.##":A
500 PRINT USING "TOTAL INTEREST PAID IS $######,#.##" P*M*N
510 PRINT
520 PRINT "PRESS ANY KEY TO CONTINUE."
530 Y$ = INKEY$ : IF Y$ = "" THEN 530
540 CLS
550 PRINT "DO YOU WANT HARD COPY Y OR N?"
560 GOSUB 1160
570 IF Y$ = "N" THEN RETURN
580 PRINT "BE SURE PRINTER IS ON."
590 LPRINT "RESULTS OF LOAN PROGRAM"
600 LPRINT "TYPE OF LOAN IS PERIODIC INTEREST PAYMENTS
FOLLOWED BY SINGLE PAYMENT OF PRINCIPAL"
610 GOSUB 2470
620 LPRINT " "
630 LPRINT "RESULTS "
640 LPRINT "PERIODIC PAYMENT IS    $#####,#.##";P
650 LPRINT "TOTAL INTEREST PAID IS $######,#.##" P*M*N
660 RETURN
670 REM NORMAL LEVEL PAYMENT LOAN
680 C1 = 0 : B = A
690 CLS
700 IF K1 <> 3 THEN K=1 ELSE K=-1
710 GOSUB 1190
720 R1 = R/100/N
730 R2 = 1 -(1+R1)[-(M*N)
740 R2 = R2/R1
750 P = A/R2
760 CLS
770 PRINT
780 PRINT USING "THE PERIODIC PAYMENT TO PAY OFF
$######,#.##";A
790 PRINT USING "BORROWED FOR ##.## YEARS WITH ## PAYMENTS PER
YEAR ";M;N
800 PRINT USING "IS $####,#.## PER PERIOD " P
810 PRINT
820 PRINT "DO YOU WANT TO SEE THE PAYMENT SCHEDULE Y OR N?"
830 GOSUB 1160
840 IF Y$ = "Y" THEN GOSUB 1470
850 PRINT "DO YOU WANT HARD COPY Y OR N?"
860 GOSUB 1160
870 IF Y$ = "Y" THEN GOSUB 1870
880 RETURN
890 REM ALL MONEY DUE AT END OF LOAN ASSUME THAT INTEREST IS
```

```
COMPOUNDED
900 PRINT "ALL PRINCIPAL PLUS INTEREST DUE AT END OF LOAN
LIFE."
910 PRINT "IT IS ASSUMED THAT THE INTEREST IS COMPOUNDED."
920 K = 1
930 GOSUB 1190
940 R1 = R/100/N
950 ID = R1*A : REM INTEREST DUE
960 P = A*(1+R1)[(M*N)
970 CLS
980 PRINT
990 PRINT USING "YOU MUST PAY $######,#.## AT THE END OF ##.##
YEARS " P,M
1000 PRINT USING "TO BORROW $######,#.## AT ##.##% INTEREST
WITH ### PERIODS/YEAR";A;R;N
1010 PRINT USING "YOU PAID $#####,#.## IN INTEREST.";P-A
1020 PRINT
1030 PRINT "DO YOU WANT HARD COPY Y OR N?"
1040 GOSUB 1160
1050 IF Y$ = "N" THEN RETURN
1060 PRINT "BE SURE PRINTER IS ON."
1070 LPRINT " "
1080 LPRINT "RESULTS OF LOAN CALCULATIONS."
1090 GOSUB 2470
1100 LPRINT " "
1110 LPRINT "RESULTS "
1120 LPRINT USING "THE FINAL PAYMENT IS $######,##.##"·P
1130 LPRINT USING "THE INTEREST PAID IS $######,##.##":P-A
1140 RETURN
1150 END
1160 REM GET A Y OR N RESPONSE
1170 Y$ = INKEY$ : IF Y$ = "" THEN 1170 ELSE IF
INSTR("YN",Y$)=0 THEN PRINT "PLEASE ANSWER Y OR N.":GOTO 1170
1180 RETURN
1190 CLS
1200 PRINT "INPUT DATA FOR LOAN PROGRAM. ENTER INFORMATION
ASKED FOR."
1210 PRINT "PRESS <ENTER> AFTER EACH ITEM. IF YOU MAKE A
MISTAKE,"
1220 PRINT "KEEP ON GOING. YOU WILL HAVE A CHANCE TO CORRECT
THE ERROR"
1230 PRINT "BEFORE CALCULATIONS BEGIN."
1240 PRINT "THE CURRENT VALUE IS SHOWN I ()"
1250 PRINT USING "AMOUNT TO BE BORROWED ($######,#.##)";A;
1260 INPUT A
```

```
1270 PRINT USING "ANNUAL INTEREST RATE  (##.##%)";R;
1280 INPUT R
1290 PRINT USING "NUMBER OF PERIODS/YEAR (###)";N;
1300 INPUT N
1310 PRINT USING "NUMBER OF YEARS        (##.##)":M;
1320 INPUT M
1330 IF K = 1 THEN 1360 : TRANSFER OUT
1340 PRINT USING "AMOUNT OF BALOON PAYMENT ($#####,#.##)";BX
1350 INPUT BX
1360 CLS
1370 PRINT "PLEASE CHECK THE INFORMATION TO INSURE THAT IT IS
CORRECT."
1380 PRINT USING "AMOUNT TO BE BORROWED      $######,#.##";A
1390 PRINT USING "ANNUAL INTEREST RATE              ##.##%";R
1400 PRINT USING "NUMBER OF PERIODS/YEAR            ###";N
1410 PRINT USING "NUMBER OF YEARS                   ##.##";M
1420 IF K = 1 THEN 1440
1430 PRINT USING "AMOUNT OF BALLOON $######,#.##";BX
1440 PRINT "ARE THESE CORRECT Y OR N"
1450 GOSUB 1160
1460 IF Y $ = "Y" THEN RETURN ELSE 1190
1470 REM
1480 B = A
1490 BZ = BX
1500 REM CRT DISPLAY OF PAYMENT SCHEDULE FOR LOAN
1510 CLS
1520 S1 = 0 : S2=0: S3 = 0
1530 IF K<>-1 THEN BX = -1:BZ=-1
1540 P = INT(100.000000*P)/100.000000000
1550 FOR J = 1 TO M
1560   CLS
1570    PRINT "PAYMENT SCHEDULE FOR YEAR ";J
1580    PRINT "PAY
#";TAB(15);"INTEREST":TAB(30);"PRINCIPAL";TAB(45);"BALANCE"
1590    FOR J1 = 1 TO N
1600            IP = B*R1
1610            IP = INT(100*IP)/100
1620            PP = P - IP
1630            C1 = C1 + PP
1640            IF C1 > A THEN PP =B : P = PP + IP
1650           IF BZ >= B THEN 1790
1660            S1 = IP + S1
1670            S2 = S2 + P
1680            S3 = S3 + PP
```

```
1690              B = B - PP
1700              PRINT J1;TAB(15);
1710              PRINT USING D$;IP;:PRINT TAB(30);
1720              PRINT USING D$;PP;:PRINT TAB(45);
1730              PRINT USING D$;B
1740     NEXT J1
1750     PRINT "PRESS ANY KEY TO CONTINUE "
1760     Y$ = INKEY$: IF Y$ = "" THEN 1760
1770 NEXT J
1780 GOTO 1840
1790 PRINT "BALLOON DUE NOW ":
1800 IF BZ > B THEN BZ = B
1810 S3 = S3 + BX
1820 S1 = IP + S1
1830 S2 = S2 + BZ + IP
1840 PRINT USING "PAID $#######,##.##  INTEREST $#####,#.##
PRINCIPAL $#####,##.##";S2;S1;S3
1850 PRINT "PRESS ANY KEY TO RETURN "
1860 Y$ = INKEY$ : IF Y$ = "" THEN 1860 ELSE RETURN
1870 REM HARD COPY FOR NORMAL LOAN
1880 LPRINT " "
1890 LPRINT "OUTPUT FOR LOAN "
1900 LPRINT " "
1910 GOSUB 2470
1920 LPRINT " "
1930 IF K <> -1 THEN BX = -1
1940 B = A :BZ = BX
1950 LC = 0
1960 S1=0
1970 S2=0
1980 S3=0
1990 PN% = 1
2000 CX = 0
2010 IF K = 1 THEN LC = 8 ELSE LC = 9
2020 FOR J = 1 TO M
2030  IF LC = 8 OR LC =9 OR LC = 0 THEN LPRINT
"PAYMENT";TAB(15);"AMOUNT";TAB(30);"INTEREST";TAB(45);"PRINCIP-
AL";TAB(60);"BALANCE"
2040    FOR J1 = 1 TO N
2050              IP = R1*B
2060              IP = INT(IP*100)/100
2070              PP = P - IP
2080             IF B <= BZ THEN 2320
2090              IF PP > B THEN PP = B: P = PP+IP
2100              S1 = S1 + IP
```

```
2110             S2 = S2 + P
2120             S3 = S3 + PP
2130             B = B - PP
2140            LPRINT TAB(5);
2150             LPRINT PN%;TAB(10);
2160            PN% = PN% + 1
2170             LPRINT USING D$;P;
2180             LPRINT TAB(30);
2190             LPRINT USING D$;IP;
2200             LPRINT TAB(45);
2210             LPRINT USING D$·PP;
2220             LPRINT TAB(60);
2230             LPRINT USING D$;B
2240            LC = LC + 1
2250            IF LC > 58 THEN PRINT"PUT NEW SHEET IN PRINTER"
ELSE 2290
2260            PRINT "PRESS ANY KEY WHEN READY."
2270            LC = 0
2280            Y$ = INKEY$ : IF Y$ = "" THEN 2280
2290   NEXT J1
2300 NEXT J
2310 GOTO 2410
2320 LPRINT TAB(20);"BALLOON DUE NOW!"
2330 IF BZ > B THEN BZ = B
2340 LPRINT TAB(5);PN%;TAB(15);:LPRINT USING D$;IP+BZ;
2350 LPRINT TAB(30);:LPRINT USING D$;IP;
2360 LPRINT TAB(45);:LPRINT USING D$;BZ;
2370 LPRINT TAB(60);:LPRINT USING D$;0.00
2380 S1 = S1 + IP
2390 S2 = S2 + BZ + IP
2400 S3 = S3 + BZ
2410 LPRINT " "
2420 LPRINT STRING$(63,"=")
2430 LPRINT TAB(20);"TOTALS"
2440 LPRINT USING "PAYMENT $######,##.##  INTEREST
$#####,#.## PRINCIPAL $######,##.##";S2;S1;S3
2450 RETURN
2460 END
2470 LPRINT " "
2480 LPRINT TAB(5);
2490 LPRINT "INPUT DATA "
2500 LPRINT TAB(5);
2510 LPRINT USING "AMOUNT OF LOAN
$#####,#.##";A
2520 LPRINT TAB(5);
```

```
2530 LPRINT USING "ANNUAL INTEREST RATE
##.##%";R
2540 LPRINT TAB(5);
2550 LPRINT USING "NUMBER OF PAYMENTS PER YEAR          ##
";N
2560 LPRINT TAB(5);
2570 LPRINT USING "LIFE OF LOAN                          ###.##
YRS";M
2580 LPRINT TAB(5);
2590 IF K = 1 THEN RETURN
2600 LPRINT USING "AMOUNT OF BALLOON
$######,#.##";BX
2610 RETURN
```

Example 1: Loan Payment Schedule

Let's assume you want to borrow $40,000 for 7 years. The bank is willing to loan you the money at 15 percent per year with quarterly payments. You want to know what the payment schedule for the loan looks like: run LOAN/BAS; data is entered and the hard copy option selected. The results are shown in Fig. 3-6. The quarterly payment is $2,331.82 and you paid $65,291 of which $25,290.50 is interest. (There is an error of $0.50 because of the limited precision math used by the computer. This is discussed later.)

Example 2: Loan Payment Schedule

Now let's rerun the above example but with the assumption that the entire loan will be paid as soon as the balance reaches $10,000. The hardcopy output is shown in Fig. 3-7. Twenty five payments were made instead of 28 and $24,797 was paid in interest instead of $25,290.50.

VARIABLE RATE LOANS

Variable rate loans have become popular with banks, who are trying to shift the risk to you. Calculation of the loan payment schedule for such loans is more complicated than the calculation for fixed rate loans. The actual loan schedule will not be known until the loan is paid off. However, it is essential to develop a forecasted loan schedule based on reasonable assumptions about future interest rates for the loan. Techniques of forecasting future loan rates are discussed in Chapter 14. The LOAN/BAS program above, can also be used to forecast the loan schedule for the following case.

One method of analyzing variable rate loans is to allow the loan payments to vary as the interest rate changes. The calculations are fairly simple. Compute the amortization schedule for the loan with the original amount. When the interest rate changes, calculate a new amortization schedule to pay off the remaining principal. If the interest rate changes again, compute a third amortization schedule to pay off the remaining principal. For this type of calculation both the principal and interest payments vary each time the interest rates change.

Example: Variable Rate Loan Calculations

Suppose you take out a $40,000.00 variable rate loan. The life of the loan is five years with quarterly payments. The bank can raise or lower the interest rate at the end of each year. The original interest rate is 16 percent. Your crystal ball tells you that the original rate will hold for two years, at which time interest rates will jump to 18 percent for two years and then drop to 12 percent for the remaining year. You would like to know what your

OUTPUT FOR LOAN

INPUT DATA	
AMOUNT OF LOAN	$ 40,000.00
ANNUAL INTEREST RATE	15.00%
NUMBER OF PAYMENTS PER YEAR	4
LIFE OF LOAN	7.00 YRS

PAYMENT	AMOUNT	INTEREST	PRINCIPAL	BALANCE
1	$ 2,331.82	$ 1,500.00	$ 831.82	$ 39,168.20
2	$ 2,331.82	$ 1,468.80	$ 863.02	$ 38,305.20
3	$ 2,331.82	$ 1,436.44	$ 895.38	$ 37,409.80
4	$ 2,331.82	$ 1,402.86	$ 928.96	$ 36,480.80
5	$ 2,331.82	$ 1,368.03	$ 963.79	$ 35,517.00
6	$ 2,331.82	$ 1,331.88	$ 999.94	$ 34,517.10
7	$ 2,331.82	$ 1,294.39	$ 1,037.43	$ 33,479.70
8	$ 2,331.82	$ 1,255.48	$ 1,076.34	$ 32,403.30
9	$ 2,331.82	$ 1,215.12	$ 1,116.70	$ 31,286.60
10	$ 2,331.82	$ 1,173.24	$ 1,158.58	$ 30,128.00
11	$ 2,331.82	$ 1,129.80	$ 1,202.02	$ 28,926.00
12	$ 2,331.82	$ 1,084.72	$ 1,247.10	$ 27,678.90
13	$ 2,331.82	$ 1,037.95	$ 1,293.87	$ 26,385.10
14	$ 2,331.82	$ 989.43	$ 1,342.39	$ 25,042.70
15	$ 2,331.82	$ 939.09	$ 1,392.73	$ 23,649.90
16	$ 2,331.82	$ 886.87	$ 1,444.95	$ 22,205.00
17	$ 2,331.82	$ 832.68	$ 1,499.14	$ 20,705.80
18	$ 2,331.82	$ 776.46	$ 1,555.36	$ 19,150.50
19	$ 2,331.82	$ 718.14	$ 1,613.68	$ 17,536.80
20	$ 2,331.82	$ 657.63	$ 1,674.19	$ 15,862.60
21	$ 2,331.82	$ 594.84	$ 1,736.98	$ 14,125.60
22	$ 2,331.82	$ 529.71	$ 1,802.11	$ 12,323.50
23	$ 2,331.82	$ 462.13	$ 1,869.69	$ 10,453.80
24	$ 2,331.82	$ 392.01	$ 1,939.81	$ 8,514.03
25	$ 2,331.82	$ 319.27	$ 2,012.55	$ 6,501.48
26	$ 2,331.82	$ 243.80	$ 2,088.02	$ 4,413.46
27	$ 2,331.82	$ 165.50	$ 2,166.32	$ 2,247.14
28	$ 2,331.82	$ 84.26	$ 2,247.14	$ 0.00

==

TOTALS

PAYMENT $ 65,291.00 INTEREST $ 25,290.50 PRINCIPAL $ 40,000.00

Fig. 3-6. Hard copy for example 1 using LOAN/BAS.

loan payments will be. Load and run LOAN/BAS. Select the normal loan and supply the data for the original loan. You want hard copy (Fig. 3-8).

The balance at the end of two years is $27,622.70. This becomes your new loan amount with a new loan interest rate of 18 percent. The loan

```
OUTPUT FOR LOAN


     INPUT DATA
     AMOUNT OF LOAN                        $  40,000.00
     ANNUAL INTEREST RATE                      15.00%
     NUMBER OF PAYMENTS PER YEAR               4
     LIFE OF LOAN                              7.00 YRS
     AMOUNT OF BALLOON                     $  10,000.00

PAYMENT        AMOUNT         INTEREST         PRINCIPAL         BALANCE
      1    $  2,331.82     $   1,500.00     $       831.82     $ 39,168.20
      2    $  2,331.82     $   1,468.80     $       863.02     $ 38,305.20
      3    $  2,331.82     $   1,436.44     $       895.38     $ 37,409.80
      4    $  2,331.82     $   1,402.86     $       928.96     $ 36,480.80
      5    $  2,331.82     $   1,368.03     $       963.79     $ 35,517.00
      6    $  2,331.82     $   1,331.88     $       999.94     $ 34,517.10
      7    $  2,331.82     $   1,294.39     $   1,037.43     $ 33,479.70
      8    $  2,331.82     $   1,255.48     $   1,076.34     $ 32,403.30
      9    $  2,331.82     $   1,215.12     $   1,116.70     $ 31,286.60
     10    $  2,331.82     $   1,173.24     $   1,158.58     $ 30,128.00
     11    $  2,331.82     $   1,129.80     $   1,202.02     $ 28,926.00
     12    $  2,331.82     $   1,084.72     $   1,247.10     $ 27,678.90
     13    $  2,331.82     $   1,037.95     $   1,293.87     $ 26,385.10
     14    $  2,331.82     $     989.43     $   1,342.39     $ 25,042.70
     15    $  2,331.82     $     939.09     $   1,392.73     $ 23,649.90
     16    $  2,331.82     $     886.87     $   1,444.95     $ 22,205.00
     17    $  2,331.82     $     832.68     $   1,499.14     $ 20,705.80
     18    $  2,331.82     $     776.46     $   1,555.36     $ 19,150.50
     19    $  2,331.82     $     718.14     $   1,613.68     $ 17,536.80
     20    $  2,331.82     $     657.63     $   1,674.19     $ 15,862.60
     21    $  2,331.82     $     594.84     $   1,736.98     $ 14,125.60
     22    $  2,331.82     $     529.71     $   1,802.11     $ 12,323.50
     23    $  2,331.82     $     462.13     $   1,869.69     $ 10,453.80
     24    $  2,331.82     $     392.01     $   1,939.81     $  8,514.03
                    BALLOON DUE NOW!
     25        $  8,833.30     $     319.27     $   8,514.03     $        0.00

===============================================================
                    TOTALS
PAYMENT $    64,797.00   INTEREST   $   24,797.00 PRINCIPAL $    40,000.00
```

Fig. 3-7. Results for example 2 of LOAN/BAS.

life is now three years (5–2), not two years. Assume that each time the interest rate is adjusted, the new rate holds for the remainder of the loan. Rerun the calculations with the new loan life, balance, and interest rate. The hard copy is shown in Fig. 3-8.

At the end of two years the balance remaining is $10,867.50. Repeat the process for the last year

```
OUTPUT FOR LOAN


     INPUT DATA
     AMOUNT OF LOAN                      $  40,000.00
     ANNUAL INTEREST RATE                       16.00%
     NUMBER OF PAYMENTS PER YEAR                4
     LIFE OF LOAN                               5.00 YRS

PAYMENT        AMOUNT          INTEREST        PRINCIPAL       BALANCE
      1    $  2,943.28      $   1,600.00    $   1,343.28    $ 38,656.70
      2    $  2,943.28      $   1,546.26    $   1,397.02    $ 37,259.70
      3    $  2,943.28      $   1,490.38    $   1,452.90    $ 35,806.80
      4    $  2,943.28      $   1,432.27    $   1,511.01    $ 34,295.80
      5    $  2,943.28      $   1,371.83    $   1,571.45    $ 32,724.40
      6    $  2,943.28      $   1,308.97    $   1,634.31    $ 31.090.10
      7    $  2,943.28      $   1,243.60    $   1,699.68    $ 29,390.40
      8    $  2,943.28      $   1,175.61    $   1,767.67    $ 27,622.70
      9    $  2,943.28      $   1,104.90    $   1,838.38    $ 25,784.30
     10    $  2,943.28      $   1,031.37    $   1,911.91    $ 23,872.40
     11    $  2,943.28      $     954.89    $   1,988.39    $ 21,884.00
     12    $  2,943.28      $     875.36    $   2,067.92    $ 19,816.10
     13    $  2,943.28      $     792.64    $   2,150.64    $ 17,665.50
     14    $  2,943.28      $     706.61    $   2,236.67    $ 15,428.80
     15    $  2,943.28      $     617.15    $   2,326.13    $ 13,102.70
     16    $  2,943.28      $     524.10    $   2,419.18    $ 10,683.50
     17    $  2,943.28      $     427.34    $   2,515.94    $  8,167.58
     18    $  2,943.28      $     326.70    $   2,616.58    $  5,551.01
     19    $  2,943.28      $     222.04    $   2,721.24    $  2,829.77
     20    $  2,943.28      $     113.19    $   2,829.77    $      0.00

===============================================================
                      TOTALS
PAYMENT $   58,865.50  INTEREST  $  18,865.20 PRINCIPAL $   40,000.00

OUTPUT FOR LOAN


     INPUT DATA
     AMOUNT OF LOAN                      $  27,622.70
     ANNUAL INTEREST RATE                       18.00%
     NUMBER OF PAYMENTS PER YEAR                4
     LIFE OF LOAN                               3.00 YRS

PAYMENT        AMOUNT          INTEREST        PRINCIPAL       BALANCE
      1    $  3,029.28      $   1,243.02    $   1,786.26    $ 25,836.40
      2    $  3,029.28      $   1,162.63    $   1,866.65    $ 23,969.80
      3    $  3,029.28      $   1,078.64    $   1,950.64    $ 22,019.10
      4    $  3,029.28      $     990.86    $   2,038.42    $ 19,980.70
      5    $  3,029.28      $     899.13    $   2,130.15    $ 17,850.60
      6    $  3,029.28      $     803.27    $   2,226.01    $ 15,624.60
      7    $  3,029.28      $     703.10    $   2,326.18    $ 13,298.40
      8    $  3,029.28      $     598.42    $   2,430.86    $ 10,867.50
```

Fig. 3-8. Results of variable rate loan example (continued on page 37).

```
      9   $   3,029.28            $       489.03    $   2,540.25     $   8,327.26
     10   $   3,029.28            $       374.72    $   2,654.56     $   5,672.70
     11   $   3,029.28            $       255.27    $   2,774.01     $   2,898.69
     12   $   3,029.28            $       130.44    $   2,898.69     $       0.00

===============================================================
                        TOTALS
PAYMENT $     36,351.40   INTEREST   $     8,728.53 PRINCIPAL $     27,622.70

RESULTS OF LOAN PROGRAM
TYPE OF LOAN IS PERIODIC INTEREST PAYMENTS FOLLOWED BY SINGLE PAYMENT OF PRINCI

     INPUT DATA
     AMOUNT OF LOAN                       $   10,867.50
     ANNUAL INTEREST RATE                        12.00%
     NUMBER OF PAYMENTS PER YEAR                  4
     LIFE OF LOAN                                 1.00 YRS

RESULTS
PERIODIC PAYMENT IS      $#####.#.## 326.02
TOTAL INTEREST PAID IS $######,#.## 1304.08
```

Fig. 3-8. Continued from page 36.

of the loan using the new balance and interest rate and a loan life of one year. The final result is shown in the total hard copy printout. Thus in a very short time you have generated the necessary forecast.

If you total all principal payments, you'll see that you actually paid slightly more than $40,000. This is because of rounding errors caused by the limited precision math used by the computer. This can be a serious problem in financial computing. Double precision can be used (look in your BASIC manual for instructions. Unfortunately, many of the functions necessary for financial calculations are limited to single precision. There are ways to program around this limitation, however the imprecision of computer math is not a serious problem in investment analysis. The problem is mentioned so you will be aware of it. The lack of precision can be a serious problem in book-keeping programs.

The major investment analysis programs use fixed interest rate loans in their calculations. This shortens the code considerably. However, if you have to use a variable interest rate loan in your analysis, just replace the loan amortization module in the program with a variable rate loan module.

Chapter 4

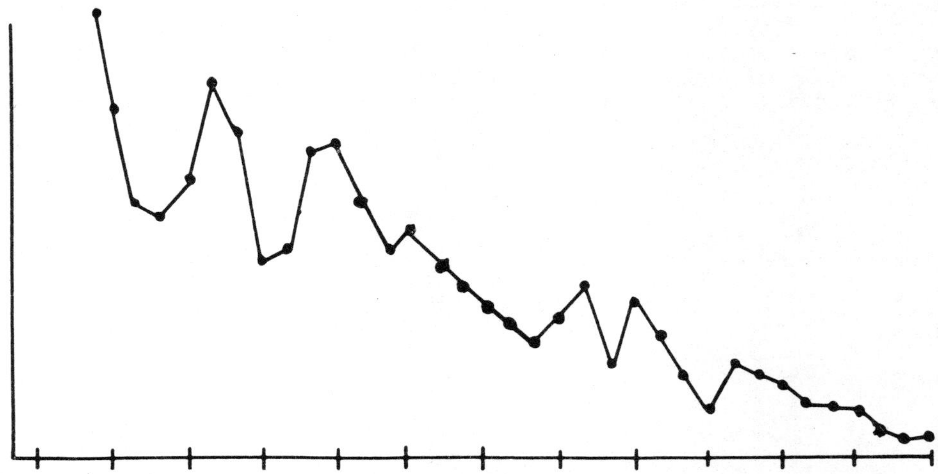

Present Value and Time Value

Time is money; an understanding of the meaning of this is crucial to sound, profitable investment decision making. Correct analysis of the time factor often makes the difference between a successful investor and one who goes broke. Once you understand the relation between time and money, you are on your way to becoming a successful investor.

Chapter 3 demonstrated that interest can turn today's dollars into more of tomorrow's dollars. This simple fact—interest can make today's dollars grow—is what the time value of money is all about. It is also why consideration of the time factor is so important.

TIMING OF CASH FLOWS

Let's use the facts about interest which were developed in the previous chapter and see how timing of cash flows from an investment affects the ultimate value of the investment. We will consider two simple investments. The cash flows from each of these investments are shown below:

Year	Investment A	Investment B
1	$100.00	$100.00
2	$0.00	$200.00
3	$400.00	$100.00
4	$100.00	$200.00
TOTAL	$600.00	$600.00

This is a fairly typical problem in investment analysis. We have two investments that each give the same total return, $600 in this case. Yet the timing of the cash flows is different. The problem is to determine which of these two investments is the more profitable.

Now let's assume that your bank will pay 10 percent interest per year on your money, and that you will put each year's cash flow into the bank. (Assume the money is received at the end of the year. Thus the first year's money earns interest during year 2, and so forth.)

Then for investment A we have the following:

Year	Cash Flow	$Bank	Interest	Total
1	$100.00		0	100.00
2	0	100.00	$10.00	$110.00
3	$400.00	$110.00	$11.00	$521.00
4	$100.00	$521.00	$52.10	$673.10
			TOTAL	$673.10

For investment B we have:

Year	Cash Flow	$Bank	Interest	Total
1	$100.00	$0.00	$0.00	$100.00
2	$200.00	$100.00	$10.00	$310.00
3	$100.00	$310.00	$31.00	$441.00
4	200.00	$441.00	$44.10	$685.10
			TOTAL	$685.10

In this simple example, the interest you can earn on the yearly cash flows allows investment B to return $12 more over the four years than does investment A. The timing of the cash flows adds an additional $12 to the value of investment B. If the cash flow timing were changed so that investment A returned zero dollars for years 1, 2, and 3 and $600.00 in year four, the difference in the returns would be $85.10.

This example clearly shows the importance of the timing of cash flows. The sooner you get your money back, the better. You have to consider the timing to insure that you select the right investment.

FUTVAL/BAS PROGRAM

The calculations above demonstrate the concept of future value. All the cash flows are compared by calculating their values at the end of the investment. A short computer program, FUTVAL/BAS, is provided below to do the arithmetic. The instructions for using the program are displayed on the crt.

FUTVAL/BAS Listing

```
10 REM PROGRAM FUTVAL BY L. E. SPARKS
20 REM REQUIRES MICROSOFT BASIC
30 REM VERSION 1.5 NOV 1981
40 REM VARIABLES A = AMOUNT INVESTED, V = FUTURE VALUE
50 REM R = INTEREST RATE % PER YEAR  N = NUMBER OF YEAR
60 REM M = NUMBER OF COMPOUNDING PERIODS
70 REM *****************************************************
80 I = 0 : J = 0 : M = 0 : R = 0 : V = 0 :REM INITIALIZE
90 CLS
100 PRINT "FUTURE VALUE PROGRAM"
110 PRINT "ENTER DATA ASKED FOR. CURRENT VALUE IS SHOWN IN ()"
120 PRINT
130 PRINT "ENTER AMOUNT INVESTED (";A;")";
140 INPUT A
150 PRINT "ENTER NUMBER OF YEARS (";N;")";
160 INPUT N
170 PRINT "ENTER INTEREST RATE % PER YEAR (";R;")";
180 INPUT R
190 PRINT "ENTER Y FOR YEARLY COMPOUNDING, M FOR
```

```
MONTHLYCOMPOUNDING, W FOR WEEKLY COMPOUNDING, D FOR DAILY
COMPOUNDING,AND C FOR CONTINUOUS COMPOUNDING"
200 INPUT Y$
210 IF INSTR("YMDWC",Y$) = 0 THEN PRINT "INCORRECT RESPONSE":
GOTO 190
220 IF Y$ ="Y" THEN M=1 ELSE IF Y$ = "M" THEN M =12 ELSE IF Y$ =
"W" THEN M = 52 ELSE IF Y$ = "D" THEN M =365 ELSE GOTO 370
230 CLS
240 PRINT
250 REM NOW KNOW COMPOUNDING PERIOD
260 IF M = 1 THEN C$="YEARLY" ELSE IF M = 12 THEN C$="MONTHLY"
ELSE IF M =52 THEN C$ = "WEEKLY" ELSE C$ ="DAILY"
270 V = A*(1 + R/100/M)[(M*N) :REM NOTE THAT [ IS THE UP ARROW
280 PRINT USING "PRESENT VALUE OF $#,######.## AT ##.##% PER
YEARFOR ### YEARS WITH %         % COMPOUNDING IS
$#,######.##";A;R;N;C$;V
290 PRINT
300 PRINT"DO YOU WANT HARD COPY Y OR N?"
310 Y$ = INKEY$: IF Y$ = "" THEN 310
320 IF Y$ ="Y" THEN LPRINT USING "THE FUTURE VALUE OF
$#,######.## INVESTED FOR### YEARS AT ##.##% WITH %          %
COMPOUNDING IS $#,######.##";A;N;R;C$;V
330 PRINT "DO YOU WANT TO DO ANOTHER ONE Y OR N?";
340 Y$=INKEY$: IF Y$="" THEN 340
350 IF Y$ ="N" THEN END ELSE IF Y$<>"Y" THEN PRINT"INCORRECT
RESPONSE":GOTO330
360 GOTO 90
370 REM HERE FOR CONTINOUS COMPOUNDING
380 V = A*EXP(R/100*N)
390 CLS
400 C$="CONTINUOUS"
410 PRINT
420 GOTO 280
```

PRESENT VALUE CONCEPT

The above example showed the importance of the timing of future cash flows from an investment. It also showed how consideration of the timing makes comparison of different investments with different timings of cash flows difficult. The example showed that one way to make valid comparisons is to assume that the cash flows could be invested at some interest rate. Then the total value of the cash flows plus possible interest earnings for the life of the investment were found and compared. In the example, the comparisons were made at the final year of the investment.

The present value concept does the same thing that was done in the example. However, instead of asking the question "How much money will I have at the end of the life of the investment, if I invest the cash flows at some predetermined interest rate?"

we ask the question "How much money would I have to set aside *now* at some predetermined interest rate, to give me the same total cash flow as the investment at the end of its life?"

The amount that we would have to set aside now is called the *present value*. The process of calculating the present value is called *discounting*. The interest rate used in the calculation is called the *discount rate*. The power of the present value concept is that it allows you to compare the value of different investments with different timings of the cash flows.

The equations used to do the present value calculations are given in Fig. 4-1.

Redoing the previous comparison by using the present value method will make the concept clear. Use the PRESVAL/BAS program below to do the necessary calculations.

Note that in the present value analysis, the present is considered to be time zero.

Investment A

Year	Cash Flow	Present Value	Cost of Investment
0		0.00	
1		$100.00	$ 90.91
2		$ 0.00	$ 0.00
3		$400.00	$300.00
4		$100.00	$ 68.30

Total present value = $459.21

1. Present value of a one time payment C.

$$P = C/(1+r)^n \text{ or } P = C(1+r)^{-n}$$

2. Present value of a series of equal cash flows.

$$P = C\{1-[1/(1+r)^n]/r\}$$

where P is the present value, C is the cash flow, r is the discount rate, and n is the number of time periods.

Fig. 4-1. Equations for calculating present value.

Investment B

Year	Cost Flow Present Value	Cost of Investment
0	0.00	
1	$100.00	$ 90.91
2	$200.00	$165.28
3	$100.00	$ 75.13
4	$200.00	$136.60

Total present value = $467.92

What does the present value tell us? What do these numbers have to do with making decisions? First, you can see that if investment A costs more than $459.21, you don't get your money back, and if investment B costs more than $467.92 you don't get your money back. Thus it would be better to bank your money at 10 percent interest than to make the investment.

If investments A and B both cost the same, say $459.21, the results tell you that you broke even with investment A and made $8.71 with investment B. In a present value analysis, you want the present value of the investment to be as high as possible.

Effect of Discount Rate on Present Value

It should be clear from the equations in Fig. 4-1 that the choice of discount rate will determine the present value of an investment. Figure 4-2 shows this effect graphically for an investment of $100.00. As we will see later, the fact that the discount rate determines the present value can greatly affect the choice of investments.

Because of the large effect of the discount rate, it is important to use reasonable values for the discount rate. Generally, the recommended value is the cost of capital for the investment. However, if you know that you can earn a risk-free return greater than the cost of capital (say long term certificate of deposit), then you should use the larger number. If you cannot do better than the certificate of deposit, why look further?

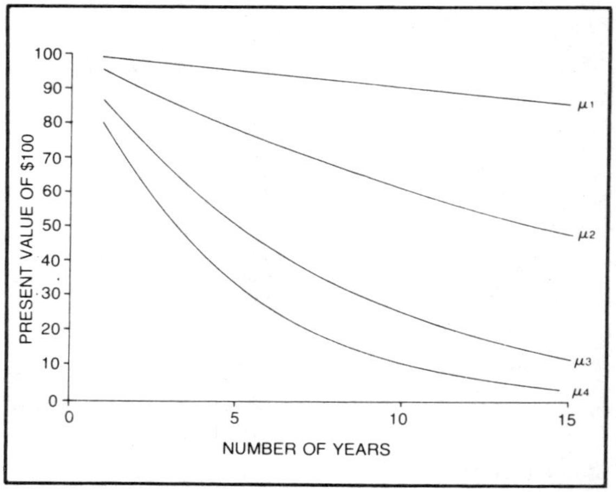

Fig. 4-2. Present value of $100 versus number years for discount rates of 1 percent, five percent, 15 percent, and 25 percent.

We'll look at the use of present value concepts for investment analysis in more detail later. The importance of the discount rate will also be discussed later.

Note that this chapter discussed the fact that a dollar today is worth more than a dollar next year because today's dollar can earn interest. This is not the same as the unpleasant fact that inflation makes a dollar tomorrow worth less than a dollar today. The effects of inflation are discussed in the next chapter.

PRESVAL/BAS PROGRAM

The PRESVAL/BAS program is used as a major module in the larger programs that follow in this book. The program listing follows. Example runs for the program are given below.

PRESVAL/BAS Listing

```
10 REM PRESENT VALUE CALCULATION PROGRAM
20 REM BY L. E. SPARKS WRITTEN IN TRS-80 BASIC
30 REM VERSION 1.5 NOV 1981
40 REM *******************************************
50 REM VARIABLES P=PRESENT VALUE, C= CASH FLOW
60 REM N = NUMBER OF YEARS R = DISCOUNT RATE
70 CLS
80 PRINT
90 PRINT "PROGRAM TO CALCULATE PRESENT VALUE OF FUTURE CASH
FLOWS"
100 PRINT
110 PRINT "<O>NE TIME CASH FLOW."
120 PRINT "<S>ERIES OF EQUAL CASH FLOWS."
130 PRINT "SELECT TYPE OF CALCULATION BY PRESSING O OR S."
140 Y$ = INKEY$ : IF Y$="" THEN 140
150 IF INSTR("OS",Y$) =0 THEN PRINT "PLEASE PRESS O OR S": GOTO
140
160 IF Y$ = "O" THEN GOSUB 220 ELSE GOSUB 330
170 PRINT "DO YOU WANT TO DO ANOTHER ONE Y OR N?"
180 Y$ = INKEY$: IF Y$="" THEN 180
190 IF INSTR("YN",Y$)=0 THEN PRINT "PLEASE ANSWER Y OR N":GOTO
170
200 IF Y$ = "N" THEN END ELSE GOTO 10
```

```
210 END
220 CLS
230 PRINT
240 PRINT "PRESENT VALUE OF ONE TIME CASH FLOW."
250 INPUT "ENTER AMOUNT OF CASH FLOW ";C
260 INPUT "ENTER DISCOUNT RATE IN PERCENT ";R
270 INPUT "ENTER NUMBER OF YEARS TO DISCOUNT ";N
280 P = C/(1+R/100)[N
290 PRINT USING "THE PRESENT VALUE OF $######.## DISCOUNTED OVER
## YEARS"; C,N
300 PRINT USING "AT A DISCOUNT RATE OF ###% IS $######.## "; R P
310 RETURN
320 END
330 REM SUBROUTINE FOR CALCULATION OF SERIES OF EQUAL CASH FLOWS
340 CLS
350 PRINT "PRESENT VALUE OF SERIES OF EQUAL CASH FLOWS."
360 INPUT "ENTER AMOUNT OF CASH FLOW ";C
370 INPUT "ENTER DISCOUNT RATE IN PERCENT ";R
380 INPUT "ENTER NUMBER OF YEARS ";N
390 R1 = R/100 ' CONVERT TO FRACTIONAL INTEREST RATE
400 P = C*(1-(1/(1+R1)[N))/R1
410 PRINT USING "THE PRESENT VALUE OF A SERIES OF EQUAL PAYMENTS
OF $######.##";C
420 PRINT USING "PAID OVER ## YEARS AND DISCOUNTED AT ##.##%
";N,R
430 PRINT USING "IS $######.##":P
440 RETURN
```

Example 1: Sam's offer

Suppose you are offered an opportunity to invest in Sam's get rich quick scheme. Sam promises to pay you $150,000 in five years if you give him $130,000 now. Should you accept Sam's offer? The first problem is to determine the discount rate. Notice that you can earn 10 percent per year on an investment with no risk. This is your opportunity cost and the cost of capital, so it is a good value to use for the discount rate.

You can now run the program since you know the discount rate. The present value of $150,000 received five years in the future with a 10 percent discount rate yields $93,138.20. So you should decline Sam's offer.

Example 2: Sam's Counter Offer

Sam is not to be denied and makes a counter offer. If you give him $35,000 now, he promises to pay back $10,000 a year for five years. Is this better than the above offer?

Run PRESVAL to find that a series of $10,000 yearly payments for five years has a present value of $37,907.90 with a 10 percent discount rate. You should accept Sam's offer. (Unless, of course, you feel that the risk is excessive.)

Chapter 5

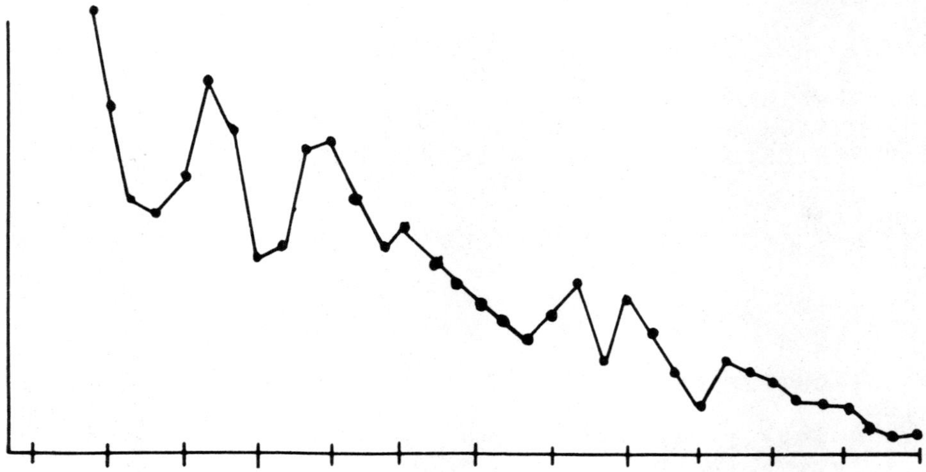

Inflation

In recent years we have all become aware of the effects of inflation. Because the objective of investment is to increase future wealth or purchasing power, it is important to know what the effects of inflation on various investments are. Once we know what the effects are, we may be able to choose investments that offer some protection against inflation.

Inflation is bad for investments for a number of reasons. First, the effect of inflation is large and generally unfavorable. Secondly, inflation is difficult if not impossible to predict. Thus, as you will see later in this chapter, one of the major effects of inflation is to increase the risk of investments, which an investor does not want.

DEFINITIONS

To discuss inflation we will use the following definitions:

- *Inflation* is the increase in the general price level. It basically means that the purchasing power of future dollars is less than the purchasing power of present dollars. The inflation rate has a major impact on the profitability of an investment. Predictions of future inflation rates are generally inaccurate.
- *Escalation* is the rise in the price of a single good or service. The combination of inflation and supply and demand is reflected in the change in price of individual items. Even with no inflation, some items will increase in price. As anyone who has looked at the price of pocket calculators can tell you, prices of some items actually decrease during periods of inflation.
- *Current year dollars* refers to dollars received in a specific year. Note that the current year dollars for any two years may or may not have the same purchasing power. The actual value, in terms of purchasing power, of current year dollars will vary from year to year as the inflation rate varies. Current year dollars are a rubber ruler and provide an

```
PROGRAM INFLAT/BAS

ENTER INFLATION RATE % PER YEAR ? 10
ENTER NUMBER OF YEARS ? 20
ENTER NUMBER OF CURRENT YEAR DOLLARS  20  YEARS FROM NOW? 1E6
THE CONSTANT YEAR DOLLAR VALUE OF $1,000,000.00
AFTER 10.00% INFLATION PER YEAR FOR 20 YEARS
IS $   148,644.00

DO YOU WANT ANOTHER ONE Y OR N?
```

Fig. 5-1. Results of example run for INFLAT/BAS.

imprecise measure of the benefits of various investments.

- *Constant year dollars* refers to dollars with a constant purchasing power referenced to some base year. Constant year dollars provide an absolute ruler for comparing the benefits of various investments. Constant year dollars tell us if we are really increasing our future wealth.

DISCOUNTING

Because the real world deals in current year dollars, it is necessary to convert current year dollars into constant year dollars to determine the effect of inflation on an investment. Current year dollars are converted to constant year dollars by the discounting process—the same way that future cash flows are converted to present value. The inflation rate is used as the discount rate.

INFLAT/BAS PROGRAM

Program INFLAT/BAS is a simple program to convert current year dollars to constant year dollars. An example run of this program is given in Fig. 5-1. The listing follows.

INFLAT/BAS Listing

```
10 REM PROGRAM INFLAT/BAS
20 REM PROGRAM TO SHOW EFFECTS OF INFLATION
30 REM VERSION 1.0 WRITTEN BY LES JAN 1982
40 REM WRITTEN IN MICROSOFT BASIC DEBUGGED ON
50 REM TRS-80 MODEL I AND III
60 REM ************************************
70 REM I = INFLATION RATE %/YEAR
80 REM A = AMOUNT OF CURRENT YEAR DOLLARS
90 REM N = NUMBER OF YEARS
100 REM C = NUMBER OF CONSTANT YEAR DOLLARS
110 REM ************************************
120 CLS
130 PRINT "PROGRAM INFLAT/BAS
140 PRINT
```

```
150 INPUT"ENTER INFLATION RATE % PER YEAR ";I
160 INPUT "ENTER NUMBER OF YEARS ";N
170 PRINT "ENTER NUMBER OF CURRENT YEAR DOLLARS ";N;
180 PRINT " YEARS FROM NOW";
190 INPUT A
200 C = A*(1+I/100)[-N : REM NOTE THAT [ IS THE UP ARROW
210 PRINT USING "THE CONSTANT YEAR DOLLAR VALUE OF $#######.##
";A
220 PRINT USING "AFTER ##.##% INFLATION PER YEAR FOR ## YEARS
";I;N
230 PRINT USING "IS $######,##.##";C
240 PRINT
250 PRINT"DO YOU WANT ANOTHER ONE Y OR N?"
260 Y$ = INKEY$: IF Y$ = "" THEN 260 ELSE IF INSTR("YN",Y$)=0
THEN PRINT "PLEASE ANSWER Y OR N":GOTO 260
270 IF Y $ = "Y" THEN 10 ELSE END
```

INCLUDING INFLATION IN INVESTMENT ANALYSIS

Inflation can be factored into investment analysis in one of two ways. The first way is to convert all future year current dollar cash flows into future year constant year dollars using the INFLAT/BAS program. Then all future year dollars are discounted using the discount rate to determine the constant year dollar present value of the investment.

A simpler way to include inflation is to add the inflation rate to the required discount rate. For example, if the discount rate is 10 percent and the inflation rate is 10 percent, the discounted cash flow calculations would be done using 20 percent as the discount rate.

Although the first method is more complicated, I prefer it because I know what is going on. When the inflation rate and the discount rate are combined, there is a real danger of forgetting that the discount rate includes an inflation component as well as a cost of capital component.

The programs in this book allow inclusion of inflation as a direct factor in the analysis. This makes it possible to clearly separate the effects of inflation from other factors affecting the investment.

Inflation has the following effects on an investment:

1. Inflation affects the profitability of all investments.
2. Inflation can change the ranking of investments.
3. High rates of inflation favor lower capital cost investments.
4. High rates of inflation may make lease alternatives more attractive compared to purchase options.
5. High rates of inflation increase the risk involved in investments by making future constant year dollar returns uncertain.

One of the major effects of inflation is that it increases the risk of an investment. Using too high an inflation rate for investment analysis results in missing good opportunities; using too low a rate can result in accepting poor investments.

Another adverse effect of inflation is that it can force too much attention to short-term payback. High rates of inflation discount the future too much.

Chapter 6

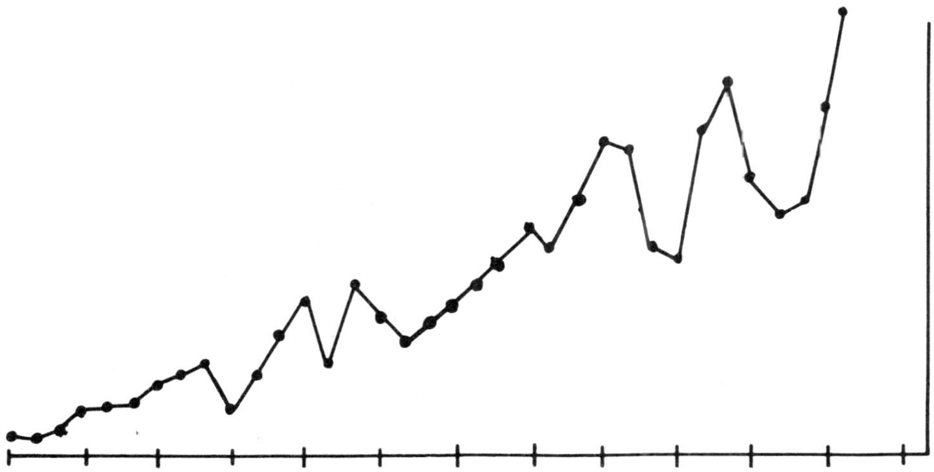

Risk

All investments involve the future, which is unknown. This fact, the unknowability of the future, leads to one fundamental problem of investment analysis: how can investment decisions be made under conditions of uncertainty?

This question must be addressed by anyone who makes investment decisions. It is especially important to consider the risk of an investment when much of the analysis is done with a computer. You must always remember that the initial data used by the computer is uncertain. Otherwise, you can be misled by the seemingly absolute accuracy of computer calculations.

In spite of its importance, the effects of uncertainty or risk are often neglected in investment analysis. Failure to consider risk can have unfortunate consequences; you can go broke.

Because risk is difficult to quantify and because risk is often neglected, we will spend some time examining the risk factor in investment analysis. Another reason for spending so much time on risk is that you must do most of the risk analysis and certainly the risk interpretation by yourself.

Before looking at how a personal computer can help analyze the risk in an investment, let's see what risk is, what the sources of risk are, what risk does to the expected return on an investment, and then try to develop some measures of risk.

DEFINITIONS

What do you mean when you say that an investment is risky? What do you mean when you say that one investment is more risky than another? These questions must be answered before we can develop computer tools to help us analyze risk.

When you talk about risk, you are really talking about uncertainty. An investment is risky because you are unsure about the actual return you will realize from your investment. So we can say that risk is related to the uncertainty of the future returns from an investment.

This definition implies that an investment with a fixed rate of return, for example a savings account, is less risky than an investment with a variable rate of return such as common stock. This is certainly correct in current year dollar terms, but may not be true in constant year dollar terms.

Thus in order to understand the risk or uncertainty in any given investment, you must know the sources of risk for that investment.

ELEMENTS OF RISK

As pointed out above, an investment may be relatively risk free in terms of one set of factors and yet be very risky in terms of other factors. The risk of any investment is made up of several individual components. These components are generally classified as *systematic* or *unsystematic risk*. Systematic risk is caused by factors that simultaneously affect the returns of all investments. Changes in the general economic and political situation are factors which affect systematic risk.

Major sources of systematic risk are: interest rate risk, inflation risk, market risk, and cyclical operating and financial risk.

Interest rate risk is caused by variability in the general level of interest rates. Bonds are an example of an investment that have a high degree of interest rate risk, yet bonds are generally regarded as low risk investments because the rate of return is fixed. Interest rate risk exists because bond prices rise and fall as interest rates change. Thus, although the yield of a bond held to maturity is fixed, the rate of return on a bond sold before maturity is uncertain because of interest rate risk.

Until recently interest rates were fairly constant for reasonable periods of time. Recently, however, interest rates have varied wildly. This means that interest rate risk has probably increased in recent years. Because interest rate risk is systematic, the increase in interest rate risk has probably increased the risk in most, if not all, investments.

Inflation risk is caused by the uncertainty of the future purchasing power of savings or invested wealth. Inflation reduces the purchasing power of savings or invested wealth. If the rate of return is less than the inflation rate, then the real value, or constant dollar value, of the investment will decrease. All fixed rate investments such as passbook savings, bonds, and life insurance have a high degree of inflation risk. With low inflation rates, the inflation risk is small and acceptable. However, when the inflation rate becomes high, the inflation risk is large and perhaps unacceptable. The current high inflation rates increase the inflation rate risk and thus the risk of most investments.

Some investments are less sensitive to inflation risk than are fixed rate savings. However, these investments are more sensitive to other types of risk than are fixed rate savings.

In general there is no perfect hedge against inflation risk. During the years 1926 to 1976 common stocks earned higher real rates of return, on the average, than other investments. Thus for this 50-year period, common stocks were the best hedge against inflation. However, as discussed below, common stocks are sensitive to other types of risks.

Market risk is caused by fluctuations in the market for a given investment. Stocks, collectibles, and real estate are examples of investments with large market risk. Fixed rate savings have very low levels of market risk.

Cyclical operating and financial risk are caused by changes in the general business cycle. These are the risks associated with the state of the general economy and affect many of the same types of investments that are affected by market risk. Cyclical operating and financial risk also affect investments in such areas as new equipment for a company and new business ventures.

In general an investment with a high degree of

systematic risk will give good returns when economic conditions are good and poor returns when economic conditions are bad.

Unsystematic risk is the risk due to factors which only affect a given investment. Examples of sources of unsystematic risk include noncyclical operating risk, management risk, industry risk.

Noncyclical operating risk is not dependent on general economic conditions, but is dependent on the operating factors that affect a particular investment.

Management risk derives from management of a business or other investment. For example, if you invest in stocks and a particular company has poor management, you can go broke even though the rest of the economy is doing well. Management risk also includes the risk involved in how you manage your investments. If you don't pay much attention to them, then you introduce a type of management risk.

Industry risk affects the industry to which your investment belongs. For example, if you invest in rental property, you are subject to the risk of the entire rental industry in your area.

In general an investor has little control over systematic risk since you have little control over the state of the economy. You can take steps to limit the systematic risk, but you don't have much control over that risk.

On the other hand, you can control unsystematic risk to some degree. You can investigate the company you invest in, to be sure it has good management. You can take an active interest in your investments.

Although it is convenient to talk about the various risk factors as if they were independent, they are not, especially for systematic risks. For example, interest rate risk is in some way related to inflation rate risk.

RELATIONSHIP OF RISK TO RETURN

Investors are compensated for assuming more risk by higher returns on their investments. This risk/return relationship is one of the more important parts of investment analysis, though it is often neglected.

The nature of the risk/return relationship will vary somewhat from investor to investor. Some investors will accept more risk for a given return than will others. A general example of the risk/return relationship is shown in Fig. 6-1. From this figure we see that the expected return on any investment is composed of two parts, interest representing the rate for a risk-free investment and a risk premium. This means that the only way to get high returns is to accept high risk. It also means that any investment offering high returns must have high risk associated with it.

Riskless investments are usually considered to be government bonds. As can be seen from Fig. 6-2, the rate of return for government bonds has varied considerably over the past several years. This could be taken to mean that the risk for these bonds has increased.

RANKING INVESTMENTS BY RISK

There have been several studies of the risk involved in various investments. These studies are based on the assumption that the risk-free rate of return is the interest paid by government bonds, and that any investment with higher returns has some element of risk. The results of one such study are shown in Fig. 6-3.

Note that the measure of increasing risk in Fig. 6-3 is the standard deviation of the returns on the investment during the period 1926-1976. The investment with the highest average return was common stock. This investment also had the highest standard deviation and thus the highest risk. The investment with the lowest return was Treasury Bills. These also had the lowest risk as measured by the standard deviation. The average inflation rate for these fifty years was 2.3 percent with a standard deviation of 4.8. The average return

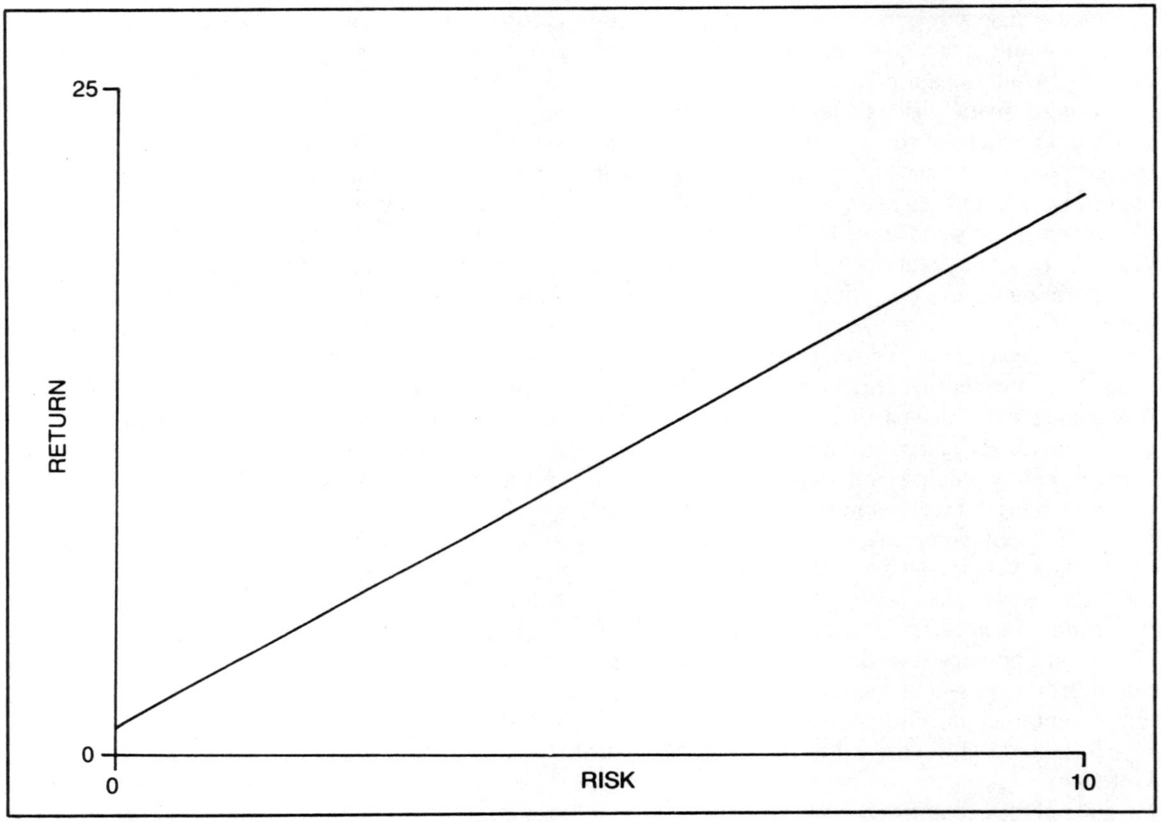

Fig. 6-1. General return versus risk. The units are arbitrary.

on Treasury Bills was 2.4 percent. Thus Treasury Bills returned only slightly more than the average rate of inflation.

These studies show that the more returns from an investment can vary, the greater the risk premium they command. The fact that the return on government bonds has at times been below the inflation rate may indicate that investors undervalue or underestimate the inflation rate risk.

MEASURES OF RISK

In order to analyze the risk in an investment, you need a measure of risk. The lack of a good measure is the major reason why many works on investment analysis neglect risk.

You could simply proceed by intuition, which is not a bad approach to risk. But intuition often finds it difficult to compete with the seemingly unbiased precision of computer calculations. You need to develop a measure of risk that can be used with the computer.

The theoretical literature on investment analysis contains considerable information on risk. The basic idea from the theoretical studies is that a risky investment can be treated as a gamble with a wide range of possible returns. Each of the possible re-

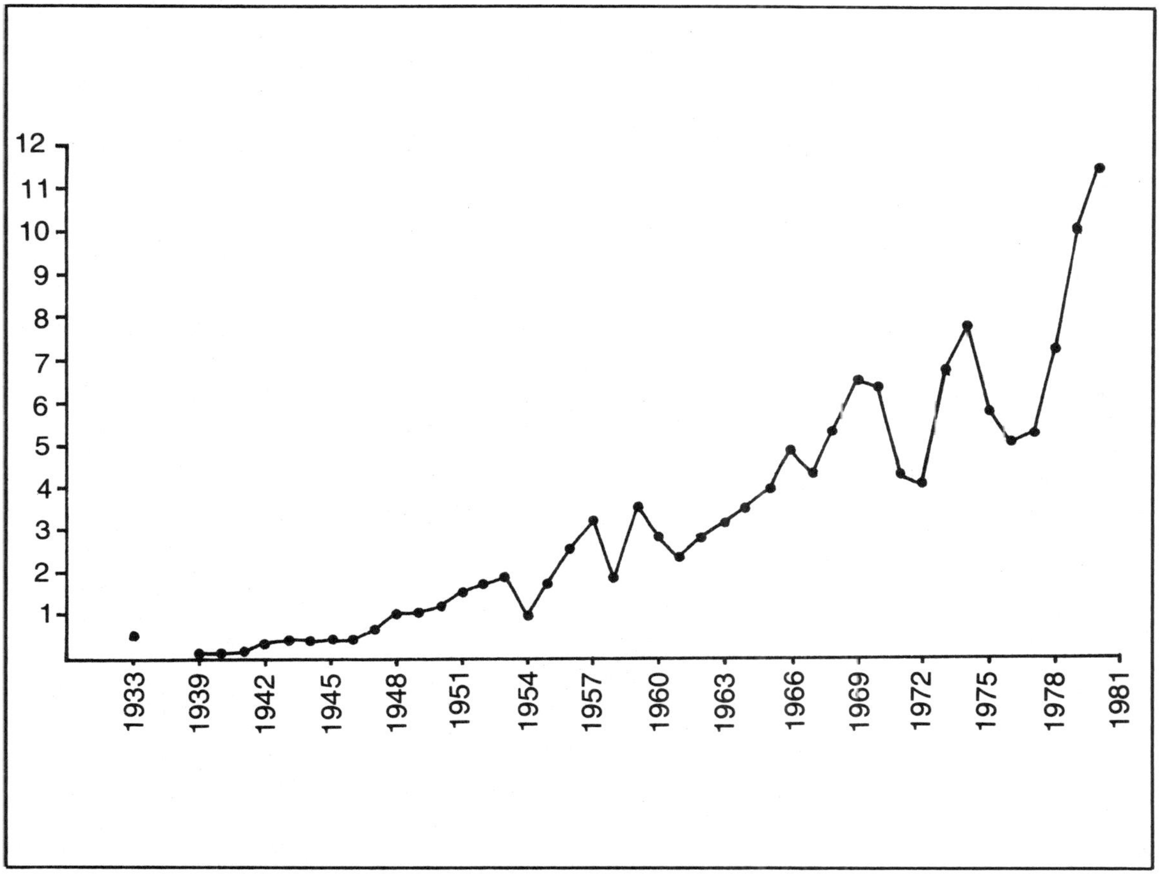

Fig. 6-2. U.S. Treasury bill rate from 1933 to 1981 (reprinted from "Multilinear Regression Analysis" by B. Flynn in *ACCESS*, January/February, 1982.

turns has a finite chance of occurring. If you knew the probability of achieving each of these returns, you could use statistical theory to calculate the expected rate of return and the probability of going broke.

Theoretical analysis along these lines has shown that under not too unrealistic assumptions, the risk in any investment can be characterized by the average and the standard deviation at the rate of return. (The standard deviation is a precise way of defining the uncertainty or spread in the rate of return.) Part of the empirical justification for this analysis is given in Fig. 6-3. Remember that Fig. 6-3 shows that the higher the standard deviation, the higher the average return, and thus the higher the risk.

If you knew the probabilities of all factors affecting your investment, you could quickly calculate the average and the standard deviation of the rate of return.

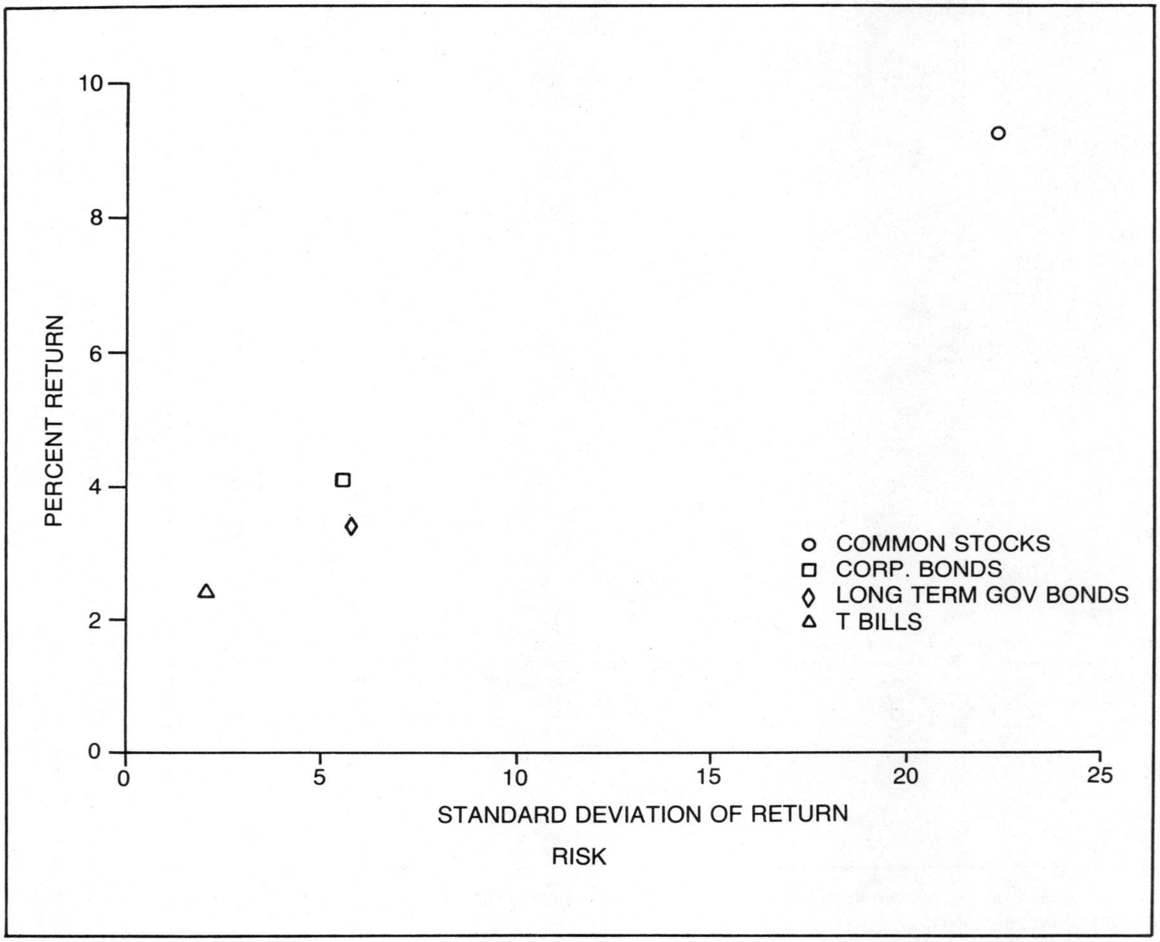

Fig. 6-3. Data showing the risk return relationship for indicated investments for the period 1926 to 1976. The risk is measured by the standard deviation of the return.

Such a situation is exactly what a gambler faces. He knows for all possible bets exactly what the odds are (if we assume an honest game), so he always knows his risk.

Unfortunately, you don't know what the exact odds are for a given investment. The more complicated the investment and the longer its life, the less confident you are. You don't have as much information about the future of your investment as the gambler has.

USING THE COMPUTER TO ANALYZE RISK

A properly designed computer analysis will force you to think about the risk in an investment. Your new tool will often confirm your intuition (if you thought about risk at all). Nevertheless, often it will show that you missed something in your initial intuitive evaluation of risk.

With a properly designed computer program you can vary the important input information affecting the investment to see how the rate of return is affected. If you do this systematically, you can discover which factors a given investment is most sensitive to. Sensitivity analysis is extremely valuable and can give you a feeling for an investment. The analysis will also remind you that computer output depends on the information you supplied.

If you give the computer a range of likely values for each of the important input parameters, and then allow the computer to choose various values of each parameter for a series of simulations, you can obtain another idea about the risk of an investment. An example program using this technique is included in this book.

Basically the technique works by asking you to provide the best estimate, best case, and worst case estimates for income, expenses, inflation rate, and interest rates of the investment. These estimates are then used to construct a probability curve for each of the parameters. The computer then picks random values of each of the parameters to be used in the calculations. The procedure is repeated several times. Then the computer calculates the mean and standard deviation of the net present value of the investment.

RISK PROGRAM

RISK is a short program demonstrating this way of studying the risk in an investment. The purpose of this program is to demonstrate the method. If you find the method useful, then you should look at the INVEST3 program given in Chapter 12. The RISK program listing follows

RISK Listing

```
10 REM PROGRAM RISK BY LES VERSION 1.0 JAN 1982
20 REM WRITTEN IN TRS-80 BASIC
30 REM DEBUGGED ON TRS-80 MODEL I AND III
40 REM DEMONSTRATION OF SIMULTION OF INVESTMENT
50 REM A1 MOST LIKELY INCOME; A2 BEST CASE, A3 WORST CASE
60 REM E1 MOST LIKELY EXPENSE; E2 BEST CASE; E3 WORST CASE
70 REM F1 MOST LIKELY INCOME ESCALATION F2 AND F3 BEST AND WORST
80 REM D1 D2 AND D3 SAME FOR EXPENSE ESCALATION
90 DEFINT I-N
100 A1=0:A2=0:A3=0:E1=0:E2=0:E3=0:D1=0:D2=0:D3=0:D4=0:EI=0:VI=0
110 EE =
0:VE=0:A=0:B=0:J=0:J1=0:X1=0:X2=0:Z1=0:Z2=0:S1=0:S2=0:A7=0:A8=0:X
=0:B2=0:B1=0
120 DIM A(100),EX(100),PR(100)
130 CLS
140 PRINT "PROGRAM RISK. SIMULATION OF RISKY INVESTMENT"
150 PRINT
160 PRINT "PLEASE ENTER DATA ASKED FOR."
170 INPUT "NAME OF INVESTMENT ";NI$
180 PRINT USING "BEST ESTIMATE OF INCOME ($######,##.##)";A1;
190 INPUT A1
200 PRINT USING "BEST CASE INCOME ($######,##.##)";A2;
```

```
210 INPUT A2
220 PRINT USING "WORST CASE INCOME ($######,##.##)";A3;
230 INPUT A3
240 PRINT USING "BEST ESTIMATE OF EXPENSES ($######,##.##)";E1;
250 INPUT E1
260 PRINT USING "BEST CASE EXPENSES ($######,##.##)";E2;
270 INPUT E2
280 PRINT USING "WORST CASE EXPENSES ($######,##.##)";E3;
290 INPUT E3
300 PRINT USING "BEST ESTIMATE INCOME ESCALATION (##.##%)";F1;
310 INPUT F1
320 PRINT USING "BEST CASE (##.##%)";F2;
330 INPUT F2
340 PRINT USING "WORST CASE (##.##%)";F3;
350 INPUT F3
360 PRINT USING "BEST ESTIMATE EXPENSE ESCALAION (##.##%)";D1;
370 INPUT D1
380 PRINT USING "BEST CASE (##.##%)";D2;
390 INPUT D2
400 PRINT USING "WORST CASE (##.##%)";D3;
410 INPUT D3
420 PRINT USING "LIFE OF INVESTMENT (## YEARS )";LF;
430 INPUT LF
440 CLS
450 PRINT "CHECK DATA TO BE SURE THEY ARE CORRECT "
460 PRINT USING "BEST ESTIMATE INCOME $######,##.##";A1
470 PRINT USING "BEST CASE INCOME     $######,##.##";A2
480 PRINT USING "WORST CASE INCOME    $######,##.##";A3
490 PRINT USING "BEST ESTIMATE EXP    $######,##.##";E1
500 PRINT USING "BEST CASE EXP        $######,##.##";E2
510 PRINT USING "WORST CASE EXP       $######,##.##";E3
520 PRINT USING "BEST ESTIMATE INCOME ESCAL         ##.##%";F1
530 PRINT USING "BEST CASE INCOME ESCAL             ##.##%";F2
540 PRINT USING "WORST CASE INCOME ESCAL            ##.##%";F3
550 PRINT USING "BEST ESTIMATE EXP ESCAL            ##.##%";D1
560 PRINT USING "BEST CASE EXP ESCAL                ##.##%";D2
570 PRINT USING "WORST CASE EXP ESCAL               ##.##%":D3
580 PRINT "ARE THESE CORRECT Y OR N?"
590 Y$ = INKEY$:IF Y$ = "" THEN 590 ELSE IF INSTR ("YN".Y$)=0
THEN PRINT "PLEASE ANSWER Y OR N.":GOTO 590
600 IF Y$ = "N" THEN 130
610 INPUT "ENTER NUMBER OF TIMES TO SIMULATE INVESTMENT
(1-100)";NS
620 IF NS = 0 THEN NS =1 ELSE IF NS >100 THEN PRINT "NUMBER OF
SIMULATIONS MUST BE LESS THAN 100.":GOTO 610
```

```
630 CLS
640 PRINT
650 PRINT "NOW WORKING ON SIMULATION. PLEASE WAIT."
660 EI = (A2 + A3 + 4*A1)/6
670 VI = ABS(A2-A3)/6
680 EE = (E2 + E3 +4*E1)/6
690 VE = ABS(E2-E3)/6
700 X1 = (F2 + F3 + 4*F1)/6
710 X2 = ABS(F2-F3)/6
720 Z1 = (D2 + D3 + 4*D1)/6
730 Z2 = ABS(D2-D3)/6
740 S1 = 0 : S2 = 0
750 FOR J = 0 TO NS
760     PRINT "SIMULATION # ";J
770     EX = EI : VX = VI
780     GOSUB 1410
790     A7 = X
800     EX = EE : VX = VE
810     GOSUB 1410
820     A8 = X :REM EXPENSE FOR SIMULATION J
830     EX = X1
840     VX = X2
850     GOSUB 1410
860     B1 = X : REM INCOME ESCALATION FOR SIMULATION J
870     EX = Z1
880     VX = Z2
890     GOSUB 1410
900     B2 = X
910    PR(J) = 0
920     FOR J1 = 1 TO LF
930             A = A7*(1+B1/100)[(J1-1) : REM INCOME
940             B = A8*(1+B2/100)[J1 : REM EXPENSE
950             PR(J) = A-B + PR(J): REM PROFIT
960     NEXT J1
970     S1 = S1 + PR(J)
980 NEXT J
990 EP = S1/(NS+1)
1000 CLS
1010 FOR J1 = 0 TO NS
1020     S2 = S2 + (PR(J1)-EP)*(PR(J1)-EP)
1030 NEXT J1
1040 SD = S2/NS
1050 SD = SQR(SD)
1060 PRINT
1070 PRINT "SIMULATION COMPLETED "
```

```
1080 PRINT "RESULTS ARE --- "
1090 PRINT USING "EXPECTED PROFIT  IS $######,##.##";EP
1100 PRINT USING "STANDARD DEVIATION IS  $###,##.##";SD
1110 PRINT "FOR HARD COPY PRESS <H>. PRESS ANY OTHER KEY TO
CONTINUE."
1120 Y$ = INKEY$: IF Y$ ="" THEN 1120 ELSE IF Y$ = "H" THEN
GOSUB 1180
1130 PRINT "DO YOU WANT ANOTHER ONE Y OR N?"
1140 Y$ = INKEY$:IF Y$="" THEN 1140 ELSE IF INSTR("YN",Y$)=0THEN
PRINT "PLEASE ANSWER Y OR N." : GOTO 1140
1150 IF Y$ = "Y" THEN 130
1160 END
1170 END
1180 LPRINT
1190 LPRINT TAB(20):"HARD COPY FOR PROGRAM RISK."
1200 LPRINT TAB(10);"NAME OF INVESTMENT = ";NI$
1210 LPRINT TAB(20);"INPUT INFORMATION "
1220 LPRINT USING "     BEST ESTIMATE OF INCOME    ........
$#####,##.##":A1
1230 LPRINT USING "     BEST CASE INCOME .................
$#####,##.##";A2
1240 LPRINT USING "     WORST CASE INCOME ................
$#####,##.##";A3
1250 LPRINT USING "     BEST ESTIMATE OF EXPENSES .........
$#####,##.##";E1
1260 LPRINT USING "     BEST CASE EXPENSES ...............
$#####,##.##";E2
1270 LPRINT USING "     WORST CASE EXPENSES ..............
$#####,##.##";E3
1280 LPRINT USING "     BEST ESTIMATE INCOME ESCALATION
.......... ##.##%";F1
1290 LPRINT USING "     BEST CASE INCOME ESCALTATION
.............. ##.##%";F2
1300 LPRINT USING "    WORST CASE INCOME ESCALATION
............... ##.##%"; F3
1310 LPRINT USING "    BEST ESTIMATE EXPENSE ESCALATION
.......... ##.##%";D1
1320 LPRINT USING "    BEST CASE EXPENSE ESCALATION
............... ##.##%";D2
1330 LPRINT USING "    WORST CASE EXPENSE ESCALATION
.............. ##.##%";D3
1340 LPRINT USING "    LIFE OF INVESTMENT
........................ ## YEARS ";LF
1350 LPRINT " "
```

```
1360 LPRINT TAB(20);"RESULTS"
1370 LPRINT USING "     EXPECTED PROFIT .... ........
$######,#.##";EP
1380 LPRINT USING "     STANDARD DEVIATION OF PROFIT .
$######,#.##";SD
1390 LPRINT USING "NUMBER OF SIMULATIONS WAS ####";NS
1400 RETURN
1410 REM NORMAL DISTRIBUTION
1420 SX = 0
1430 FOR K1 = 1 TO 12
1440    SX = SX + RND(0)
1450 NEXT K1
1460 X = VX*(SX-6)+EX
1470 RETURN
1480 END
```

Example: Using RISK

Let's use program RISK to see how the method works, using the information about two possible investments given in Fig. 6-4. You have two investments with the same estimated profit, but the range of possible costs and expenses is much different. The problem is to determine which of these two risky investments is the least risky.

You can use program RISK to answer this question. Enter the data the program asks for, then wait a few minutes until the necessary calculations are done. The output from the program is shown in Fig. 6-5. Note that for investment A the average

DATA FOR EXAMPLE OF RISK		
ITEM	A	B
MOST LIKELY INCOME	$10,000	$10,000
BEST CASE	14,000	$18,000
WORST CASE	$6,000	$4,000
BEST ESTIMATE EXP	$7,000	$7,000
BEST CASE	$5,000	$3,000
WORST CASE	$9,000	$10,000
BEST ESTIMATE ESCAL INCOME	12%	12%
BEST CASE	14%	16%
WORST CASE	8%	4%
BEST ESTIMATE ESCAL EXP	8%	8%
BEST CASE	5%	3%
WORST CASE	12%	15%
LIFE OF INVESTMENT	5	5

Fig. 6-4. Data for example of RISK.

```
            NAME OF INVESTMENT = A
                      INPUT INFORMATION
     BEST ESTIMATE OF INCOME     ........ $  10,000.00
     BEST CASE INCOME .................. $  14,000.00
     WORST CASE INCOME ................. $   6,000.00
     BEST ESTIMATE OF EXPENSES ......... $   7,000.00
     BEST CASE EXPENSES ................ $   5,000.00
     WORST CASE EXPENSES ............... $   9,000.00
     BEST ESTIMATE INCOME ESCALATION  ......... 12.00%
     BEST CASE INCOME ESCALTATION ............. 14.00%
    WORST CASE INCOME ESCALATION ..............  8.00%
    BEST ESTIMATE EXPENSE ESCALATION ..........  8.00%
    BEST CASE EXPENSE ESCALATION ..............  5.00%
    WORST CASE EXPENSE ESCALATION ............. 12.00%
    LIFE OF INVESTMENT ........................  5 YEARS

                      RESULTS
     EXPECTED PROFIT ............. $  17,433.10
    STANDARD DEVIATION OF PROFIT . $  10,261.90
NUMBER OF SIMULATIONS WAS    50

                      HARD COPY FOR PROGRAM RISK.
            NAME OF INVESTMENT = B
                      INPUT INFORMATION
     BEST ESTIMATE OF INCOME     ........ $  10,000.00
     BEST CASE INCOME .................. $  18,000.00
     WORST CASE INCOME ................. $   4,000.00
     BEST ESTIMATE OF EXPENSES ......... $   7,000.00
     BEST CASE EXPENSES ................ $   3,000.00
     WORST CASE EXPENSES ............... $  10,000.00
     BEST ESTIMATE INCOME ESCALATION  ......... 12.00%
     BEST CASE INCOME ESCALTATION ............. 16.00%
    WORST CASE INCOME ESCALATION ..............  4.00%
    BEST ESTIMATE EXPENSE ESCALATION ..........  8.00%
    BEST CASE EXPENSE ESCALATION ..............  3.00%
    WORST CASE EXPENSE ESCALATION ............. 15.00%
    LIFE OF INVESTMENT ........................  5 YEARS

                      RESULTS
     EXPECTED PROFIT ............. $  18,110.30
    STANDARD DEVIATION OF PROFIT . $  15,406.30
NUMBER OF SIMULATIONS WAS    50
```

Fig. 6-5. Hard copy for program RISK.

profit is $17,433.10 with a standard deviation of $10,110.30, and for investment B the average profit is $18,110.30 with a standard deviation of $15,406.30.

Examine a statistics book to learn how to interpret your results. Statistics tells us that about 95 percent of all results will be within two standard deviations of the mean (mean is another word for average). More than 99 percent of all results will be within three standard deviations of the mean.

For these two investments it is very unlikely that investment A will return more than $37,000, whereas the upper limit for investment B is $48,000. The likely lower limit for investment A is a loss of $3,000, investment B might lose as much as $12,000. Thus investment B seems to be much riskier than investment A.

The added risk for investment B means that the cost of acquiring investment B should be much less than the cost of acquiring investment A.

The computer simulation provides valuable insight into the risk of an investment. You are forced to consider the risk factors and cannot ignore them.

However, the method still depends on the data you supply and is at best only a crude simulation of the actual risk. A serious issue that must be faced is the likely bias in the estimates.

There is considerable empirical evidence that we all are optimistic, and tend to overestimate the good in an investment and underestimate the bad. There doesn't seem to be a whole lot one can do about this built-in optimistic bias. At best we should recognize it.

This concludes the discussion of risk. The main ideas to remember are that risk exists in all investments, and that the only way to get high returns is to assume high risks. Beware if someone promises you large risk-free returns. High risk has to be hidden somewhere to justify the high rate of return.

Chapter 7

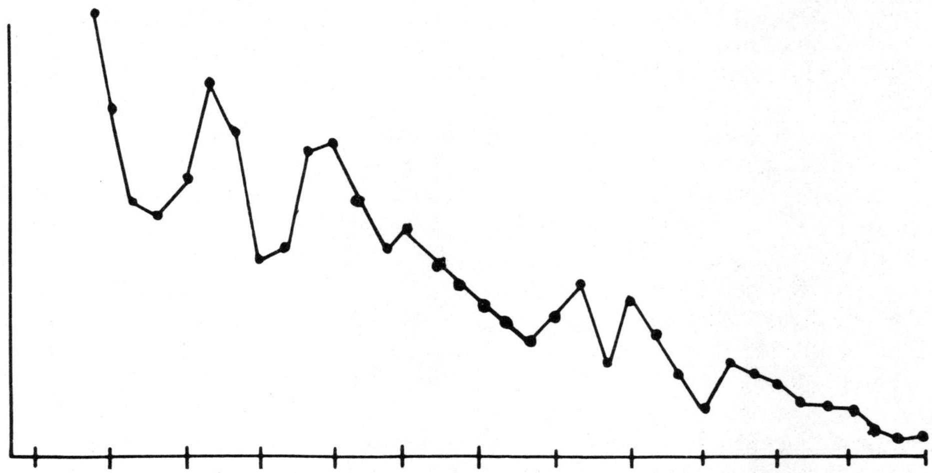

Effects of Taxes

This discussion is based on 1981 tax laws that still haven't been completely implemented. If an investment you're analyzing is strongly affected by taxes, you should get professional help before investing.

There are two problems with taxes: first, to determine the effects on the added expense on the investment; to minimize taxes that must be paid. Let's look at some features of the new tax that affect investment analysis.

DEPRECIATION

As mentioned earlier in this book, depreciation is an expense for tax purposes. Actually depreciation is how the government lets you recover the capital cost of your investment. The new tax law recognizes this and has replaced the word depreciation with something called *Accelerated Cost Recovery System* (ACRS). In addition to the name change, the rules of the game have also changed. The main impact of ACRS is that the capital cost of an asset can be recovered much faster under the new rules.

The new rules divide property into four categories according to the type of asset. The time for depreciating the asset is fixed for all items in each category, thus greatly simplifying the task of determining how long you have to use assets. These time periods for depreciation are generally much shorter than the time periods under previous tax laws, thus providing major tax savings.

Items in the first category can be written off over three years. Items in this category include cars, light duty trucks, research and experimentation equipment, and other short-lived property. Most business property (except buildings) is included in the five-year category. This includes machinery, computers, and other such items. Most public utility property, "theme park" structures, and railroad tank cars are included in the ten-year category.

If you don't want to write off an asset quite as fast as allowed, you have other options. Items in the three-year category can be written off over five or 12 years. Items in the five-year category can be written off over 12 or 25 years. Items in the ten-year category can be written off over 35 or 45 years. If you elect to use one of the optional time periods for any item in a given category, all items in that category must use the same time period.

The allowable percentage cost that can be deducted for each item is given in Tables 7-1, 7-2, and 7-3. There is no table for 15-year real estate property. Tables for this category have not yet been published. The depreciation for these assets uses the 175 percent declining balance method. The tables are based on the half-year convention which assumes that property was placed in service on the first day of the second half of the first year.

Tables 7-1, 7-2, and 7-3 are built into the programs that follow. You can use the straight line method of depreciation in place of these tables. The option is included in the programs.

SELLING A DEPRECIATED ASSET

When you sell an asset that has been depreciated, the IRS recovers the depreciated amount at your normal income tax rates, not at the capital gains tax rate. This means that the profit from the sale will be taxed as ordinary income to the extent of your ACRS deductions.

The IRS does not recover ACRS in the following cases:

- Fifteen-year real estate that is residential rental property.
- Fifteen-year real estate that is outside the United States.

Table 7-1. Cost Recovery Percentages 1981-1984 for Property Placed in Service Anytime During 1981-1984.

For property placed in service anytime during the period 1981-1984.

Year	3 Year	5 Year	10 Year	15 Year PU
1	25	15	8	5
2	38	22	14	10
3	37	21	12	9
4		21	10	8
5		21	10	7
6			10	7
7			9	6
8			9	6
9			9	6
10			9	6
11-15				6

Table 7-2. Cost Recovery Percentages for 1985 for Property Placed in Service in 1985.

For property placed in service in 1986.

Year	3 Year	5 Year	10 Year	15 Year PU
1	29	18	9	6
2	47	33	19	12
3	24	25	16	12
4		16	14	11
5		8	12	10
6			10	9
7			8	8
8			6	7
9			4	6
10			2	5
11				4
12				4
13				3
14				2
15				1

Table 7-3. Cost Recovery Percentages for 1986 for Property Placed in Service in 1986.

For property placed in service in 1986.

Year	3 Year	5 Year	10 Year	15 Year PU
1	33	20	10	7
2	45	32	18	12
3	22	24	16	12
4		16	14	11
5		8	12	10
6			10	9
7			8	8
8			6	7
9			4	6
10			2	5
11				4
12				3
13				3
14				2
15				1

- Fifteen-year real estate that is depreciated using straight line methods.
- Fifteen-year real estate that is subsidized low-income housing.

Since ACRS is not recovered from real estate if you use straight line depreciation, I believe you should use straight line depreciation when you get involved in real estate.

EXPENSING PRIVILEGE

The new tax law eliminated the additional first year depreciation that could be claimed under the old law. Shortened depreciation periods make up for this. In addition, the new law allows you to deduct ("expense") in one year the entire cost of certain property which is placed in service after 1981. For 1982 and 1983, you can deduct up to $5,000 of qualifying property. For 1984 and 1985 the limit increases to $7,500. For 1986 and thereafter, the limit is $10,000.

In general, qualified property is tangible personal property you acquire by purchase which is used in your business or trade. The property must be eligible for the investment tax credit (which you lose). Your personal computer is an example of an item that could be expensed at once.

You must tell the IRS that you are taking advantage of this part of the tax law. Also note that if you sell the property, the IRS treats the deduction from expensing as depreciation and recovers it the same way that it recovers depreciation.

INVESTMENT TAX CREDIT

The investment tax credit is another part of the tax law that affects investments. The tax credit is not a deduction; i.e., it is not deducted as an expense from income. It is a credit and is deducted directly from the amount that you owe the IRS.

Under the new law you are allowed a credit of 10 percent of the total cost of five-, ten-, and fifteen-year public utility property. The investment tax credit for three-year property is 10 percent of 60 percent of the total cost of the property. For example, if you purchase five-year property for $10,000, then you are allowed a credit of $1,000; if you purchase three-year property for $10,000 you are allowed a $600 credit (amount eligible for credit = .6 × $10,000 = $6,000. Credit = .1 × $6,000 = $600.)

Of course there are rules that allow the IRS to recover the investment tax credit if you sell your property. The IRS doesn't let you get away with much.

MARGINAL TAX RATES

When you run the programs, notice that one of the input items is marginal tax rate. This is the tax rate that you would pay if you earned one more dollar. This is not your average tax rate. For many people, the marginal tax rate will be in the range of 40 to 50 percent. The new tax law may result in a slight reduction in marginal tax rate. But if you consider combined federal and state taxes, the marginal tax rate for many of us will exceed 50 percent and will likely remain so.

This completes the short discussion of taxes. The tax code is complicated; if large amounts of money are involved, you should consult an expert. The purpose of this discussion was to provide you with enough information to evaluate an investment in light of the new tax law.

I did not discuss all-savers certificates or IRA accounts. These may both be good investments for you. The IRA most surely is one. You should investigate further.

The concepts and programs in this book can help you evaluate the many IRA plans that are being offered. You can select the one most likely to meet your need. You can make your own estimates of likely returns and risk. If you do make your own estimates, you'll be in better shape than the person who goes by what a particular financial institution says.

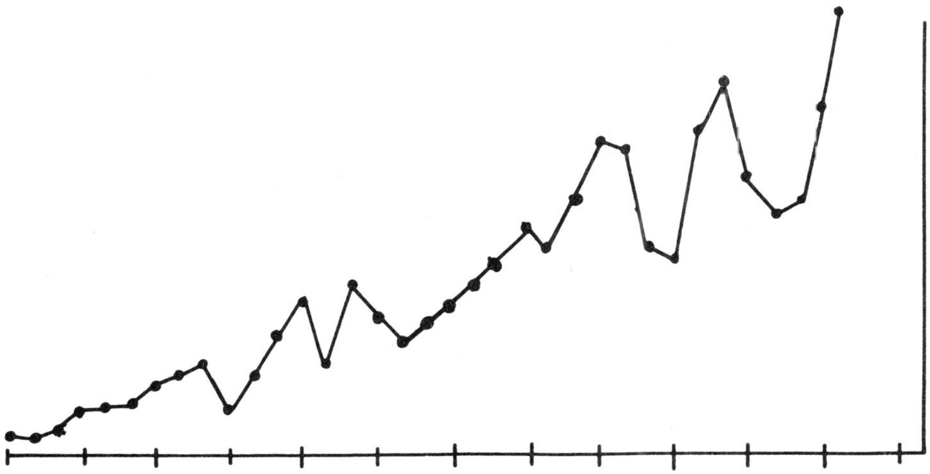

Chapter 8

Methods of Investment Analysis

Several methods of analyzing investments have been developed. Some have been found useful and have survived; others have not. Some of the more common methods of investment analysis and their advantages and disadvantages are presented in this chapter.

SIMPLE RETURN ON INVESTMENT

Simple return on investment, or ROI, is one of the more common methods for evaluating an investment. Simple return on investment is the sum of all profits from the investment, divided by the capital cost of the investment times the number of year of the investment.

Example: Simple ROI

For example, let's assume that the total cost of the investment is \$50,000. The profits from the investment are \$10,000 the first year, \$20,000 in both the second and third years, and \$5,000 the fourth and final year. The return on investment is:

$$\text{ROI} = (\$10{,}000 + 20{,}000 + 20{,}000 + 5{,}000) / (4 \times 50{,}000)$$
$$= 55{,}000/(200{,}000) = 0.275 \text{ or } 27.5 \text{ percent}$$

The advantages claimed for the simple ROI method are:

- The calculation of simple ROI is easy.
- Simple ROI involves profit, and investors are used to thinking in terms of profit.
- It considers all profits in the life of the investment. (The payback method discussed below does not do this.)

The major disadvantages of the method are:

- There are no universal definitions of invested capital or profits so there is no assurance that everyone is talking about the same things.
- The method provides for a single initial investment followed by a series of yearly profits or

losses. It does not provide for additional investment during the life of the investment.

- It does not include the time value of money. Profits earned during the early years are given the same weight as profits earned later. This is a poor way to treat cash flows for two reasons. First, future cash flows are more uncertain than near-term cash flows and thus are riskier. Second, the time value of money shows that near-term cash flows are more valuable than long-term cash flows.

Because the simple ROI method neglects the timing of the cash flows, it must be considered a very crude tool for investment analysis and decision making.

PAYBACK PERIOD

The payback method is a popular way of analyzing investments. You simply ask how soon the income from an investment equals the cost of the investment. Investments with the shortest payback period are selected.

The payback period is calculated from the annual cash flows for each year of the investment. The annual cash flow is given by:

profit for year + depreciation − tax paid.

For example, assume you have a chance to invest $10,000 in a new business. The investment will earn $2,000 a year. The payback period is then five years.

The main advantage of the payback period is that it tells you how soon you will get your money back. The main disadvantages of the payback period method are:

- It does not identify the profitability of an investment, which is what really matters. I don't know anyone who invests to minimize payback time.
- It ignores the timing of cash flows.
- It completely ignores all cash flows that occur after the payback period. Thus an investment with a two-year payback period followed by no income would be preferred to an investment with a three-year payback period followed by three years of high profits. This doesn't sound like a choice most people would make.
- It does not apply to many types of investments in which the main profit is from capital gains, for example a real estate investment.

Despite all its disadvantages, the payback period method is favored by many investors. It is useful as a rough screening method. However, the fact that it totally ignores the time value of money must be considered a fatal flaw.

DISCOUNTED CASH FLOW RETURN ON INVESTMENT

The discounted cash flow return on investment or *the internal rate of return method* is one of two methods of investment analysis which consider the time value of money. The basic idea is to find the discount rate that makes the present value of total cash flows for the life of the investment equal to the present value of the cost of the investment. The method requires trial-and-error calculations, but these are easy with a computer. Without a computer the calculations would be tedious and probably make the method unusable, especially if several investments must be examined.

The major advantage of the discounted cash flow return on investment method is that you don't have to assume a discount rate. The method produces a number that has real meaning and is useful for decision making. To use the discounted cash flow return on investment method to rank investments, choose the investment with the highest discounted cash flow return on investment.

The major problems with the discounted cash flow return on investment method are:

- Good investments might be missed when funds are limited. To see how this might happen consider the case shown in Fig. 8-1. Note that

Total amount to invest is $100,000.			
	A	B	C
CAPITAL	$70,000	$100,000	$30,000
DCFROI	15%	14.5%	10%

Fig. 8-1. Example of problem of applying discounted cash flow rate of return method when funds are limited.

investment A has the highest internal rate of return. You want to invest all available funds, so you will select investments A and C. However, an examination of the combined rate of return from A and C shows that investment B is best for all your money. There are ways to modify the discounted cash flow rate of return method to allow for the case shown in Fig. 8-1. However, these make the computations even more difficult.

- The method can produce two values of discounted cash flow return on investment. This is a serious problem if some of the cash flows during the life of the investment are negative and some are positive. Figure 8-2 shows this.

NET PRESENT VALUE

The final method is the net present value method. This is the other method that considers the time value of money. In the net present value method, all future cash flows from the investment are discounted with a predetermined discount rate. If the net present value of all future cash flows is greater than the present value of the cost of the investment, the investment is considered profitable.

The biggest problem with the method is in determining the value of the discount rate to be used. The general advice, as discussed in Chapter 4 is to use the larger of the cost of capital and the maximum risk free return. The investment criterion is that an investment with a present value greater than or equal to the cost of the investment will be accepted. If more than one acceptable investment is found, then the investment with the greatest net present value will be selected.

When the present value of future cash flows is less than the cost of the investment, the earnings from the investment were less than you would receive, had you put your money into the investment represented by the discount rate. If you consistently find that your investments are not producing a high present value, you should be sure that you are using the correct discount rate.

THE EFFECT OF DISCOUNT RATE CHOICE

As you saw in Chapter 4, the value used for the discount rate has a large effect on the calculated net present value. The effect of this on investment decision making is discussed in this section.

The *net present values* (present value of all cash flows less present value of cost of investment) for two investments are plotted as a function of discount rate in Fig. 8-3. At low discount rates investment A is superior; at high discount rates investment B is superior. Investment B's ranking improves as the discount rate increases because investment B has higher early cash flows than does investment A. At low discount rates, the value of investment A's later year cash flows is still high. However, as the discount rate increases, the value of future year cash flows greatly decreases.

This example is meant to show the importance of selecting the correct discount rate. To do this you must know the cost of capital and the available returns on risk free investments.

HIDDEN ASSUMPTION

There is one significant assumption made in the discounted cash flow methods that needs to be discussed. This assumption is that incoming cash flows from the investment can be reinvested at the discount rate. For the discounted cash flow return on investment method this means that you are assuming you can invest all profits at the discounted cash flow return on investment rate.

For the net present value method the assumption is that one can reinvest at the cost of capital. This should be fairly close to the truth, which means that in the long run the assumption in the net

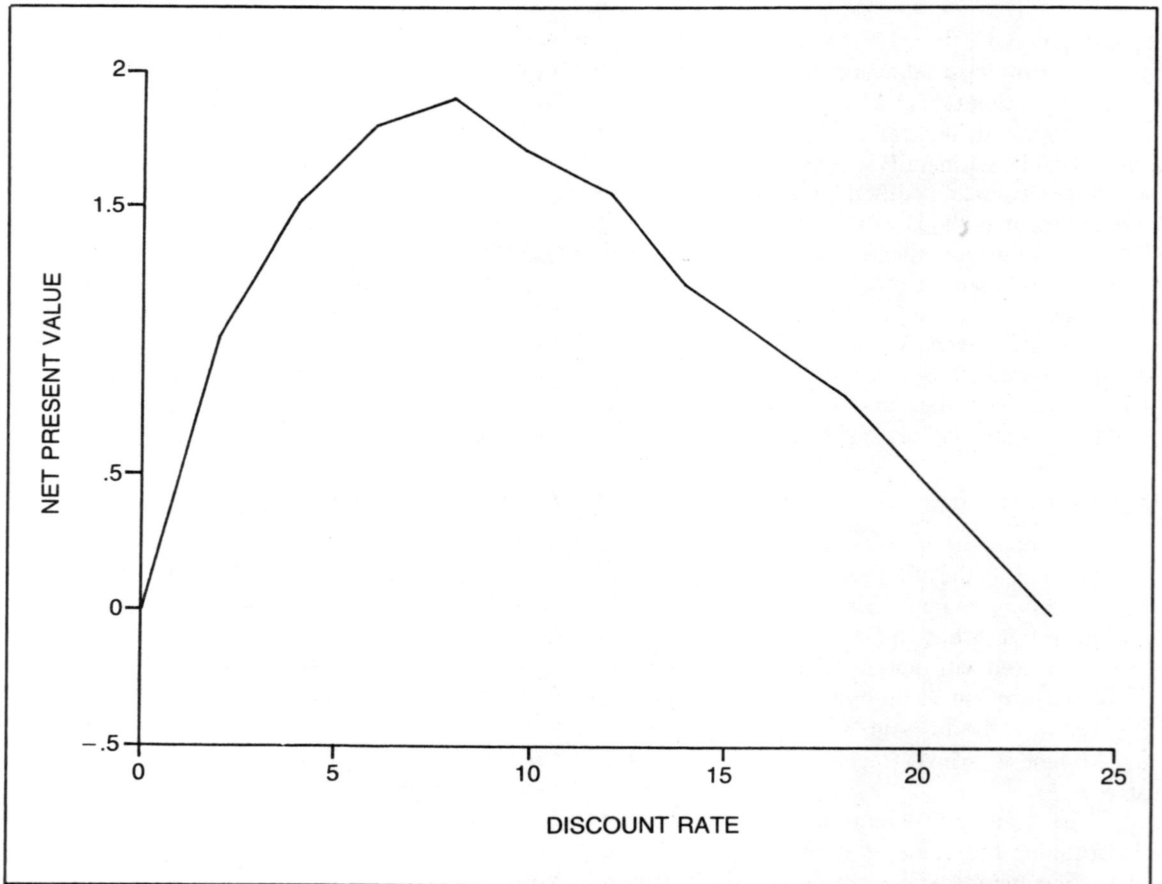

Fig. 8-2. Curve showing the two rates of return possible with the discounted cash flow rate of return method when both positive and negative cash flows are encountered.

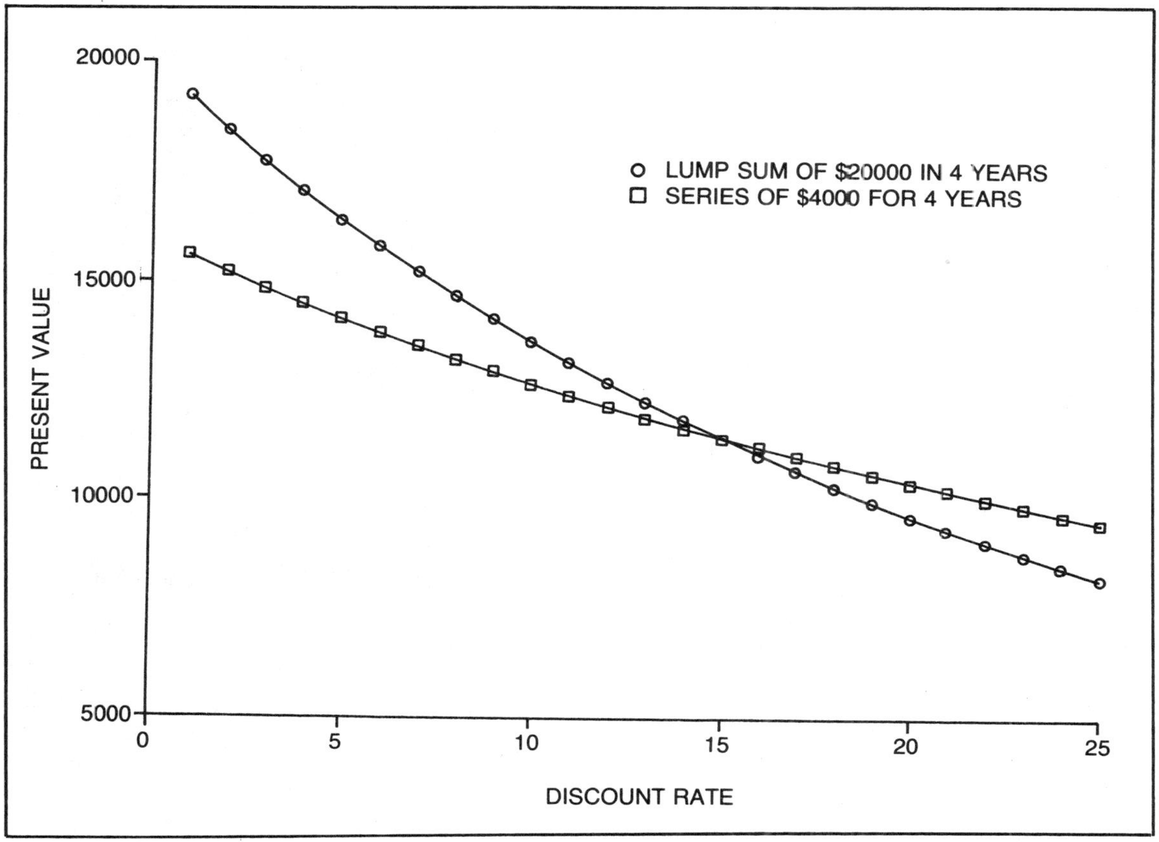

Fig. 8-3. Comparison of the present value of two investments as a function of discount rate.

present value method is not as radical as the assumption in the discounted cash flow return on investment method.

The main danger of using the discounted cash flow methods of investment analysis is that you can be so confident of the details of the calculations that you forget other important factors. The programs in this book use the present value method.

Chapter 9

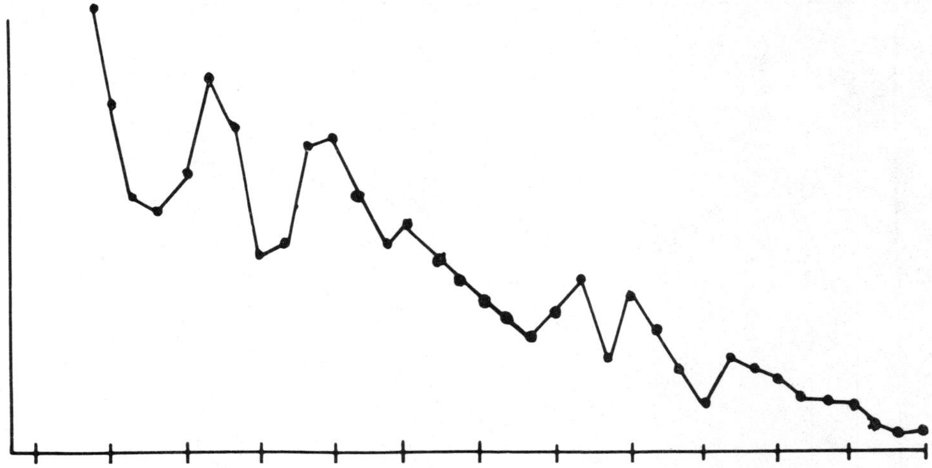

Introduction to INVEST Programs

The INVEST programs are written in Microsoft BASIC as implemented on the TRS-80 Model I and Model III computers. They are designed to use the level II and disk BASIC versions of TRS-80 BASIC. Complete listings for all programs in this book are provided. INVEST1, INVEST2, and INVEST3 require 48K RAM to run as written. They will run in 32K RAM if most of the remarks are removed and multistatements are used on individual lines.

The programs are written in modules. For most cases the input module and the output modules are the main modules that must be changed if the programs are to be used on a computer other than the Model I or Model III—especially if Microsoft BASIC is not used by the other computer. The input and output modules for each of the programs should run in Microsoft BASIC 80 version 5.2. This means that the programs should run as written, with the possible exception of the CLS command, on any computer using CP/M v2.0 and BASIC 80 version 5.2.

All programs provide the option of hard copy output, which gives a complete copy of all input information, a summary of the calculated results, and detailed results for each year of the investment.

All programs use the present value method of investment evaluation. Three programs are supplied: program INVEST1, program INVEST2, and program INVEST3.

INVEST1/BAS is a general-purpose investment analysis program best suited for investments in which the income is expected to pay for the investment. INVEST1 does not provide for cases when the investment is resold for a profit.

INVEST2 is intended for general evaluation of an investment in which most or all of the profit is expected to come from capital gains, for example an investment in real estate. INVEST2 can be used to evaluate most investments where the majority of the return is expected from capital gains.

INVEST3 is designed to help you get an idea of the risk involved in an investment evaluated by

INVEST2. It is really an enhanced version of INVEST2.

Each program requires considerable information about the investment. How well the programs serve you depends mostly on the quality of this information; you should spend time obtaining all necessary information.

An efficient way to use the program is to run them with your best estimate of all required information. If the investment appears favorable after this step, review your estimates and refine them if possible. (If the investment looks bad, don't try to find data that makes it look good.) Now rerun the program with your new information. If the results still look good, run the sensitivity analysis, if INVEST1 is being used, or INVEST3 if a real estate investment is being studied.

After all this, if the investment still looks good, play with the programs. Change various assumptions and see what happens. You will often find that you've overlooked something important.

Pay careful attention to the yearly details. They often contain important information that can help you make a decision and help you manage an investment better. Pay special attention to spendable cash flow, which usually shows you how much working capital you need to maintain an investment and keep the bank happy.

Chapter 10

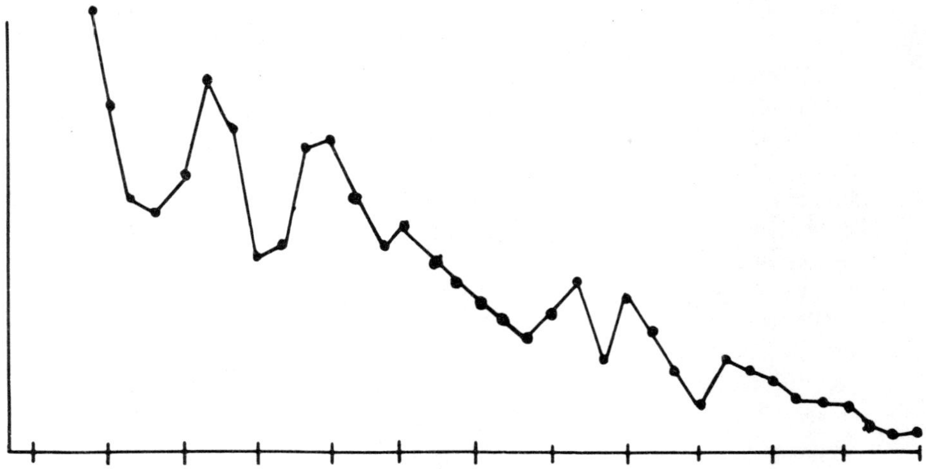

INVEST1 Program

In the first type of investment to be examined, income pays for the investment. We do not expect to sell property for capital gain, but rather to earn ordinary income from the investment.

This is the situation typically faced by many of us. Should we buy a business? Should our business buy a new tool or expand? These are the types of questions that program INVEST1 can help answer.

OVERVIEW

The program is organized in modules. The first module is used to enter data about the investment. The second module calculates loan payment schedules for one or two loans which may have different interest rates, lengths, number of payments per year, and amounts. The third module computes yearly cash flows. All present value and inflation discounting are done by this module. The fourth module is used to display results on the crt. The final module provides a hard copy of the investment calculations.

Data Input Module

Requirements for the data input module are:

- Information will be entered from the keyboard and displayed on the crt.
- Information will be entered as pages, with the user given a chance to correct information.
- The user will be able to move from one page of the input to another.
- The computer will not begin calculations until receiving a specific command from the user.

The input module for the programs meets these requirements. However, some sacrifices were required in order to insure program compatibility with most computers using Microsoft BASIC 80.

Specific information required from you is displayed on the crt along with the current value of the variable. Brief instructions for using the data entry module are printed on the crt. These instructions are intended to help you use the program without having to constantly refer to the documentation.

All data are entered into the computer as strings. Numeric data are converted to single precision numbers if necessary. The use of strings for input allows you to move from page to page and to correct data. Specific computers can provide the same capabilities by using hardware-specific programming. However, this limits the number of computers that can use the programs.

Twenty five different items of data must be entered. As soon as all data are entered, the computer can begin the calculations.

LOAN MODULES

Modules are provided to amortize two different loans. Two was picked as a more or less typical value of the number of loans that might be used to finance an investment. If you need more loans, you can modify the program accordingly.

The loan schedule is calculated on the assumption it will be paid off in fixed payments that pay off principal and interest. If you have a different type of loan, you should replace the loan module with the appropriate loan calculations. See Chapter 3 of this book for BASIC programs that might be used in a new loan module.

The loan module calculates the payment schedule for the entire life of the loan, even if the life of the investment is less than the life of the loan. Yearly interest and principal payments are sorted for later use. As soon as the loans are calculated, the program moves to the module to calculate the yearly cash flows.

Cash Flow Module

The cash flow module is the most essential part of the program. In this module the year-to-year activities of the business are accounted for. The first step is to determine yearly income and expenses, escalated as per the user's instructions. The program then calculates depreciation using the new tables supplied by the IRS. Real estate is depreciated over 15 years using straight line depreciation. (This seems like the best way to depreciate real estate and avoid the IRS's recovery process.)

The program then determines the yearly profit before taxes. If the profits are negative, i.e., the investment lost money, the program adds the loss to any previous tax loss and then calculates the cash flows. If the investment made a profit, that profit is reduced by any previous tax losses, and state income tax is calculated. The state income tax is deducted from the profit and the federal income tax is calculated.

The program next checks to see whether there is investment tax credit to be taken. If there is, federal income tax is reduced by the amount of the investment tax credit. If the available investment tax credit is greater than the tax due, the program subtracts the tax from the credit and sets the tax to zero.

Now the program calculates the current year dollar and constant year dollar cash flows. The program also calculates the spendable cash flow. The cash flows are discounted at the specific discount rate, and the program loops back to do the next year.

The Display Module

The crt display module is used to display the results of the calculation. First, a summary of the results is displayed along with the present value of the investment, in terms of current year dollars and constant year dollars. If the present value of the investment is less than the cost of the investment, an appropriate message is printed.

The program then asks if you want to see the yearly details of the calculations. If you do, the results of each year are shown. These figures are useful for managing the investment. You can determine if your investment is working as you assumed it would. If not, you can determine what action might be taken to improve the situation.

Hard Copy Module

The hard copy module is used to provide hard copy on a line printer. The first item printed is a complete list of all input. This is absolutely necessary to permit subsequent use of the information from the program.

The next item printed is the summary results. These are checked to be sure you made a profit. If the investment did not make money, i.e., if the present value of the cash flows is less than the present value of the cost of the investment, the computer will print an appropriate message. Finally, the yearly details of the investment are printed.

When the printout is completed, the computer asks if you want to make another run. If you answer Y, then you are returned to the data input module. All previous information is still stored in the computer, so you can analyze the same investment with a different set of assumptions or you can analyze a completely new investment. The choice is yours.

USER INSTRUCTIONS

As soon as the program is run, you are asked if you want instructions. If you do, press <I> (there is no need to press <ENTER>). The screen will clear and the first page of the brief user instructions will be displayed. When you have read the instructions, press any key to go to the next page. The screen will clear and the second page of the user instructions will be displayed. When you have read the instructions, press any key and return to the main program.

User instructions are shown in Fig. 10-1.

When you return to the program, the name of the investment will be displayed and you will be asked to enter a new name. If you do want to enter a new name, type in the name. This name is used as an identifier so you can keep track of various investments. When you have entered the name, you must press <ENTER> to move on.

After you have entered the name of the investment, you will be transferred to the data input module. Data is entered by filling in three pages of information. The information you are required to enter is shown in Fig. 10-2. Each of the important data input items is discussed below.

Enter data by typing in the requested information. You must press <ENTER> when you have completed entering the item. When you enter a datum, the next piece of information is displayed along with all previous data for that page. When you have completed entering all the data for a given page, a message is displayed at the bottom of the screen telling you to review the data.

When you are ready to move to the next page, type > and press <ENTER>. You are then shown the first datum for the next page. If you want to move back to a previous page, type < and press <ENTER>. You will be shown all the data for that page.

When all data is entered, a message directing you to review the data is displayed. When you are ready to start calculations, type G and press <ENTER>. The program then transfers to the loan payment module.

If you notice a mistake in the data, you can correct it by typing C and pressing <ENTER>. As soon as you press <ENTER>, the screen is cleared and all data for the page you're working on is displayed. To correct an item, type the number of the item and press <ENTER>. The item you wish to correct is displayed, along with the current value. If you wish to keep the current value, type C and press <ENTER>. If you wish to change the value, type in the correct value and press <ENTER>. As soon as you press <ENTER>, the screen will clear and all data on the page will be displayed along with the corrected value.

When you have completed your corrections, type R and press <ENTER>. You will be returned to your former position in the data entry.

As soon as you have completed data entry,

```
INSTRUCTIONS

THIS PROGRAM CALCULATES THE PRESENT VALUE OF THE

CASH FLOWS FROM AN INVESTMENT. IN ORDER TO USE

THE PROGRAM, YOU MUST SUPPLY THE INPUT INFORMATION.

DATA ENTRY IS A MATTER OF SUPPLYING THE INFORMATION

ASKED FOR. DATA ARE ENTERED IN A THREE PAGE FORM.

YOU MOVE FROM PAGE TO PAGE WITH THE < AND > KEYS.

AND THEN FOLLOWING THE INSTRUCTIONS.

WHEN ALL THE DATA ARE CORRECT, YOU CAN START THE

CALCULATIONS BY ENTERING G.

PRESS ANY KEY TO CONTINUE

INSTRUCTIONS PAGE 2

ALL DATA ASKED FOR IS SELF EXPLANATORY, WITH THE

POSSIBLE EXCEPTION OF YEARS AFTER INVEST BEFORE REC

INCOME. THIS QUESTION IS BASED ON THE FACT THAT MANY

INVESTMENTS DO NOT START PAYING UNTIL SOME TIME

AFTER THE MONEY IS SPENT. YOU ENTER THE NUMBER OF

YEARS YOU ESTIMATE IT WILL TAKE FOR INCOME TO START

COMING AFTER THE INVESTMENT IS MADE. FOR EXAMPLE IF

YOU KNOW IT WILL TAKE ONE YEAR, ENTER 1. IF IT WILL

TAKE HALF A YEAR, ENTER 0.5.

PRESS ANY KEY TO CONTINUE
```

Fig. 10-1. User instructions shown on crt for INVEST1 /BAS.

These are the input data required for the investment analysis program.	
Total amount of investment	$__________
Amount of first loan	$__________
Yearly interest rate 1st loan	__________ %
Life of 1st loan	__________years
Number of paymnts per yr	__________
Time after invest before rec income	__________yrs
Amount of second loan	$__________
Yearly interest rate 2nd loan	__________ %
Life of second loan	__________ years
Number of payments per yr	__________
Estimated annual income	$__________
Estimated annual expenses	$!
Escalation for income	__________ %
Escalation for expenses	__________
Federal income tax rate	__________ %
State income tax rate	__________ %
Discount rate	__________ %
Life of investment	__________ years
Value of 3 yr property	$__________
Value of 5 yr property	$__________
Value of 10 yr property	$__________
Value of 15 yr PU property	$__________
Value of 1st line real estate	$__________
Year property placed in svc	__________
Inflation rate	__________ %

Fig. 10-2. Input data worksheet for INVEST1/BAS.

type G and press <ENTER>. Program control is then transferred to the main program. You are asked if you want to take the investment tax credit. You must press Y or N. You do not need to press <ENTER>. The computer will display its activities. This is to let you know that the computer is working.

First, the computer reads the depreciation schedules. Then the computer calculates loan schedules for the first and second loans. Finally, the computer calculates yearly cash flows.

As soon as calculations for the last year are completed, the screen is cleared and a summary is displayed. You are then asked if you want to display the detailed results. Answer by pressing Y or N. You do not need to press <ENTER>. If you select Y, detailed results for the first year are shown on the crt. Move to the next year by pressing any key. You do not need to press <ENTER>.

If you did not elect to see detailed results, and also after the last year is displayed, you are asked if you want hard copy. Answer by pressing Y or N. You do not have to press <ENTER>.

If you press Y, you are reminded to turn the printer on. Hard copy output is printed; first, input information, next the summary results, and finally yearly details.

After all results have been printed, and also if you declined hard copy, you are asked if you want to run another case. Answer by pressing Y or N. You do not have to press <ENTER>.

If you want to run another case, press Y. You will then be transferred to the first page, first item of the input module. All information previously entered is still stored. You can change as many times as desired. You can move from page to page at any time by typing > and pressing <ENTER>.

INPUT DATA

Total amount of the investment is the capital cost of the investment. This includes commissions and all other costs involved in purchasing the investment.

Amount of first loan is the amount that is borrowed as a first mortgage, for example.

Yearly interest rate for first loan is the percentage interest charged for the first loan.

Life of first loan is the number of years allowed to pay back the first loan.

Number of loan payments per year is self-explanatory: 1 for yearly, 2 for two times a year, 4 for quarterly, and so on.

Time after investing before receiving income: Some investments do not earn money as soon as they are purchased. For example, a major piece of equipment won't earn money for some time. This data item takes care of such situations. Enter the number of years or decimal fraction of a year that you estimate will be required before the investment produces income. The program assumes that interest, principal, and depreciation apply to an investment even when income is not produced. However, no expenses are incurred.

The next several items are merely listed with no discussion. *Amount of first loan, Yearly interest rate for 2nd loan, Life of second loan, Number of payments per year 2nd loan.*

Estimated annual income is your best estimate of the total income (gross income) that will be produced by the investment.

Estimated annual expenses is your best estimate of all expenses, except interest on the two loans and depreciation, required by an investment.

Escalation for income is the estimated yearly percentage increase in income. The program assumes that increases in income lag behind increases in expenses by one year.

Escalation for expenses is the estimated yearly percentage increase in expenses. In general the escalation for income and expenses will not be the same as the general inflation rate entered later. Most industries have cost indices that can be used to estimate income and expense escalation rates.

Federal income tax rate is the rate at which the next dollar you earn will be taxed.

State income tax is the same as above applied to state income tax.

Discount rate is one of the most important data items. If you have doubts about what to use, reread the chapter on present value. An appropriate value to use is the greater of your average cost of capital and the return you can get on a risk free investment.

Life of investment is the useful life of the investment, which has nothing to do with depreciation (covered by the next data item).

Value of three year property is the value of the property in your investment that can be depreciated over three years under the new tax laws.

Value of five year property is the dollar value of the property involved in your investment that can be depreciated over five years.

Value of 10 year property is the value of the property that can be depreciated over ten years.

Value of 15 year Pu property is the value of the public utility property that can be depreciated over 15 years under the new 1981 tax laws.

Value of St Line real estate is the value of the real estate that will be depreciated over 15 years using straight line depreciation.

Inflation rate is the estimated yearly inflation rate. The cost of living index published by the government is a good approximation.

OUTPUT DATA

Summary results are the major output data. These results tell you how an investment will perform. There are only four items:

- *Current year dollar present value of cash flows* is the discounted value of the total cash flow from an investment, not corrected for inflation. It is better to have higher values for cash flows. If you are analyzing several investments, all of equal risk, the best investment is the one with the highest present value.
- *Constant year dollar present value of cash flows* is the discounted value of the cash flows, corrected for inflation.
- *Current year dollar net present value (discounted cash cost)* is the discounted cash flows minus the cost of the investment. A good investment will have a positive net present value. If the value is negative, the investment did not recover its costs. Note that no correction for inflation is made.
- *Constant year dollar net present value* is the net present value of the investment, corrected for inflation. The net present value of a good investment is positive.

Detailed results for the yearly calculations are a year-by-year score card of the investment. Income, expenses, depreciation, taxes, tax credits, loan payments, and cash flows are all shown. The results are most useful as tools for managing an investment after it has been made.

The essential thing to examine in the yearly printout is the spendable cash flow. If it is negative, then no matter what the other cash flows are, you must find additional funds to keep the investment going. Remember that spendable cash flow is a measure of how much cash goes into or out of your pocket. It includes interest plus principal payments on your loans. No matter how good the investment, negative spendable cash flow is an indication of possible trouble.

INVEST1/BAS LISTING

```
10 CLEAR 200
20 REM
*****************************************************
30 REM PROGRAM INVEST1/BAS
40 REM PROGRAM TO ANALYZE AN INVESTMENT THAT IS EXPECTED
50 REM TO EARN INCOME AND PAY FOR ITSELF WITH THE INCOME
60 REM EARNED BY THE INVESTMENT
70 REM WRITTEN BY L. E. SPARKS VERSION 2.9 NOVEMBER 1981
80 REM WRITTEN IN TRS-80 DISK BASIC RUNS ON TRS-80
90 REM MODEL I AND MODEL III REQUIRES 48K RAM. FOR LESS RAM
100 REM REMOVE REMARKS, REDIMENSION ARRAYS, ELIMINATE
SPACES,
```

```
110 REM AND USE MULTIPLE STATEMENTS PER LINE.
120 REM IF THE CLS STATEMENT FOR CLEARING THE SCREEN IS
CHANGED
130 REM THE PROGRAM WILL RUN IN MBASIC OR BASIC 80
140 REM FOR CP/M SYSTEMS
150 REM AS WRITTEN REQUIRES 48K RAM FOR LESS RAM REDUCE
DIMENSIONS OF ARRAYS.
160 REM FOR LESS RAM REMOVE REMARK STATEMENTS
170 REM
*****************************************************
180 CLS
190 PRINT "=============================================="
200 PRINT "  INVESTMENT ANALYSIS PROGRAM INVEST1/BAS"
210 PRINT "  REFERENCE INVESTMENT ANALYSIS ON MICROCOMPUTER
TAB BOOKS"
220 PRINT "   BY LES VERSION 2.9 NOV 1981"
230 PRINT "=============================================="
240 PRINT "IF YOU WANT INSTRUCTIONS PRESS I ELSE PRESS ANY
KEY TO CONTINUE"
250 Y$=INKEY$: IF Y$="" THEN 250 ELSE IF Y$="I" THEN GOSUB
6470
260 CLS
270 DEFINT K,M,N
280 I=0:J=0:K=0:M=0:N=0:P=0:PV=0:PI=0:SP=0:CS=0
290 D$="$#,######.##"
300 PM = 3
310 I9 = 25 : REM MAXIMUM NUMBER OF ITEMS TO BE READ IN
320 IP=0 PP=0:A=0:B=0:V=0:SI=0:F=1:FL=0:TC=0
330 DIM F$(30),V(30),DP(4,15),D(30),SF(30),PV(4,3) PI(4,3)
340 REM D(I) IS DEPRECIATION FOR ITH YEAR, SF IS SPENDABLE
CASH FLOW
350 REM TC IS ALLOWABLE TAX CREDIT TC(I) IS TAX CREDIT
TAKEN IN ITH YEAR.
360 REM DP IS DEPRECIATION FOR NEW 1981 TAX LAW
370 DIM A1(30),A2(30),E1(30),E2(30),EX(30),T1(30),T2(30)
380 REM A1=PRINCIPAL  OF LOAN 1, A1=PRINCIPAL  OF LOAN 2,
E1=INCOME
390 REM E2=INCOME 2, EX=EXPENSES, T1=FEDERAL TAX, T2=STATE
TAX
400 DIM
B1(30),B2(30),CF(30),DF(30),DI(30),DY(30),IP(30),IZ(30),TC(3
0)
410 REM B1=BALANCE ON LOAN 1, B2=BALANCE ON LOAN 2
420 REM CF=CURRENT YEAR CASH FLOW, DF = DISCOUNTED CASH
FLOW
```

```
430 REM DI = CONSTANT DOLLAR CASH FLOW DY=DISCOUNTED
CONSTANT
440 REM DOLLAR CASH FLOW
450 REM IP INTEREST PAID LOAN 1, IZ INTEREST PAID LOAN 2
460 GOTO 580
470 REM SUBROUTINE TO DO LOAN CALCULATIONS
480 REM SUBROUTINE IS HERE FOR SPEED
490 FOR J1 = 1 TO NP
500     IP = I1 * A
510     IP = INT(IP*100)/100
520    SI = SI + IP
530     PP = P - IP
540     A = A - PP
550     B = B + PP
560 NEXT J1
570 RETURN
580 REM TRANSFER TO INITIALIZATION
590 GOSUB 6200
600 REM
610 PV=0:B=0:SI=0:A=0:DI=0:PI=0:REM INITIALIZE COUNTERS FOR
SUMS
620 TC = 0: F = 0 : FL = 0 : F1 = 1
630 SP = 0 : CS = 0
640 REM SP IS TOTAL SPENABLE CASH FLOW LOSS CS IS NUMBER OF
YEARS WITH SPENDABLE LOSS.
650 REM INITIALIZE ALL ARRAYS TO ZERO
660 CLS
670 PRINT "INITIALIZING EVERYTHING"
680 FOR I = 1 TO 30
690     PRINT I;
700      D(I) = 0
710      CF(I) = 0
720      EX(I) = 0
730      E1(I) = 0
740      E2(I) = 0
750      TC(I) = 0
760      T1(I) = 0
770      T2(I) = 0
780     SF(I) = 0
790 NEXT I
800 CLS
810 PRINT "NAME OF INVESTMENT IS ";NI$
820 INPUT" ENTER NEW NAME ";NI$
830 GOSUB 5160 : REM TRANSFER TO DATA INPUT
```

```
840 CLS
850 PRINT
"================================================="
860 PRINT"DO YOU WANT TO TAKE INVESTMENT TAX CREDIT ?"
870 PRINT
"================================================="
880 Y$=INKEY$:IF Y$="" THEN 880 ELSE IF
INSTR("YN",Y$)=0THEN PRINT "ANSWER Y OR N PLEASE ":GOTO 860
890 IF Y$="Y" THEN TC = 1 ELSE TC = 0
900 CLS
910 REM NOW READ IN DEPRECIATION TABLE
920 RESTORE
930 CLS
940 PRINT "READING DEPRECIATION TABLE"
950 GOSUB 5910
960 GOSUB 1650
970 REM CALCULATE INVESTMENT TAX CREDIT ALLOWED
980 REM TAX CREDIT IS ALLOWED ON 100% OF FIVE AND TEN YEAR
PROPERTY
990 REM TAX CREDIT IS ALLOWED ON 60% OF THREE YEAR PROPERTY
1000 TC =TC*0.1*(V(20)+V(21)+0.6*V(19))
1010 REM ALL LOANS TAKEN CARE OF NOW LETS DO YEARLY CASH
FLOWS
1020 KD = 0
1030 CLS
1040 PRINT "NOW WORKING ON YEARLY CASH FLOWS."
1050 REM K IS THE YEAR NUMBER ASSUME THAT INCOME LAGS
EXPENSES
1060 IF V(6) = 0 THEN F = 1 ELSE F = 0
1070 REM THE INVESTMENT MAY NOT EARN INCOME FOR SOME TIME
AFTER
1080 REM THE INITIAL MONEY IS SPENT
1090 FOR K=1 TO V(18)
1100     PRINT K, : REM SHOW USER THAT SOMETHING IS GOING ON
1110    IF (K-V(6))>0 THEN KA =1 ELSE KA =0
1120      IF F = 1 THEN 1180
1130      IF FL = -1 THEN F = 1:F1=F:GOTO 1180
1140      IF V(6) > K THEN F = 0 : GOTO 1180 : REM NO INCOME
YET
1150      F = K - V(6)
1160     F1 = 0
1170      FL = -1
1180     E1(K) = F * V(11)*(1+V(13)/100)[(K-1)
1190     EX(K) = F * V(12)*(1+V(14)/100)[(K)
```

```
1200    KD = KD + KA
1210    IF KD = 0 THEN 1240
1220     IF KD > 15 THEN 1240 :REM BYPASS DEPRECIATION
1230     D(K) = DP(1,KD)*V(19) + V(20)*DP(2,KD) +
V(21)*DP(3,KD) + V(22)*DP(4,KD) + V(23)/15
1240     E2(K) = E1(K) - D(K) - EX(K) - IP(K) - IZ(K)
1250      IF TL = 0 AND K>1 THEN 1420 :REM CHECK TO SEE IF
HAVE LOSS CARRY FORWARD
1260     IF E2(K)<0 THEN TL = TL + (-1*E2(K)) :
T1(K)=0:T2(K)=0:GOTO 1530
1270     IF E2(K) >TL THEN 1300
1280     TL = TL - (-1*E2(K)) : T1(K)=0:T2(K)=0
1290      GOTO 1530
1300     E2 = E2(K)-TL : TL = 0
1310     T2(K) = V(16)/100 * E2 : REM STATE TAX PAID
1320     T1(K) = V(15)/100*(E2-T2(K)) : REM FED TAX PAID
1330      IF TC = 0 THEN 1530
1340      IF TC < T1(K) THEN 1380 ELSE TC(K) = T1(K)
1350      TC = TC - T1(K)
1360      T1(K) = 0
1370      GOTO 1530
1380      TC(K) = TC
1390      T1(K) = T1(K) - TC
1400      TC = 0
1410     GOTO 1530
1420     IF E2(K) > 0 THEN T2(K) = V(16)/100*E2(K) ELSE
T2(K) = 0
1430     IF E2(K)>=0 THEN T1(K) = (E2(K)-T2(K))*V(15)/100
ELSE T1(K) =0
1440     IF E2(K) < 0 THEN TL = -1*E2(K) :GOTO 1530
1450      IF TC = 0 THEN 1530
1460      IF TC < T1(K) THEN 1500 ELSE TC(K) = T1(K)
1470      TC = TC - T1(K)
1480      T1(K) = 0
1490      GOTO 1530
1500      TC(K) = TC
1510      T1(K) = T1(K) - TC
1520      TC = 0
1530     CF(K) = E2(K)-T1(K)-T2(K)+D(K) : REM CASH FLOW FOR
YR K
1540     DF(K) = CF(K)*(1+V(17)/100)[-K : REM DISCOUNTED
CASH FLOW
1550     DI(K) = CF(K)*(1+V(25)/100)[-K
1560     DY(K) = DI(K)*(1+V(17)/100)[-K
```

```
1570     SF(K) =
E1(K)-EX(K)-T1(K)-T2(K)-IP(K)-IZ(K)-A1(K)-A2(K):REM
SPENDABLE CASH FLOW
1580    IF SF(K)<0 THEN SP = SP +(-1)*SF(K): CS = CS + 1
1590 REM KEEP TRACK OF WHEN SPENDABLE CASH FLOW IS NEGATIVE
AND THE NUMBER OF YEARS WITH NEGATIVE CASH FLOW.
1600     PV = DF(K)+PV
1610     PI = DY(K)+PI
1620 NEXT K
1630 GOSUB 2240 :REM PRINT IT OUT
1640 END
1650 REM NOW TAKE CARE OF LOANS
1660 CLS
1670 PRINT "NOW WORKING ON FIRST LOAN"
1680 REM FIRST LOAN
1690 IF V(2) = 0 THEN 1890 :REM TRANSFER IF NO FIRST LOAN
1700 REM FIRST CALCULATE PAYMENT
1710 I1 = V(3)/100/V(5) : REM INTEREST PER PERIOD
1720 S=0
1730 S2 = 0
1740 A = V(2)
1750 V = (I1+1)[(V(4)*V(5))
1760 P = V(2)*(I1*V)/(V-1)
1770 P = INT(100*P)/100
1780 NP = V(5)
1790 J2 = 1
1800 GOSUB 470
1810 A1(J2) = B
1820 IP(J2) = SI
1830 IF J2 = V(4) THEN 1950
1840 PRINT J2,
1850 SI=0
1860 B = 0
1870 J2=J2+1
1880 GOTO 1800
1890 REM HERE BECAUSE NO FIRST LOAN V(2)=0
1900 IF IP(1)=0 THEN 1950 : REM CHECK TO SEE IF ARRAYS
ZEROED
1910 FOR JZ = 1 TO 30
1920     IP(JZ)=0
1930   A1(JZ) = 0
1940 NEXT JZ
1950 REM NOW DO SECOND LOAN
1960 CLS
```

```
1970 PRINT "NOW WORKING ON SECOND LOAN"
1980 IF V(7) = 0 THEN 2170 : REM TRANSFER IF NO SECOND LOAN
1990 A = V(7)
2000 SI = 0
2010 B = 0
2020 I1 = V(8)/100/V(10)
2030 V = (I1+1)[(V(9)*V(10))
2040 P = V(7)*(I1*V)/(V-1)
2050 P = INT(P*100)/100
2060 NP = V(10)
2070 J2 = 1
2080 PRINT  J2,
2090 GOSUB 470
2100 A2(J2) = B
2110 IZ(J2) = SI
2120 IF J2 = V(9) THEN RETURN
2130 SI = 0
2140 B = 0
2150 J2 = J2 + 1
2160 GOTO 2080
2170 REM HERE BACAUSE NO SECOND LOAN
2180 IF IZ(1) AND A2(1) = 0 THEN RETURN
2190 FOR JZ = 1 TO 30
2200    IZ(JZ) = 0
2210    A2(JZ) = 0
2220 NEXT JZ
2230 RETURN
2240 REM NOW PRINT OUT THE RESULTS
2250 CLS
2260 PRINT "RESULTS OF CALCULATIONS "
2270 PRINT" SUMMARY"
2280 PRINT "================================================"
2290 PRINT USING"PRESENT VALUE OF CASH FLOWS
$###,####.##";PV
2300 PRINT USING "PRESENT VALUE CONSTANT YR
$###,####.##";PI
2310 IF PV<V(1) THEN PRINT "NOTE THAT PRESENT VALUE IS LESS
THAN INVESTMENT"
2320 PRINT
"================================================"
2330 PRINT "DO YOU WANT TO SEE YEARLY DETAILS Y OR N?"
2340 Y$=INKEY$:IF Y$="" THEN 2340 ELSE IF INSTR("YN",Y$)=0
THEN PRINT"TRY AGAIN":GOTO 2330
2350 IF Y$="N" THEN 2560
2360 FOR K=1 TO V(18)
```

```
2370   CLS
2380    PRINT USING"INCOME
$#,######.##":E1(K)
2390    PRINT USING"EXPENSES
$#,######,##";EX(K)
2400    PRINT USING"DEPRECIATION
$#,######.##";D(K)
2410    PRINT USING"INTEREST FIRST LOAN
$#,######.##";IP(K)
2420    PRINT USING"INTEREST SECOND LOAN
$#,######.##";IZ(K)
2430    PRINT USING"PRINCIPAL FIRST LOAN
$#,######.##";A1(K)
2440    PRINT USING"PRINCIPAL SECOND LOAN
$#,######.##";A2(K)
2450    PRINT USING"TAXABLE INCOME
$#,######.##";E1(K)-EX(K)-D(K)-IP(K)-IZ(K)
2460    PRINT USING"STATE TAXES PAID
$#,######.##";T2(K)
2470   PRINT USING"FEDERAL TAX PAID
$#,######.##";T1(K)
2480    PRINT USING"AFTER TAX CASH FLOW
$#,######.##";CF(K)
2490    PRINT USING"DISCOUNTED CASH FLOW
$#,######.##";DF(K)
2500    PRINT USING"CONSTANT DOLLAR CASH
$#,######.##";DY(K)
2510    PRINT USING"SPENDABLE CASH FLOW
$#,######.##";SF(K)
2520    PRINT"THIS IS YEAR ";K;" PRESS  ANY KEY FOR NEXT
YEAR"
2530    Y$=INKEY$:IF Y$="" THEN 2530
2540 NEXT K
2550 CLS
2560 PRINT"DO YOU WANT HARD COPY Y OR N "
2570 Y$=INKEY$:IF Y$="" THEN 2570 ELSE IF INSTR("YN",Y$)=0
THEN PRINT"TRY AGAIN":GOTO 2560
2580 IF Y$="Y" THEN GOSUB 2690
2590 CLS
2600 PRINT "DO YOU WANT TO RUN A SENSITIVITY ANALYSIS Y OR
N?"
2610 Y$=INKEY$: IF Y$="" THEN 2610 ELSE IF INSTR("YN",Y$)=0
THEN PRINT "PLEASE TRY AGAIN.":GOTO 2610
2620 IF Y$="Y" THEN GOSUB 3210
2630 PRINT"DO YOU WANT TO RUN ANOTHER CASE Y OR N?"
```

```
2640 Y$=INKEY$:IFY$=""THEN 2640 ELSE IF INSTR("YN",Y$)=0
THEN PRINT"TRY AGAIN":GOTO 2080
2650 IF Y$="Y" THEN 600
2660 PRINT"SESSION OVER. PLEASE REMOVE DISKS BEFORE
TURNING"
2670 PRINT"SYSTEM OFF."
2680 END
2690 PRINT"HARD COPY ROUTINE. PLEASE BE SURE PRINTER IS ON"
2700 LPRINT TAB(5);"RESULTS OF INVESTMENT ANALYSIS PROGRAM
V 2.9"
2710 LPRINT TAB(5) ; "NAME OF INVESTMENT ";NI$
2720 LPRINT " "
2730 LPRINT TAB(30);"INPUT DATA SUMMARY"
2740 FOR I = 1 TO 25
2750    LPRINT TAB(10);
2760    LPRINT USING F$(I);V(I)
2770 NEXT I
2780 LPRINT TAB(5);
"============================================"
2790 LPRINT" "
2800 LPRINT TAB(30);"SUMMARY RESULTS"
2810   LPRINT TAB(9);
2820 LPRINT USING "CURRENT YEAR DOLLARS PRESENT VALUE OF
CASH FLOWS $#,######.##";PV
2830 LPRINT TAB(9);
2840 LPRINT USING"CONSTANT YEAR DOLLAR PRESENT VALUE OF
CASH FLOWS  $#,######.##";PI
2850 LPRINT TAB(9);
2860 LPRINT USING"NET PRESENT VALUE (DISCOUNTED CASH -
COST) =      $#,######.##";PV-V(1)
2870 LPRINT TAB(9);
2880  LPRINT USING"CONSTANT YEAR NET PRESENT VALUE =
        $#,######.##";PI-V(1)
2890 IF V(1)>PV THEN LPRINT TAB(10);:LPRINT USING"YOU LOST
$#,######.## IN PRESENT VALUE ";V(1)-PV
2900 IF V(1)>PI THE LPRINT TAB(10);:LPRINT USING "YOU LOST
$#,######.## IN PURCHASING POWER ";V(1)-PI
2910 LPRINT TAB(5)
"================================================"
2920 PRINT "PRESS ANY KEY WHEN READY WITH NEW SHEET OF
PAPER."
2930 Y$=INKEY$:IF Y$="" THEN 2930
2940 LPRINT TAB(30);"RESULTS OF EACH YEARS OPERATION "
2950 FOR I=1 TO V(18)
2960   LPRINT TAB(30);"RESULTS FOR YEAR ";I
```

```
2970  LPRINT
TAB(5);"----------------------------------------"
2980   LPRINT USING"    GROSS INCOME
........................$#,######.##";E1(I)
2990   LPRINT USING"    EXPENSES
.............................$#,######.##";EX(I)
3000   LPRINT USING"    DEPRECIATION
........................$#,######.##";D(I)
3010   LPRINT USING"    INTEREST 1ST LOAN
....................$#,######.##";IP(I)
3020   LPRINT USING"    PRINCIPAL 1ST LOAN
...................$#,######.##";A1(I)
3030   LPRINT USING"    INTEREST 2ND LOAN
....................$#,######.##";IZ(I)
3040   LPRINT USING"    PRINCIPAL 2ND LOAN
...................$#,######.##";A2(I)
3050   LPRINT USING"    TAXABLE INCOME
.......................$#,######.##";E2(I)
3060   LPRINT USING"    STATE TAX PAID
.......................$#,######.##";T2(I)
3070  LPRINT USING"    INVESTMENT TAX CREDIT TAKEN
.........$#,######.##";TC(I)
3080   LPRINT USING"    FEDERAL TAX PAID
.....................$#,######.##";T1(I)
3090   LPRINT USING"    AFTER TAX CASH FLOW
..................$#,######.##";CF(I)
3100   LPRINT USING"    CONSTANT DOLLAR CASH FLOW
...........$#,######.##";DI(I)
3110   LPRINT USING"    DISCOUNTED CURRENT YEAR CASH FLOW
...$#,######.##";DF(I)
3120   LPRINT USING"    DISCOUNTED CONSTANT YR CASH FLOW
....$#,######.##";DY(I)
3130   LPRINT USING"    SPENDABLE CASH FLOW
..................$#,######.##";SF(I)
3140   IF SF(I)<0 THEN LPRINT "     NOTE THAT SPENDABLE
CASH IS NEGATIVE. YOU NEED TO BORROW MONEY."
3150  LPRINT
TAB(5);"========================================"
3160  IF INT(I/3)-I/3 = 0 THEN PRINT"PRESS ANY KEY WHEN
READY WITH NEW SHEET OF PAPER IN PRINTER " ELSE 3180
3170  Y$=INKEY$ : IF Y$ = "" THEN 3170
3180 NEXT I
3190  LPRINT
TAB(5);"========================================"
3200 RETURN
```

```
3210 REM SUBROUTINE FOR SENSITIVITY ANALYSIS
3220 CLS
3230 PRINT "YOU HAVE SELECTED A SENSITIVITY ANALYSIS."
3240 PRINT "PLEASE NOTE THAT ONLY A FEW ITEMS ARE CHECKED."
3250 PRINT "THE ITEMS THAT ARE CHECKED ARE:"
3260 PRINT "ESTIMATED INCOME. +/- 10% VARIATION.
3270 PRINT "ESTIMATED EXPESNE. +/- 10 % VARIATION."
3280 PRINT "ESCALATION OF INCOME. +/- 10"
3290 PRINT "ESCALATION OF EXPENSE. +/- 10%"
3300 PRINT "THE LONGER THE LIFE OF THE INVESTMENT, THE
LONGER"
3310 PRINT "THE CALCULATIONS TAKE."
3320 PRINT
3330 PRINT "DO YOU WANT THE INVESTMENT TAX CREDIT Y OR N?"
3340 Y$=INKEY$:IF Y$="" THEN 3340 ELSE IF INSTR("YN",Y$)=0
THEN PRINT "TRY AGAIN. ":GOTO 3330
3350 IF Y$="Y" THEN T1=1 ELSE T1=0
3360 PRINT "STARTING BY VARYING INCOME."
3370 PV(1,1)=PV
3380 PI(1,1)=PI
3390 TEMP = V(11)
3400 V(11)=TEMP*1.1
3410 GOSUB 4010
3420 PV(1,2)=PV
3430 PI(1,2)=PI
3440 V(11)=TEMP*.9
3450 GOSUB 4010
3460 PV(1,3)=PV
3470 PI(1,3)=PI
3480 V(11)=TEMP
3490 TEMP = V(12)
3500 V(12)=TEMP*1.1
3510 GOSUB 4010
3520 PV(2,2)=PV
3530 PI(2,2)=PI
3540 V(12)=0.9*TEMP
3550 GOSUB 4010
3560 PV(2,3)=PV
3570 PI(2,3)=PI
3580 V(12)=TEMP
3590 TEMP = V(13): REM ESCALATION FOR INCOME
3600 V(13)=TEMP*1.1
3610 GOSUB 4010
3620 PV(3,2)=PV
3630 PI(3,2)=PI
```

```
3640 V(13)=TEMP*0.9
3650 GOSUB 4010
3660 PV(3,3)=PV
3670 PI(3,3)=PI
3680 V(13)=TEMP
3690 TEMP=V(14)
3700 V(14)=1.1*TEMP
3710 GOSUB 4010
3720 PV(4,2)=PV
3730 PI(4,2)=PI
3740 V(14)=0.9*TEMP
3750 GOSUB 4010
3760 PV(4,3)=PV
3770 PI(4,3)=PI
3780 V(14)=TEMP
3790 CLS
3800 PRINT "SENSTIVITY ANALYSIS IS COMPLETE "
3810 PRINT "THE RESULTS ARE AS FOLLOWS"
3820 PRINT "A 10% INCREASE IN INCOME CHANGES THE PRESENT
VALUE"
3830 PRINT "FROM ";
3840 PRINT USING D$;PV(1,1);
3850 PRINT USING "TO "+D$;PV(1,2)
3860 PRINT "A 10% DECREASE IN INCOME CHANAGES THE PRESENT
VALUE TO ";
3870 PRINT USING D$;PV(1,3)
3880 PRINT "A 10% INCREASE IN EXPENSES CHANGES PRESENT
VALUE TO ";
3890 PRINT USING D$;PV(2,2)
3900 PRINT "A 10% DECREASE IN EXPENSES CHANAGES PRESENT
VALUE TO ";
3910 PRINT USING D$;PV(2,3)
3920 PRINT "A 10% INCREASE IN THE GROWTH RATE OF INCOME
CHANGES THE"
3930 PRINT USING"PRESENT VALUE TO $#,######.##";PV(3,2)
3940 PRINT USING"A 10% DECREASE IN INCOME GROWTH GIVES
$#,######.##";PV(3,3)
3950 PRINT USING"A 10% INCREASE IN EXPENSE GROWTH GIVE
$#,######.##";PV(4,2)
3960 PRINT USING "A 10% DECREASE IN EXPENSE GROWTH GIVES
$#,#####.##";PV(4,3)
3970 PRINT"DO YOU WANT HARD COPY Y OR N"
3980 Y$=INKEY$: IF Y$="" THEN 3980 ELSE IF INSTR("YN",Y$)=0
THEN PRINT"TRY AGAIN.":GOTO 3970
3990 IF Y$="Y" THEN GOSUB 4690
```

```
4000 RETURN
4010 REM
4020 REM CALCULATE INVESTMENT TAX CREDIT ALLOWED
4030 REM TAX CREDIT IS ALLOWED ON 100% OF FIVE AND TEN YEAR
PROPERTY
4040 REM TAX CREDIT IS ALLOWED ON 60% OF THREE YEAR
PROPERTY
4050 TC =T1*0.1*(V(20)+V(21)+0.6*V(19))
4060 REM ALL LOANS TAKEN CARE OF NOW LETS DO YEARLY CASH
FLOWS
4070 CLS
4080 PRINT "NOW WORKING ON YEARLY CASH FLOWS."
4090 REM K IS THE YEAR NUMBER ASSUME THAT INCOME LAGS
EXPENSES
4100 IF V(6) = 0 THEN F = 1 ELSE F = 0
4110 IF F=0 THEN F1=0 ELSE F1=1
4120 REM THE INVESTMENT MAY NOT EARN INCOME FOR SOME TIME
AFTER
4130 PV=0:DY=0:TL=0:SP=0:CS=0:PI=0:FL=0 : KA = 0: KD = 0
4140 REM THE INITIAL MONEY IS SPEND
4150 FOR K=1 TO V(18)
4160    PRINT K : REM SHOW USER THAT SOMETHING IS GOING ON
4170   IF (K - V(6)) > 0 THEN KA = 1 ELSE KA = 0
4180     IF F = 1 THEN 4240
4190     IF FL = -1 THEN F = 1:F1=F:GOTO 4240
4200     IF V(6) > K THEN F = 0 : GOTO 4240 : REM NO INCOME
YET
4210     F = K - V(6)
4220    F1 = 0
4230     FL = -1
4240    E1(K) = F * V(11)*(1+V(13)/100)[(K-1)
4250    EX(K) = F * V(12)*(1+V(14)/100)[(K)
4260   KD = KD +KA
4270   IF KD = 0 OR KD > 15 THEN 4290 : REM BYPASS
DEPRECIATION
4280    D(K) = DP(1,KD)*V(19) + V(20)*DP(2,KD) +
V(21)*DP(3,KD) + V(22)*DP(4,KD) + V(23)/15
4290    E2(K) = E1(K) - D(K) - EX(K) - IP(K)
4300     IF TL = 0 AND K>1 THEN 4470 :REM CHECK TO SEE IF
HAVE LOSS CARRY FORWARD
4310    IF E2(K)<0 THEN TL = TL + (-1*E2(K)) :
T1(K)=0:T2(K)=0:GOTO 4580
4320    IF E2(K) >TL THEN 4350
4330    TL = TL - (-1*E2(K)) : T1(K)=0:T2(K)=0:PRINT TL
4340     GOTO 4580
```

```
4350     E2 = E2(K)-TL : TL = 0
4360     T2(K) = V(16)/100 * E2 : REM STATE TAX PAID
4370     T1(K) = V(15)/100*(E2-T2(K)) : REM FED TAX PAID
4380      IF TC = 0 THEN 4580
4390      IF TC < T1(K) THEN 4430 ELSE TC(K) = T1(K)
4400      TC = TC - T1(K)
4410      T1(K) = 0
4420      GOTO 4580
4430      TC(K) = TC
4440      T1(K) = T1(K) - TC
4450      TC = 0
4460     GOTO 4580
4470     IF E2(K) > 0 THEN T2(K) = V(16)/100*E2(K) ELSE
T2(K) = 0
4480     IF E2(K) > 0 THEN T1(K) = (E2(K)-T2(K))*V(15)/100
ELSE T1(K) =0
4490    IF E2(K)<0 THEN TL = E2(K)*(-1):GOTO 4580
4500      IF TC = 0 THEN 4580
4510      IF TC < T1(K) THEN 4550 ELSE TC(K) = T1(K)
4520      TC = TC - T1(K)
4530      T1(K) = 0
4540      GOTO 4580
4550      TC(K) = TC
4560      T1(K) = T1(K) - TC
4570      TC = 0
4580     CF(K) = E2(K)-T1(K)-T2(K)+D(K) : REM CASH FLOW FOR
YR K
4590     DF(K) = CF(K)*(1+V(17)/100)[-K : REM DISCOUNTED
CASH FLOW
4600     DI(K) = CF(K)*(1+V(25)/100)[-K
4610     DY(K) = DI(K)*(1+V(17)/100)[-K
4620     SF(K) =
E1(K)-EX(K)-T1(K)-T2(K)-IP(K)-IZ(K)-A1(K)-A2(K):REM
SPENDABLE CASH FLOW
4630    IF SF(K)<0 THEN SP = SP +(-1)*SF(K): CS = CS + 1
4640 REM KEEP TRACK OF WHEN SPENDABLE CASH FLOW IS NEGATIVE
AND THE NUMBER OF YEARS WITH NEGATIVE CASH FLOW.
4650     PV = DF(K)+PV
4660     PI = DY(K)+PI
4670 NEXT K
4680 RETURN
4690 REM HARD COPY FOR SENSTIVITY ANALYSIS
4700 CLS
4710 PRINT "BE SURE PRINTER IS ON"
4720 LPRINT TAB(10);"RESULTS OF SENSITIVITY ANALYSIS FOR"
```

```
4730 LPRINT TAB(10);NI$
4740 LPRINT TAB(5);
"============================================="
4750 LPRINT TAB(5);"NOTE THAT IN THE SENSITIVITY ANALYSIS
ONLY ONE VARIABLE IS VARIED AT A TIME"
4760 LPRINT
TAB(5);"=================================================="
4770 LPRINT TAB(10);"RESULTS OF VARYING INCOME"
4780 LPRINT TAB(10);"INCOME";TAB(20):"CURRENT $
PV";TAB(35);"CONSTANT $ PV"
4790 LPRINT TAB(10);V(11):TAB(20):PV(1,1);TAB(35):PI(1,1)
4800 LPRINT
TAB(10);V(11)*1.1;TAB(20):PV(1,2);TAB(35):PI(1,2)
4810 LPRINT
TAB(10);V(11)*0.9;TAB(20);PV(1,3);TAB(35):PI(1,3)
4820 LPRINT  TAB(10)"========================="
4830 LPRINT TAB(10);"RESULTS OF VARYING EXPENSES "
4840 LPRINT TAB(10);"EXPENSE";TAB(20);"CURRENT $
PV";TAB(35);"CONSTANT $ PV"
4850 LPRINT TAB(10);V(12);TAB(20);PV(1,1);TAB(35):PI(1,1)
4860 LPRINT
TAB(10);V(12)*1.1;TAB(20);PV(2,2);TAB(35);PI(2,2)
4870 LPRINT
TAB(10);V(12)*0.9;TAB(20);PV(2,3);TAB(35);PI(2,3)
4880 LPRINT TAB(10);"========================"
4890 LPRINT TAB(10); "RESULTS OF VARYING RATE OF INCOME
GROWTH"
4900 LPRINT TAB(10);"INCOME GROWTH ";TAB(20):"CURRENT $
PV";TAB(35):"CONSTANT $ PV"
4910 LPRINT TAB(10);V(13):TAB(20);PV(1,1);TAB(35) PI(1,1)
4920 LPRINT
TAB(10);V(13)*1.1;TAB(20);PV(3,2):TAB(35) PI(3,2)
4930 LPRINT
TAB(10);V(13)*0.9;TAB(20);PV(3,3):TAB(35):PI(3,3)
4940 LPRINT TAB(10);"========================"
4950 LPRINT TAB(10); "RESULTS OF VARYING RATE OF COST
GROWTH"
4960 LPRINT TAB(10);"COST GROWTH";TAB(20);"CURRENT $ PV
";TAB(35);"CONSTANT $ PV"
4970 LPRINT TAB(10);V(14);TAB(20);PV(1,1);TAB(35) PI(1,1)
4980 LPRINT
TAB(10);V(14)*1.1;TAB(20);PV(4,2);TAB(35);PI(4,2)
4990 LPRINT
TAB(10);V(14)*.9;TAB(20);PV(4,3);TAB(35);PI(4,3)
5000 LPRINT TAB(10);"======================="
```

```
5010 LPRINT TAB(10);
5020 LPRINT USING "COST OF INVESTMENT $#,######.##";V(1)
5030 LPRINT TAB(10); "======================="
5040 RETURN
5050 END
5060 REM ERROR SUBROUTINE
5070 CLS
5080 PRINT "******************************"
5090 PRINT "INPUT DATA ERROR!!!"
5100 IF V(18) >30 THEN PRINT "MAXIMUM LIFE ALLOWED IS 30
YEARS"
5110 IF V(19)+V(20)+V(21)+V(22)>V(1) THEN PRINT
"DEPRECIATION TAKEN EXCEEDS VALUE OF INVESTMENT "
5120 PRINT "PLEASE CORRECT DATA ENTRY "
5130 FOR KQ = 1 TO 400
5140 NEXT KQ
5150 RETURN
5160 REM DATA ENTRY SUBROUTINE
5170 P1=1
5180 IZ=1: IX=9
5190 I=IZ:IQ=1
5200 CLS
5210 PRINT"INVESTMENT ANALYSIS DATA INPUT PAGE ";P1
5220 PRINT"PROVIDE DATA ASKED FOR. CURRENT VALUE SHOWN IN
()"
5230 PRINT"IF YOU WISH TO CORRECT A PREVIOUS ENTRY ENTER C"
5240 PRINT"TO GO TO NEXT PAGE ENTER >"
5250 PRINT STRING$(63,"=")
5260 IF I = IZ THEN 5280 ELSE FOR IQ=IZ TO I-1:PRINT USING
F$(IQ);V(IQ):NEXT IQ
5270 IF I > I9 THEN 5400
5280    PRINT USING F$(I);V(I);
5290 V$=""
5300    INPUT V$
5310   IF V$="" THEN 5380
5320    IF V$=">" THEN 5540 ELSE IF V$="C" THEN 5670
5330   IF V$="<" THEN 5610
5340   V(I)=VAL(V$):V$=""
5350   IF V(18)>30 THEN GOSUB 5060 : GOTO 5200
5360  IF V(19)+V(20)+V(21)+V(22)>V(1) THEN GOSUB 5060: GOTO
5200
5370  IF I = I9 THEN 5400
5380 I=I+1:IF I<=IX THEN 5200
5390  GOTO 5490
5400 PRINT STRING$(63,"=")
```

```
5410 PRINT"END OF DATA ENTRY. PLEASE CHECK DATA ON THIS
PAGE."
5420 PRINT"TO CORRECT DATA ENTER C. TO REVIEW PREVIOUS PAGE
ENTER <"
5430 PRINT"TO REVIEW ALL DATA ENTER R. TO START
CALCULATIONS ENTER G.";
5440 Y$=""
5450 INPUT Y$
5460 IF Y$="G" THEN RETURN ELSE IF Y$="C" THEN 5500 ELSE IF
Y$="<" THEN 5610
5470 IF Y$ <> "R" THEN PRINT "PLEASE ENTER C,<,R,OR
G.":GOTO 5410
5480 CLS
5490 PRINT "END OF PAGE ";P1;" REVIEW DATA ENTER > TO GO TO
NEXT PAGE"
5500 PRINT"ENTER C TO CORRECT ENTRY AND ENTER R TO RETURN
TO MAIN PROGRAM";
5510 Y$="":INPUT Y$
5520 IF Y$ = "<" THEN 5610
5530 IF Y$=">" THEN 5540 ELSE IF Y$="C" THEN 5670 ELSE IF
Y$<>"R" THEN PRINT"PLEASE ANSWER >,C,OR R":GOTO 5490
5540 REM
5550 IF P1 = PM THEN 5400
5560 P1=P1+1
5570 IZ=IZ+9
5580 IX =IZ+8
5590 I=IZ:IQ=IZ
5600 GOTO 5200
5610 IF P1>1 THEN P1=P1-1 ELSE GOTO 5200
5620 IF P1 =1 THEN IZ = 1 : IX =8
5630 IF P1 = 2 THEN IZ = 9 : IX = 16
5640 IF P1 = 3 THEN IZ = 17 : IX = 24
5650 IF I > IX THEN I = IX
5660 GOTO 5200
5670 REM CORRECTION PAGE
5680 CLS
5690 V$=""
5700 PRINT "ROUTINE TO CORRECT ENTRY ON PAGE ";P1
5710 PRINT STRING$(63,"=")
5720 IF IX > I9 THEN IX = I9
5730 FOR J=IZ TO IX
5740   PRINT J;
5750    PRINT USING F$(J);V(J)
5760 NEXT J
5770 PRINT STRING$(63,"=")
```

```
5780 PRINT "IF YOU WANT TO CORRECT ALL ENTRIES ENTER A
ELSE"
5790 INPUT "ENTER ITEM NUMBER TO CORRECT R TO RETURN ";YI$
5800 IF YI$="A" THEN GOTO 5160
5810 IF YI$="R" THEN 5880 ELSE J=VAL(YI$)
5820 IF J>IX THEN PRINT "NOT ON THIS PAGE ":GOTO 5790
5830 IF J<=0 THEN J = IX
5840 PRINT USING F$(J);V(J):INPUT"ENTER CORRECT VALUE C IF
OK ";C$
5850 IF C$="C" THEN GOTO 5670 ELSE V(J)=VAL(C$)
5860 GOTO 5670
5870 END
5880 REM
5890 GOTO 5200
5900 IF V(24)<1982 THEN V(24)=1982
5910 REM READ IN NEW DEPRECIATION
5920 FOR I=1 TO 4
5930   IF I = 1 THEN JM = 3 ELSE IF I = 2 THEN JM = 5 ELSE
IF I = 3 THEN JM = 10 ELSE JM = 15
5940    FOR J = 1 TO JM
5950            READ DP(I,J)
5960           DP(I,J)=DP(I,J)/100 : REM CONVERT TO DECIMAL
FRACTION
5970    NEXT J
5980 NEXT I
5990 IF V(24) <1985 THEN RETURN
6000 JZ = JZ +1
6010 IF V(24) = 1985 AND JZ = 1 THEN 5920 ELSE IF V(24) =
1985 THEN RETURN
6020 IF JZ <= 2 THEN 5920 ELSE RETURN
6030 REM DEPRECIATION FOR 3  YEAR
6040 DATA 25,38,37
6050 REM DEPRECIATION FOR 5 YEAR
6060 DATA 15,22,21,21,21
6070 REM DEPRECIATION DATA FOR 10 YEAR
6080 DATA 8,14,12,10,10,10,9,9,9,9
6090 REM FOR 15 YEAR
6100 DATA 5,10,9,8,7,7,6,6,6,6,6,6,6,6,6
6110 REM DATA FOR 1985
6120 DATA 29,47,24,18,33,25,16,8
6130 DATA 9,19,16,14,12,10,8,6,4,2
6140 DATA 6,12,12,11,10,9,8,7,6,5,4,4,3,2,1
6150 REM DATA FOR 1986
6160 DATA 33,45,22,20,32,24,16,8
6170 DATA 10,18,16,14,12,10,8,6,4,2
```

```
6180 DATA 7,12,12,11,10,9,8,7,6,5,4,3,3,2,1
6190 END
6200 REM INITIALIZATION SUBROUTINE
6210 F$(1)="TOTAL AMOUNT OF INVESTMENT
$#,######.##"
6220 F$(2)="AMOUNT OF FIRST LOAN
$#,######.##"
6230 F$(3)="YEARLY INTEREST RATE FOR 1ST LOAN
##.##%
6240 F$(4)="LIFE OF FIRST LOAN YEARS
##.##  YRS"
6250 F$(5)="NUMBER OF LOAN PAYMENTS PER YEAR
##"
6260 F$(6)="TIME AFTER INVESTING BEFORE REC. INCOME
#.## YRS"
6270 F$(7)="AMOUNT OF SECOND LOAN
$#,######.##
6280 F$(8)="YEARLY INTEREST RATE FOR 2ND LOAN
##.##%"
6290 F$(9)="LIFE OF SECOND LOAN YEARS
## YRS"
6300 F$(10) ="NUMBER OF PAYMENTS PER YEAR  2ND LOAN
##"
6310 F$(11)="ESTIMATED ANNUAL INCOME
$#,######.##"
6320 F$(12)="ESTIMATED ANNUAL EXPENSES
$#,######.##"
6330 F$(13)="ESCALATION FOR INCOME
 ##.##%"
6340 F$(14)="ESCALATION FOR EXPENSES
##.##%"
6350 F$(15)="FEDERAL INCOME TAX RATE
##.##%"
6360 F$(16)="STATE INCOME TAX RATE
##.##%"
6370 F$(17)="DISCOUNT RATE
##.## %"
6380 F$(18)="LIFE OF INVESTMENT
## YRS"
6390 F$(19) = "VALUE OF 3 YEAR PROPERTY
$#,######.##"
6400 F$(20) = "VALUE OF 5 YEAR PROPERTY
$#,######.##"
6410 F$(21) = "VALUE OF 10 YEAR PROPERTY
$#,######.##"
```

```
6420 F$(22) = "VALUE OF 15 YEAR PU PROP
$#,######.##"
6430 F$(23) = "VALUE OF ST LINE REAL ESTATE
$#,######.##"
6440 F$(24) = "YEAR PROPERY PLACED IN SVC
####"
6450 F$(25) = "INFLATION RATE
##.##%"
6460 RETURN
6470 CLS
6480 PRINT
"=================================================="
6490 PRINT "INSTRUCTIONS "
6500 PRINT "THIS PROGRAM CALCULATES THE PRESENT VALUE OF
THE"
6510 PRINT "CASH FLOWS FROM AN INVESTMENT. IN ORDER TO USE"
6520 PRINT "THE PROGRAM, YOU MUST SUPPLY THE INPUT
INFORMATION."
6530 PRINT "DATA ENTRY IS A MATTER OF SUPPLYING THE
INFORMATION"
6540 PRINT "ASKED FOR. DATA IS ENTERED IN A THREE PAGE
MENU.
6550 PRINT "YOU MOVE FROM PAGE TO PAGE WITH THE < AND >
KEYS."
6560 PRINT "YOU CAN CORRECT A WRONG ENTRY BY ENTERING C
AND"
6570 PRINT "THEN FOLLOWING THE INSTRUCTIONS."
6580 PRINT "WHEN ALL THE DATA ARE CORRECT, YOU CAN START
THE"
6590 PRINT "CALCULATIONS BY ENTERING G."
6600 PRINT "YOU MUST ENTER ALL THE DATA BEFORE YOU CAN RUN
THE PROGRAM."
6610 PRINT "PRESS ANY KEY TO CONTINUE"
6620 Y$=INKEY$:IF Y$="" THEN 6620
6630 CLS
6640 PRINT "INSTRUCTIONS PAGE 2"
6650 PRINT "ALL DATA ASKED FOR IS SELF EXPLANATORY, WITH
THE
6660 PRINT "POSSIBLE EXCEPTION OF YEARS AFTER INVEST BEFORE
REC
6670 PRINT "INCOME. THIS QUESTION IS BASED ON THE FACT THAT
MANY
6680 PRINT "INVESTMENTS DO NOT START PAYING UNITIL SOME
TIME
```

```
6690 PRINT "AFTER THE MONEY IS SPENT. YOU ENTER THE NUMBER
OF"
6700 PRINT "YEARS YOU ESTIMATE IT WILL TAKE FOR INCOME TO
START"
6710 PRINT "COMING AFTER THE INVESTMENT IS MADE. FOR
EXAMPLE IF"
6720 PRINT "YOU KNOW IT WILL TAKE ONE YEAR ENTER 1. IF IT
WILL
6730 PRINT "TAKE HALF A YEAR, ENTER 0.5."
6740 PRINT "PRESS ANY KEY TO CONTINUE"
6750 Y$=INKEY$:IF Y$="" THEN 6750
6760 RETURN
```

Example: Using INVEST1/BAS

Input data are shown in Fig. 10-3.

Remember that this investment is expected to pay for itself from income it generates. You do not expect to make your profit from resale. This is the type of investment that a cursory examination of the input data reveals little. The investment appears fine. The estimated $85,000 (income minus expenses) should cover all loan payments and give you a profit. Results of the line printer output are shown in Fig. 10-4.

All of the hard copy output is shown in Figs. 10-3 and 10-4. First there is the data you entered, which is shown here so you can verify that the program used the data you wanted it to. A quick review shows the data is correct (Fig. 10-3).

The next item in the output is the summary results (Fig. 10-3). The present value of the current year (not corrected for inflation) cash flows is less than your investment. You lost more than $7,800 in current year value on the investment, indicating that the investment was a poor one.

The inflation corrected information is even worse. The constant year present value of the cash flows is only $135,679. This is more than $64,000 below the cost of the investment. The computer printed a message to warn us that the investment was a money loser.

Now let's look at the yearly details (Fig. 10-4). First, spendable cash flow is negative for the first year of the investment. This means that you would have to find an additional $51,730.40 to keep the investment going. The cost of this money would reduce the return on the investment even further.

There aren't any other surprises in the printout. The investment doesn't earn taxable income until the second year; this is somewhat offset by the tax loss carried forward from the first year. In the second year you pay some state tax, but because of the investment tax credit you do not have to pay federal tax. In the third year you still have enough of the investment tax credit remaining to offset the federal tax. In the fourth year you pay both federal and state tax.

The program assumes that all tax losses can be carried forward for as long as necessary to earn income to offset tax losses. The tax laws limit the time that you can carry tax losses forward; however, I think that any good investment will earn income before the tax losses expire.

The program also assumes that the investment tax credit can be taken at any time. There are limits to the time you have available to take the investment tax credit. Consult the IRS to be sure.

SENSITIVITY ANALYSIS

After the hard copy is printed, you are asked if you want to run a sensitivity analysis of the investment. If so, press Y. You do not have to press <ENTER>. The sensitivity analysis determines

```
                    INPUT DATA SUMMARY
     TOTAL AMOUNT OF INVESTMENT                     $ 200,000.00
     AMOUNT OF FIRST LOAN                           $ 100,000.00
     YEARLY INTEREST RATE FOR 1ST LOAN                    15.00%
     LIFE OF FIRST LOAN YEARS                              5.00   YRS
     NUMBER OF LOAN PAYMENTS PER YEAR                     1
     TIME AFTER INVESTING BEFORE REC. INCOME              1.00 YRS
     AMOUNT OF SECOND LOAN                          $   50,000.00
     YEARLY INTEREST RATE FOR 2ND LOAN                    15.00%
     LIFE OF SECOND LOAN YEARS                              3 YRS
     NUMBER OF PAYMENTS PER YEAR  2ND LOAN               1
     ESTIMATED ANNUAL INCOME                        $ 115,000.00
     ESTIMATED ANNUAL EXPENSES                      $  35,000.00
     ESCALATION FOR INCOME                                 12.00%
     ESCALATION FOR EXPENSES                                8.00%
     FEDERAL INCOME TAX RATE                               40.00%
     STATE INCOME TAX RATE                                 10.00%
     DISCOUNT RATE                                         12.00 %
     LIFE OF INVESTMENT                                    5 YRS
     VALUE OF 3 YEAR PROPERTY                     $   40,000.00
     VALUE OF 5 YEAR PROPERTY                     $  160,000.00
     VALUE OF 10 YEAR PROPERTY                    $         0.00
     VALUE OF 15 YEAR PU PROP                     $         0.00
     VALUE OF ST LINE REAL ESTATE                 $         0.00
     YEAR PROPERY PLACED IN SVC                          1982
     INFLATION RATE                                        10.00%
============================================

                    SUMMARY RESULTS
   CURRENT YEAR DOLLARS PRESENT VALUE OF CASH FLOWS $ 192,184.00
   CONSTANT YEAR DOLLAR PRESENT VALUE OF CASH FLOWS  $ 135,679.00
   NET PRESENT VALUE (DISCOUNTED CASH - COST) =      $   -7,816.09
   CONSTANT YEAR NET PRESENT VALUE =                 $  -64,321.40
    YOU LOST $    7,816.09 IN PRESENT VALUE
    YOU LOST $   64,321.40 IN PURCHASING POWER
============================================
```

Fig. 10-3. Results of investment analysis program INVEST1 for Example 1.

the current year dollar and constant year dollar present values of all cash flows for the following cases:

1. Estimated income 10 percent higher than the initial value.

2. Estimated income 10 percent lower than the initial value.

3. Estimated expenses 10 percent higher than the initial value.

4. Estimated expenses 10 percent lower than the initial value.

5. Estimated income growth rate 10 percent greater than the initial estimate.

6. Estimated income growth rate 10 percent less than the initial estimate.

```
                      RESULTS FOR YEAR  1
 ----------------------------------------
GROSS INCOME ........................$          0.00
EXPENSES ............................$          0.00
DEPRECIATION ........................$          0.00
INTEREST 1ST LOAN ...................$     15,000.00
PRINCIPAL 1ST LOAN ..................$     14,831.60
INTEREST 2ND LOAN ...................$      7,500.00
PRINCIPAL 2ND LOAN ..................$     14,398.80
TAXABLE INCOME ......................$    -22,500.00
STATE TAX PAID ......................$          0.00
INVESTMENT TAX CREDIT TAKEN .........$          0.00
FEDERAL TAX PAID ....................$          0.00
AFTER TAX CASH FLOW .................$    -22,500.00
CONSTANT DOLLAR CASH FLOW ...........$    -20,454.50
DISCOUNTED CURRENT YEAR CASH FLOW ...$    -20,089.30
DISCOUNTED CONSTANT YR CASH FLOW ....$    -18,263.00
SPENDABLE CASH FLOW .................$    -51,730.40
 NOTE THAT SPENDABLE CASH IS NEGATIVE. YOU NEED TO BORROW MONEY.
 ========================================
                      RESULTS FOR YEAR  2
 ----------------------------------------
GROSS INCOME ........................$ 128,800.00
EXPENSES ............................$  40,824.00
DEPRECIATION .. .....................$  34,000.00
INTEREST 1ST LOAN ...................$  12,775.30
PRINCIPAL 1ST LOAN ..................$  17,056.30
INTEREST 2ND LOAN ...................$   5,340.17
PRINCIPAL 2ND LOAN ..................$  16,558.70
TAXABLE INCOME ......................$  35,860.60
STATE TAX PAID ......................$   1,336.06
INVESTMENT TAX CREDIT TAKEN .........$   4,809.80
FEDERAL TAX PAID ....................$        0.00
AFTER TAX CASH FLOW .................$  68,524.50
CONSTANT DOLLAR CASH FLOW ...........$  56,631.80
DISCOUNTED CURRENT YEAR CASH FLOW ...$  54,627.30
DISCOUNTED CONSTANT YR CASH FLOW ....$  45,146.60
SPENDABLE CASH FLOW .................$  34,909.50
 ========================================
                      RESULTS FOR YEAR  3
 ----------------------------------------
GROSS INCOME ........................$ 144,256.00
```

Fig. 10-4. Results of operation for each year (continued on pages 99 and 100).

```
EXPENSES ..............................$  44,089.90
DEPRECIATION ..........................$  50,400.00
INTEREST 1ST LOAN ....... ............$  10,216.80
PRINCIPAL 1ST LOAN ...................$  19,614.70
INTEREST 2ND LOAN ....................$   2,856.37
PRINCIPAL 2ND LOAN ...................$  19,042.50
TAXABLE INCOME .......................$  36,692.80
STATE TAX PAID .......................$   3 669.28
INVESTMENT TAX CREDIT TAKEN ..........$  13,209.40
FEDERAL TAX PAID .....................$       0.00
AFTER TAX CASH FLOW ..................$  83,423.60
CONSTANT DOLLAR CASH FLOW ............$  62,677.40
DISCOUNTED CURRENT YEAR CASH FLOW ...$  59,379.30
DISCOUNTED CONSTANT YR CASH FLOW ....$  44,612.50
SPENDABLE CASH FLOW ..................$  44,766.40
 ========================================
                          RESULTS FOR YEAR  4
 ----------------------------------------
GROSS INCOME .........................$ 161,567.00
EXPENSES .............................$  47,617.10
DEPRECIATION .........................$  48,400.00
INTEREST 1ST LOAN ....................$   7,274.61
PRINCIPAL 1ST LOAN ...................$  22,556.90
INTEREST 2ND LOAN ....................$       0.00
PRINCIPAL 2ND LOAN ...................$       0.00
TAXABLE INCOME .......................$  58,274.90
STATE TAX PAID .......................$   5,827.49
INVESTMENT TAX CREDIT TAKEN ..........$     380.77
FEDERAL TAX PAID .....................$  20,598.20
AFTER TAX CASH FLOW ..................$  80,249.20
CONSTANT DOLLAR CASH FLOW ............$  54,811.30
DISCOUNTED CURRENT YEAR CASH FLOW ...$  50,999.90
DISCOUNTED CONSTANT YR CASH FLOW ....$  34,833.60
SPENDABLE CASH FLOW ..................$  57,692.30
 ========================================
                          RESULTS FOR YEAR  5
 ----------------------------------------
GROSS INCOME .........................$ 180,955.00
EXPENSES .............................$  51,426.50
DEPRECIATION .........................$  33,600.00
INTEREST 1ST LOAN ....................$   3,891.07
PRINCIPAL 1ST LOAN ...................$  25,940.50
```

```
INTEREST 2ND LOAN ....................$          0.00
PRINCIPAL 2ND LOAN ...................$          0.00
TAXABLE INCOME .......................$     92,037.10
STATE TAX PAID .......................$      9,203.71
INVESTMENT TAX CREDIT TAKEN .........$          0.00
FEDERAL TAX PAID .....................$     33,133.30
AFTER TAX CASH FLOW ..................$     83,300.00
CONSTANT DOLLAR CASH FLOW ............$     51,722.80
DISCOUNTED CURRENT YEAR CASH FLOW ...$     47,266.70
DISCOUNTED CONSTANT YR CASH FLOW ....$     29,348.90
SPENDABLE CASH FLOW ..................$     57,359.50
 ======================================
 ======================================
```

Fig. 10-4. Continued from page 99.

7. Estimated expense growth rate 10 percent greater than the initial estimate.

8. Estimated expense growth rate 10 percent less than the initial estimate.

This tells you how sensitive the profitability of the investment is to each of these items. The calculations are done by changing only one variable at a time. All other variables remain at their original values. For example, the calculations with 10 percent lower expenses are done with the original values of income, income and expense, growth, and all other data.

The benefit of a sensitivity analysis is that it warns you about the important variables and tells you which of the variables not to worry about. If a 10 percent change in a variable produces a major change in the net present values, then considerable effort should be made to insure that the value of the variable is the best available. However, if a 10 percent change doesn't produce any significant change in the present values, there isn't much sense in spending time to obtain better data.

The sensitivity analysis for the example is shown in Fig. 10-5. A 10 percent change in the income estimate had a significant impact on the investment. A 10 percent increase in income made the investment profitable, in current year dollar terms. A change in the expense estimate didn't show much.

Changes in the growth rate of expenses and income had considerable impact. The fact that changes in the cost and income growth rates are important suggests ways to make the investment more attractive. For example, any steps that will increase income growth will make the investment more attractive. Furthermore, cost growth must be carefully managed. If the costs grow faster than estimated, the investment becomes very unattractive.

So what can be concluded? First, the investment is unattractive. Even the best of the conditions in the sensitivity analysis shows that in constant year dollar terms the investment doesn't pay. The analysis does suggest ways to make the investment more attractive—mainly by increasing income growth and controlling cost growth. But in the final analysis, I would say that the investment is over priced.

You can modify the program to include other items in the sensitivity analysis. The items I included are generally the most important. If you include the cost of the investment in the sensitivity

```
     RESULTS OF SENSITIVITY ANALYSIS FOR
     EXAMPLE 1 USING INVEST1
=============================================
NOTE THAT IN THE SENSITIVITY ANALYSIS ONLY ONE VARIABLE IS VARIED AT A TIME
=============================================
     RESULTS OF VARYING INCOME
     INCOME     CURRENT $ PV    CONSTANT $ PV
      115000     192184          135679
      126500     222525          159383
      103500     177028          125817
     ==========================
     RESULTS OF VARYING EXPENSES
     EXPENSE    CURRENT $ PV    CONSTANT $ PV
      35000      192184          135679
      38500      193163          137827
      31500      206738          147832
     =========================
     RESULTS OF VARYING RATE OF INCOME GROWTH
     INCOME GROWTH CURRENT $ PVCONSTANT $ PV
      12         192184          135679
      13.2       205998          147010
      10.8       194031          138733
     =========================
     RESULTS OF VARYING RATE OF COST GROWTH
     COST GROWTHCURRENT $ PV    CONSTANT $ PV
      8          192184          135679
      8.8        198209          141600
      7.2        201656          144036
     ========================
     COST OF INVESTMENT $ 200,000.00
     ========================
```

Fig. 10-5. Results of sensitivity analysis for example 1.

analysis, you must modify the depreciable property also.

OTHER USES OF THE PROGRAM

The fact that the example investment does not pay for itself (even with a significantly higher estimate of expected income) suggests another use for the program: you can determine what a reasonable price would be. (By reasonable I mean a price that at least allows the investment to pay for itself.) To answer this question, just answer the question "DO YOU WANT TO RUN ANOTHER CASE?" by pressing Y. You get to the first of the data entry form; change the cost of the investment to (say) $150,000. Leave the amount of the first loan at $100,000 and change the amount of the second loan to $50,000. Leave everything else on the page unchanged.

Leave page two alone. On page three, change the depreciation values by reducing the five year property to $100,000. This completes all changes in the input data. (You could have reduced both the three and five year property; I decided to change the five year property.)

Now run the program again. As can be seen from the summary output shown in Fig. 10-6, the investment still didn't pay for itself in terms of constant year dollars. Try $120,000 as the amount of the investment. The first loan stays at $100,000 and the second loan goes to $20,000. The value of

```
RESULTS OF INVESTMENT ANALYSIS PROGRAM V 2.9
NAME OF INVESTMENT EXAMPLE 1 USING INVEST1

                    INPUT DATA SUMMARY
    TOTAL AMOUNT OF INVESTMENT                  $ 150,000.00
    AMOUNT OF FIRST LOAN                        $ 100,000.00
    YEARLY INTEREST RATE FOR 1ST LOAN                  15.00%
    LIFE OF FIRST LOAN YEARS                            5.00  YRS
    NUMBER OF LOAN PAYMENTS PER YEAR                    1
    TIME AFTER INVESTING BEFORE REC. INCOME            1.00 YRS
    AMOUNT OF SECOND LOAN                       $  50,000.00
    YEARLY INTEREST RATE FOR 2ND LOAN                  15.00%
    LIFE OF SECOND LOAN YEARS                            3 YRS
    NUMBER OF PAYMENTS PER YEAR  2ND LOAN              1
    ESTIMATED ANNUAL INCOME                     $ 115,000.00
    ESTIMATED ANNUAL EXPENSES                   $  35,000.00
    ESCALATION FOR INCOME                                12.00%
    ESCALATION FOR EXPENSES                               8.00%
    FEDERAL INCOME TAX RATE                              40.00%
    STATE INCOME TAX RATE                                10.00%
    DISCOUNT RATE                                        12.00 %
    LIFE OF INVESTMENT                                   5 YRS
    VALUE OF 3 YEAR PROPERTY                  $  50,000.00
    VALUE OF 5 YEAR PROPERTY                  $ 100,000.00
    VALUE OF 10 YEAR PROPERTY                 $       0.00
    VALUE OF 15 YEAR PU PROP                  $       0.00
    VALUE OF ST LINE REAL ESTATE              $       0.00
    YEAR PROPERY PLACED IN SVC                     1982
    INFLATION RATE                                  10.00%
==============================================

                   SUMMARY RESULTS
   CURRENT YEAR DOLLARS PRESENT VALUE OF CASH FLOWS $ 177,217.00
   CONSTANT YEAR DOLLAR PRESENT VALUE OF CASH FLOWS  $ 125,018.00
   NET PRESENT VALUE (DISCOUNTED CASH - COST) =      $  27,217.20
   CONSTANT YEAR NET PRESENT VALUE =                 $ -24,981.90
    YOU LOST $  24,981.90 IN PURCHASING POWER
=================================================
```

Fig. 10-6. Results of investment analysis program using INVEST1.

```
                    INPUT DATA SUMMARY
TOTAL AMOUNT OF INVESTMENT                      $ 120,000.00
AMOUNT OF FIRST LOAN                            $ 100,000.00
YEARLY INTEREST RATE FOR 1ST LOAN                      15.00%
LIFE OF FIRST LOAN YEARS                                5.00  YRS
NUMBER OF LOAN PAYMENTS PER YEAR                        1
TIME AFTER INVESTING BEFORE REC. INCOME                1.00 YRS
AMOUNT OF SECOND LOAN                           $  20,000.00
YEARLY INTEREST RATE FOR 2ND LOAN                      15.00%
LIFE OF SECOND LOAN YEARS                                3 YRS
NUMBER OF PAYMENTS PER YEAR  2ND LOAN                  1
ESTIMATED ANNUAL INCOME                         $ 115,000.00
ESTIMATED ANNUAL EXPENSES                       $  35,000.00
ESCALATION FOR INCOME                                   12.00%
ESCALATION FOR EXPENSES                                  8.00%
FEDERAL INCOME TAX RATE                                 40.00%
STATE INCOME TAX RATE                                   10.00%
DISCOUNT RATE                                           12.00 %
LIFE OF INVESTMENT                                      5 YRS
VALUE OF 3 YEAR PROPERTY                      $   20,000.00
VALUE OF 5 YEAR PROPERTY                      $  100,000.00
VALUE OF 10 YEAR PROPERTY                     $        0.00
VALUE OF 15 YEAR PU PROP                      $        0.00
VALUE OF ST LINE REAL ESTATE                  $        0.00
YEAR PROPERY PLACED IN SVC                          1982
INFLATION RATE                                       10.00%
============================================

                    SUMMARY RESULTS
CURRENT YEAR DOLLARS PRESENT VALUE OF CASH FLOWS $ 170,960.00
CONSTANT YEAR DOLLAR PRESENT VALUE OF CASH FLOWS  $ 121,188.00
NET PRESENT VALUE (DISCOUNTED CASH - COST) =      $  50,959.80
CONSTANT YEAR NET PRESENT VALUE =                 $   1,187.94
================================================
```

Fig. 10-7. Results of investment analysis program using INVEST1.

the three year property becomes $20,000 and the value of the five year property becomes $100,000. Rerun the program.

The summary is shown in Fig. 10-7. You finally reduced the cost of the investment enough to get your money back.

The program has told you that based on expected income and expenses, this particular investment that is being offered for $200,000 is worth only $120,000. If you pay much more than this, you lose purchasing power. All of these calculations took less than 15 minutes, including keying in the data and deciding how to rearrange things. You can see what a powerful tool this program can be.

Chapter 11

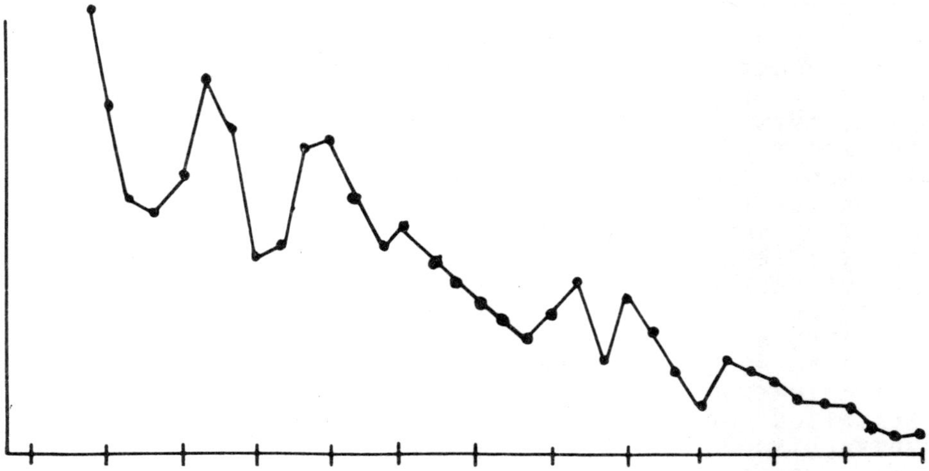

INVEST2 Program

Program INVEST1 is a very powerful tool but it is limited to investments that pay for themselves from income generated. The program cannot analyze investments in which much, if not all, of the expected profit comes from selling the property. Program INVEST2 is designed for cases in which the property is expected to appreciate during the life of the investment and is then sold at a profit, generally called a *capital gain.*

The profits from investments such as the one modeled by INVEST2 receive favorable tax treatment because they are taxed at a much lower rate than ordinary income. This favorable tax treatment makes investments that yield capital gains very attractive.

The investment modeled by INVEST2 is an investment in rental real estate, which is one of the most common types of investments for capital gains. Rental real estate is usually purchased with mostly borrowed money. The investor has little of his own money tied up. The idea is for the rental income to pay all out of pocket costs. Any capital gains are "gravy." This is what books on "how to make a million in 2 days in real estate" say.

Unfortunately, the hard facts are that real estate investments are like all other investments. You can gain very high returns from real estate investments, but only if you are willing to accept high risk. The same evaluation procedures should be used. The profit from an investment must have a higher present value than the present value of the money it cost to purchase the property.

The amount of your money tied up in typical real estate investment is the *down payment*—the difference between the purchase cost (which may be more than the price of the property) and all loans—and the accumulated principal payments or accumulated equity. If you assume that the principal payments and accumulated principal or equity could be invested at the discount rate (the basic assump-

Number of 1 bedroom unfur	
Rent	$ ________
Number of 1 bedroom furnished	________
Rent	$ ________
Number of 2 bedroom unfur	________
Rent	$ ________
Number of 2 bedroom furnished	________
Rent	$ ________
Number of 3 bedroom unfurn	________%
Rent	$ ________
Number of 3 bedroom fur	________
Rent	$ ________
Vacancy allowance	________ %

Fig. 11-1. Worksheet for data entry program INVEST2.

tion of present value analysis), then the present value of the total after tax profits from the investment must exceed the present value of the down payment and the present value of the accumulated equity. If not, then you should put your money into the investment represented by the discount rate.

THE REAL ESTATE INVESTMENT

Let's look at an investment in rental real estate. Assume that the investment is purchased with borrowed money. The property will have both a first mortgage and a second mortgage so as to minimize the amount of your money that is tied up.

A worksheet is needed to help with the analysis of the investment. The worksheets for the computer analysis are shown in Figs. 11-1, 11-2, and 11-3.

Figure 11-1 is the worksheet for rental income from an apartment building with one, two, and three bedroom apartments. For each type of unit, you must know the number of units and the expected monthly or yearly rent.

The last item Fig. 11-1 is the vacancy allowance, which accounts for the fact that some units will be vacant part of the time. The vacancy allowance for existing rental property should be well known. The vacancy allowance for any type of rental property in any area should also be known. The vacancy allowance for your investment should be in line with that of similar property in your city. You should not expect to have a significantly lower vacancy allowance than that of similar rental units. If you have a significantly higher than average vacancy allowance, you have a serious problem and should look for reasons why the vacancy allowance is so high. Special care should be paid to determining what the vacancy allowance actually is. It can be the difference between a good and bad investment. Of course if you make the investment, you should pay special attention to keeping the actual vacancy rate as low as possible.

Figure 11-2 is used as the worksheet for estimating expenses. Most of the expenses are self explanatory; however, the management expense

Insurance	$______ per year or month
Licenses	$______
Property tax	$ ______
Utilities	$ ______
Management	$ ______
Janitor	$ ______
Advertising	$ ______
Maintenance	$ ______
Miscel. Expenses	$ ______

Fig. 11-2. Data entry worksheet for expenses.

deserves comment. Even if you manage the property yourself, you have a management expense; your time is worth something. Be sure to include an allowance for the time you have to spend managing the property.

Also be sure to include social security, unemployment insurance, and any other similar costs in addition to salary that you may pay for janitor service, management, and so forth. These costs can be significant and are often overlooked until they have to be paid.

Figure 11-3 is very similar to the worksheet used with INVEST1. This worksheet defines the expected costs of purchasing the investment; the loan information; income and capital gains tax information; the discount rate; the escalation in property value income and expenses; the inflation rate; and the depreciation information. I will only comment on those items that were not required for INVEST1.

Escalation for value of property is the rate at which you expect the value of your investment to appreciate per year. If this value doesn't exceed the discount rate, you may be in trouble. The only way the investment will be worthwhile if the escalation rate is less than the discount rate is if income from the property is high.

Escalation rate for rents is the rate at which you think you can increase rents. Because most rental properties involve leases which fix the rent, increases in rents are assumed to lag behind increases in expenses by one year.

Federal capital gains tax rate is the capital gains tax rate. It is substantially less than your ordinary income tax rate.

State capital gains tax rate is the same as above, applied to the state (not all states have it).

All other information is the same as required for INVEST1. See Chapter 9 for information if you have questions about the data.

Because of the 1981 tax law, depreciation calculations have changed. For rental real estate, only structures can be depreciated. Land does not depreciate. The real question is which of the methods of depreciation allowed under the 1981 tax law is best. In general, it appears that straight line 15-year depreciation is best. In this case the taxable profit from the sale of the property is calculated by subtracting the accumulated depreciation from the original cost of the property to obtain the taxable basis. The taxable profit is then the selling price less cost of selling less the taxable basis. Or the selling price less the cost of selling less the price you paid less accumulated depreciation. Then profit is taxed at the capital gains rate (which is less than the tax rate for ordinary income).

Your real profit is less than the IRS profit. If the accelerated cost recovery method is used instead of straight line depreciation, some or perhaps all of the profit from the sale may be taxed as ordinary income. Generally, the amount of depreciation in excess of the straight line depreciation will be taxed as ordinary income. For example, suppose you sell an asset for $10,000. You pur-

Total amount of investment	$ ________
Amount of first loan	$ ________
Interest rate 1st loan	________ %
Life of 1st loan	________ yrs
Number of payments/yr	________
Time after investing before receive income	________ yrs
Amount of second loan	$ ________
Interest rate 2nd loan	________ %
Life of second loan	________ yrs
Number of payments per year	________
Escalation for value of property	________ %
Cost of selling as % of price	________ %
Escalation for rents	________ %
Escalation for expenses	________ %
Federal income tax rate	________ %
Federal capital gains tax rate	________ %
State capital gains tax rate	________ %
State income tax rate	________ %
Discount rate	________ %
Life of investment	________ yrs
Value of 3 year property	$ ________
Value of 5 year property	$ ________
Value of 10 year property	$ ________
Value of 15 year PU property	$ ________
Value of 15 yr st line real estate	$ ________
Year property placed in service	
Inflation rate	________ %

Fig. 11-3. Data entry for remaining data for INVEST2.

chased the asset for $8,000 and depreciated it using an accelerated method. Straight line depreciation would have given you (say) $3,000 in depreciation, whereas the accelerated method gave you (say) $5,000 in depreciation. The IRS will tax the $2,000 difference as ordinary income, which is all of your capital gain. Because the capital gains tax rates are lower than ordinary income tax rates, it thus appears that straight line depreciation is best. It is certainly the method I would use in analyzing an investment.

If you make an investment you should perform detailed calculations to determine your best depreciation method. Your personal tax rate and situation may mean that you should use an accelerated depreciation method, or you may even want to use more than 15 years to depreciate the property. Get professional help if necessary.

OUTPUT DATA

Information provided by the computer for INVEST2 is similar to information provided by INVEST1. INVEST2 provides information about capital gains for an investment in addition to cash flow information provided by INVEST1.

A summary of the important output information is provided on the crt and on hard copy. Because the hard copy is more complete, the following discussion will emphasize the hard copy output.

The first page of the hard copy gives a complete listing of all information provided to the program. This information is provided to be sure there are no errors in the input data.

The important part of the output information is the summary results on the second page of the hard copy. These results indicate how an investment performed.

The first item in the summary is the present value of all rental profits, which tells you whether the property produced income during the time it was held. If the present value of all rental profits is low, the investment probably isn't doing well.

The next several items of the hard copy summary are the details of the final transaction where the property was sold. The selling price, cost of selling, balance due on outstanding loans, taxable basis, taxable profit, and taxes paid are all shown. The final after tax profit is shown last.

The important item from the selling transaction is the present value of the profit from the sale, less the balance due on outstanding loans. This tells you if you made any money on the sale of the property.

Next, the present value of all profits minus the outstanding loan balances is shown. This value should exceed the present value of accumulated equity.

The accumulated equity, the present value of the accumulated equity, and the constant year dollar value of the accumulated equity are shown.

Finally the important net present value (profit less outstanding loan balances less present value of equity) is shown. This must be positive for the investment to be a good one. If the net present value is negative, you should invest your money in the investment represented by the discount rate.

The final result is the constant year value of all profits.

The next several pages of the output give year-to-year details of the profit and loss from rents. These should be examined to assure that spendable cash flow is positive. Whenever spendable cash flow is negative, you have to add money to the investment to keep it going. The program will print out a warning message if spendable cash flow is negative.

USER INSTRUCTIONS

As with INVEST1, a brief set of user instructions is displayed on the crt if desired. To display user instructions, press <I> (you don't have to press <ENTER>) when you are asked if you want user instructions. The user instructions as they appear on the crt are shown in Fig. 11-4.

```
INSTRUCTIONS
THIS PROGRAM CALCULATES THE PRESENT VALUE OF THE
CASH FLOWS FROM AN INVESTMENT. IN ORDER TO USE
THE PROGRAM, YOU MUST SUPPLY THE INPUT INFORMATION.
FIRST DATA TO ENTER ARE INCOME ESTIMATES. THEN ENTER
THE EXPENSES. THESE TWO TYPES OF INFORMATION ARE ENTERED
ON A TWO PAGE FORM - 1 PAGE FOR INCOME AND 1 FOR EXPENSES.
FINALLY DATA ON COST ETC ARE ENTERED USING A 3 PAGE FORM.
FOR THESE PAGES YOU CAN MOVE WITH THE < AND > KEYS.
YOU CAN CORRECT A WRONG ENTRY BY ENTERING C AND
THEN FOLLOWING THE INSTRUCTIONS.
WHEN ALL DATA ARE CORRECT, YOU CAN START THE
CALCULATIONS BY ENTERING G.
YOU MUST ENTER ALL THE DATA BEFORE YOU CAN RUN THE PROGRAM.
PRESS ANY KEY TO CONTINUE
INSTRUCTIONS PAGE 2
ALL DATA ASKED FOR IS SELF EXPLANATORY, WITH THE
POSSIBLE EXCEPTION OF YEARS AFTER INVEST BEFORE REC
INCOME. THIS QUESTION IS BASED ON THE FACT THAT MANY
INVESTMENTS DO NOT START PAYING UNTIL SOME TIME
AFTER THE MONEY IS SPENT. YOU ENTER THE NUMBER OF
YEARS YOU ESTIMATE IT WILL TAKE FOR INCOME TO START
COMING AFTER THE INVESTMENT IS MADE. FOR EXAMPLE IF
YOU KNOW IT WILL TAKE ONE YEAR, ENTER 1. IF IT WILL
TAKE HALF A YEAR, ENTER 0.5.
PRESS ANY KEY TO CONTINUE
```

Fig. 11-4. Crt instructions for calculation of present value of cash flows from an investment.

DATA ENTRY

Data entry for INVEST2 is somewhat different from data entry for INVEST1; more data is required. Income and expense data are entered in more detail than for INVEST1.

For rental data entry the first items entered are the data for the income from the property. The important items are number of rental units of various types and the monthly or yearly rental expected. Entering the number of units is straightforward; just enter the appropriate number. However, entering the rents is more involved. The program allows you to enter monthly or yearly rents, depending on which are known. To enter a monthly rent you must precede the amount of rent by an M. For example, a monthly rent of $400 is entered as M400. If you wish to enter a yearly rent, you must precede the amount by a Y. For example, a yearly rent of $4,800 is entered as Y4800. The program checks to see if you used the correct format. If you did not, an error message is printed and you are asked to reenter the data. Instructions for data entry are shown on the crt while you are entering data. The crt display is shown in Fig. 11-5.

After you have entered all data, the crt is cleared and all data on income are displayed for you to check. At this point you are asked if the data is correct. If not, you should press <N>; otherwise you should press <Y> (you do not have to press <ENTER>). The program will only accept Y or N. If you press any other key, an error message is displayed. The crt display for this step is shown in Fig. 11-6.

If you find an error in the data and press <N>, the crt is cleared and you are returned to the income data entry form. You are asked to check each item and make necessary corrections. The current value of the item is displayed in parentheses. If you want to keep that value, press <ENTER>. Otherwise enter the correct values.

The process of data entry and review is repeated until you certify that your data is correct by pressing <Y>. Then you are allowed to move to the expense data entry form.

EXPENSE DATA ENTRY

Information on expected expenses is entered in much the same way as was the rental information.

```
INCOME ESTIMATES  FOR RENTAL PROPERTY

ENTER DATA ASKED FOR. DO NOT WORRY IF YOU MAKE AN ERROR.

YOU WILL HAVE A CHANCE TO CORRECT IT LATER.

TO ENTER MONTHLY EXPENSES PRECEED AMOUNT WITH <M> AND

FOR YEARLY PRECEED WITH <Y>.

EG M100 IS $100 PER MONTH Y2000 IS  $2000 PER YEAR.

NUMBER OF 1 BEDROOM UNFOR       0?
```

Fig. 11-5. Crt display for data entry of income estimates.

```
NUMBER OF 1 BEDROOM UNFUR              0

RENT $        0.00/MO    $             0.00/YR

NUMBER OF 1 BEDROOM FUR                0

RENT $        0.00/MO    $             0.00/YR

NUMBER OF 2 BEDROOM UNFUR              0

RENT $        0.00/MO    $             0.00/YR

NUMBER OF 2 BEDROOM FUR                0

RENT $        0.00/MO    $             0.00/YR

NUMBER OF 3 BEDROOM UNFUR              0

RENT $        0.00/MO    $             0.00/YR

NUMBER OF 3 BEDROOM FUR                0

RENT $        0.00/MO    $             0.00/YR

ALLOWANCE FOR VACANCIES     0.00%

TOTAL YEARLY INCOME    $          0.00

ARE THESE CORRECT Y OR N?
```

Fig. 11-6. Crt display for data check.

Each item of expense is displayed on the crt with the current value shown in parentheses. If you want to keep the current value, press <ENTER>; otherwise enter the correct information.

As for rental information, you can enter costs either as costs per month or costs per year. You must precede the amount with either an M or a Y. If you don't, an error message is displayed.

When you have entered the last expense item, the screen is cleared and all expense data are displayed. You are asked to review the data and to press <Y> if it is correct and <N> if it is not.

If you press <N>, the expense data entry process starts over. You are shown each expense item and may either keep the item by pressing <ENTER> or change the item by entering a new value.

The crt display for expense data entry is shown in Fig. 11-7. As with the rental income data entry, you must certify that the data is correct by pressing <Y> before you can leave the expense data entry module.

OTHER DATA ENTRY

The remaining information is entered using a three-page form in Fig. 11-8, in a manner similar to the data entry process for INVEST1/BAS. User instructions shown on the crt tell you how to use the data entry forms. Additional information is provided in the previous discussion of INVEST1.

The best way to see how to use program INVEST2 is to look at an example. The example is a multiapartment rental property. The purchase of the property will be financed with two loans. You expect to hold the property for six years and then sell it. The asking price for the property is $300,000.00; $240,000.00 is the estimated value of the building; $60,000.00 is the estimated value of the land. The question is, "Is this a good investment? Let's run the program to find out.

The entire hard copy output from the program is given in Figs. 11-9 and 11-10. All input data (Fig. 11-9) are printed first, followed by summary results and yearly details (Fig. 11-10).

Summary results show that you made a profit on rents as well as on the resale of the property.

```
ENTER EXPENSES. PRECEDE BY M FOR MONTHLY, Y FOR YEARLY

INSURANCE                $     0.00/MO        $     0.00/YR?

LICENSES                 $     0.00/MO        $     0.00/YR?

PROP TAX                     0.00/MO          $     0.00/YR

UTILITIES                $     0.00/MO        $     0.00/YR?

MANAGEMENT               $     0.00/MO        $     0.00/YR

JANITOR                  $     0.00/MO        $     0.00/YR?

ADVERTIS                 $     0.00/MO        $     0.00/YR?

MAINT EXP                $     0.00/MO        $     0.00/YR

MISC EXP                 $$     0.00/MO       $     0.00/YR
```

Fig. 11-7. Crt display for entering expenses.

```
INVESTMENT ANALYSIS DATA INPUT PAGE 1

PROVIDE DATA ASKED FOR. CURRENT VALUE SHOWN IN ()

IF YOU WISH TO CORRECT A PREVIOUSLY ENTRY ENTER C

TO GO TO THE NEXT PAGE ENTER >

============================================================

TOTAL AMOUNT OF INVESTMENT                        $0.00

AMOUNT OF FIRST LOAN                              $0.00

YEARLY INTEREST RATE FOR 1ST LOAN                 00.00%

LIFE OF FIRST LOAN YEARS                          0.00 YEARS

NUMBER OF LOAN PAYMENTS PER YEAR                  0

TIME AFTER INVESTING BEFORE REC INCOME            0.00YRS

AMOUNT OF SECOND LOAN                             $0.00

YEARLY INTEREST RATE FOR 2ND LOAN                 00.00%

LIFE OF SECOND LOAN YEARS                         0 YRS

INVESTMENT ANALYSIS DATA INPUT PAGE 2

PROVIDE DATA ASKED FOR. CURRENT VALUE SHOWN IN ()

IF YOU WISH TO CORRECT A PREVIOUS ENTRY ENTER C

TO GO TO NEXT PAGE ENTER >.

==========================================================

NUMBER OF PAYMENTS PER YEAR 2ND LOAN              0
```

Fig. 11-8. Investment analysis data input (continued on page 114).

```
ESCALATION FOR VALUE OF PROPERTY                 00.00%

COST OF SELLING AS % OF PRICE                    0.00%

ESCALATION FOR RENTS                             00.00%

ESCALATION FOR EXPENSES                          00.00%

FEDERAL INCOME TAX RATE                          00.00%

FEDERAL CAPITAL GAINS TAX RATE                   00.00%

STATE CAPITAL GAINS TAX RATE                     00.00%

STATE INCOME TAX RATE                            00.00%

DISCOUNT RATE                                    00.00%
INVESTMENT ANALYSIS DATA INPUT PAGE 3

PROVIDE DATA ASKED FOR. CURRENT VALUE SHOWN IN ()

IF YOU WISH TO CORRECT A PREVIOUS ENTRY ENTER C

TO GO TO PREVIOUS PAGE ENTER <.
======================================================
LIFE OF INVESTMENT                               00YRS

VALUE OF 3 YEAR PROPERTY                         $00.00

VALUE OF 5 YEAR PROPERTY                         $00.00

VALUE OF 10 YEAR PROPERTY                        $00.00

VALUE OF 15 YEAR PU PROPERTY                     $00.00

VALUE OF ST LINE REAL ESTATE                     $00.00

YEAR PROPERTY PLACED IN SVC

INFLATION RATE                                   00.00%
```

Fig. 11-8. Continued from page 113.

```
                         INPUT DATA SUMMARY
   TOTAL AMOUNT OF INVESTMENT                   $ 300,000.00
   AMOUNT OF FIRST LOAN                         $ 175,000.00
   YEARLY INTEREST RATE FOR 1ST LOAN                   15.50%
   LIFE OF FIRST LOAN YEARS                            15.00  YRS
   NUMBER OF LOAN PAYMENTS PER YEAR                    12
   TIME AFTER INVESTING BEFORE REC. INCOME              0.00 YRS
   AMOUNT OF SECOND LOAN                        $  75,000.00
   YEARLY INTEREST RATE FOR 2ND LOAN                   13.00%
   LIFE OF SECOND LOAN YEARS                            2 YRS
   NUMBER OF PAYMENTS PER YEAR  2ND LOAN                2
   ESCLATION FOR VALUE OF PROPERTY                     16.00%
   COST OF SELLING AS % OF PRICE                        6.00%
   ESCALATION FOR RENTS                                12.00%
   ESCALATION FOR EXPENSES                              8.00%
   FEDERAL INCOME TAX RATE                             50.00%
   FEDERAL CAPITAL GAINS TAX RATE                      25.00%
   STATE CAPITAL GAINS TAX RATE                         0.00%
   STATE INCOME TAX RATE                               10.00%
   DISCOUNT RATE                                       12.00 %
   LIFE OF INVESTMENT                                   6 YRS
   VALUE OF 3 YEAR PROPERTY                      $          0.00
   VALUE OF 5 YEAR PROPERTY                      $          0.00
   VALUE OF 10 YEAR PROPERTY                     $          0.00
   VALUE OF 15 YEAR PU PROP                      $          0.00
   VALUE OF ST LINE REAL ESTATE                  $ 240,000.00
   YEAR PROPERY PLACED IN SVC                          1982
   INFLATION RATE                                      10.00%
========================================================
               INCOME ESTIMATES.
========================================================

NUMBER OF 1 BEDROOM UNFUR    5 RENT $   350.00/MO   $    4,200.00/YR
NUMBER OF 1 BEDROOM FUR      0 RENT $     0.00/MO   $        0.00/YR
NUMBER OF 2 BEDROOM UNFUR    4 RENT $   500.00/MO   $    6,000.00/YR
NUMBER OF 2 BEDROOM FUR      2 RENT $   600.00/MO   $    7,200.00/YR
NUMBER OF 3 BEDROOM UNFUR    5 RENT $   700.00/MO   $    8,400.00/YR
NUMBER OF 3 BEDROOM FUR      2 RENT $   850.00/MO   $   10,200.00/YR
ALLOWANCE FOR VACANCIES  8.00% OR $  9,744.00/YR
TOTAL YEARLY INCOME $ 112,056.00
==================================================================
                    EXPENSES
INSURANCE  $  150.00/MO   $ 1,800.00/YR
LICENSES   $  125.00/MO   $ 1,500.00/YR
```

Fig. 11-9. Results of investment analysis using INVEST2 (continued on page 116).

```
               PROP TAX    $   250.00/MO    $ 3,000.00/YR
               UTILITIES   $   150.00/MO    $ 1,800.00/YR
               MANAGEMENT  $   550.00/MO    $ 6,600.00/YR
               JANITOR     $     0.00/MO    $      0.00/YR
               ADVERTIS    $   120.00/MO    $ 1,440.00/YR
               MAINT EXP   $   250.00/MO    $ 3,000.00/YR
               MISC EXP    $   100.00/MO    $ 1,200.00/YR
                    TOTAL EXPENSES PER YEAR $   20,340.00

                        *** SUMMARY RESULTS ***

   CURRENT YEAR DOLLARS PRESENT VALUE OF RENT PROFIT $ 205,861.00
   SELLING PRICE .......... $ 730,918.00
   COST OF SELLING ........ $  43,855.10
   BALANCE DUE ON LOANS ... $ 145,700.00
   BASIS FOR TAX PURPOSE .. $ 204,000.00
   TAXABLE PROCEEDS ....... $ 483,063.00
   TOTAL CAPITAL GAINS TAX  $ 120,766.00
   NET PROFIT FROM SALE ... $ 266,297.00
   PRESENT VALUE OF PROFIT FROM SALE - BALANCE DUE   $  61,098.60
   PRESENT VALUE OF TOTAL PROFITS - BALANCE DUE      $ 266,959.00
   ACCUMULATED EQUITY ...... $154,300.00
   PRESENT VALUE EQUITY .... $132,239.00
   CONSTANT YR DOLLAR   .... $118,484.00
   NET PRESENT VALUE (PROFIT  -EQUITY) =             $ 134,721.00
   CONSTANT YEAR NET PRESENT VALUE ALL PROFIT-BALANCE $  63,789.10
:==================================================================
```

Fig. 11-9. Continued from page 115.

The present value results show that the investment made a profit even allowing for inflation. This looks like a good investment.

Now let's examine yearly details. The first bad news appears in the spendable cash flow for the first year, which is negative. You need slightly more than $5,000 in working capital just to keep going during the first year. Spendable cash flow for the second year is also negative. Spendable cash flow for all remaining years is positive.

What is the impact of the negative spendable cash flows on the investment? The easiest way, and the most conservative, is to assume you need about $8,000 in working capital in addition to the $50,000 down payment. You can subtract the working capital from the present value of the profit and the inflation corrected present value to find the final return from the investment. The investment still earns money. Thus even with conservative assumptions about working capital, this looks like a good investment.

By using INVEST1 and INVEST2 you can analyze almost any investment. The main changes required to analyze investments other than the examples given concern interpretation of the input data. For example, if you want to analyze an office building instead of an apartment house, replace the one, two, and three bedroom apartments with the appropriate office sizes. The one instance where additional help would be useful is in assessment of risk. The next chapter discusses a modification of INVEST2 that allows you to get an idea about the risk involved in an investment.

```
                         RESULTS FOR YEAR  1
 ----------------------------------------
GROSS INCOME ........................$ 112,056.00
EXPENSES ............................$  21,967.20
DEPRECIATION ........................$  16,000.00
INTEREST 1ST LOAN ...................$  26,903.20
PRINCIPAL 1ST LOAN ..................$   3,210.71
INTEREST 2ND LOAN ...................$   8,643.85
PRINCIPAL 2ND LOAN ..................$  35,141.50
TAXABLE INCOME ......................$  38,541.80
STATE TAX PAID ......................$   3,854.18
INVESTMENT TAX CREDIT TAKEN .........$       0.00
FEDERAL TAX PAID ....................$  17,343.80
AFTER TAX CASH FLOW .................$  33,343.80
CONSTANT DOLLAR CASH FLOW ...........$  30,312.50
DISCOUNTED CURRENT YEAR CASH FLOW ...$  29,771.30
DISCOUNTED CONSTANT YR CASH FLOW ....$  27,064.80
SPENDABLE CASH FLOW .................$  -5,008.43
 NOTE THAT SPENDABLE CASH IS NEGATIVE. YOU NEED TO BORROW MONEY.
 ========================================
                         RESULTS FOR YEAR  2
 ----------------------------------------
GROSS INCOME ........................$ 125,503.00
EXPENSES ............................$  23,724.60
DEPRECIATION ........................$  16,000.00
INTEREST 1ST LOAN ...................$  26,368.60
PRINCIPAL 1ST LOAN ..................$   3,745.26
INTEREST 2ND LOAN ...................$   3,926.97
PRINCIPAL 2ND LOAN ..................$  39,858.40
TAXABLE INCOME ......................$  55,482.60
STATE TAX PAID ......................$   5,548.26
INVESTMENT TAX CREDIT TAKEN .........$       0.00
FEDERAL TAX PAID ....................$  24,967.10
AFTER TAX CASH FLOW .................$  40,967.20
CONSTANT DOLLAR CASH FLOW ...........$  33,857.20
DISCOUNTED CURRENT YEAR CASH FLOW ...$  32,658.80
DISCOUNTED CONSTANT YR CASH FLOW ....$  26,990.70
SPENDABLE CASH FLOW .................$  -2,636.51
 NOTE THAT SPENDABLE CASH IS NEGATIVE. YOU NEED TO BORROW MONEY.
 ========================================
                         RESULTS FOR YEAR  3
 ----------------------------------------
GROSS INCOME ........................$ 140,563.00
EXPENSES ............................$  25,622.50
DEPRECIATION ........................$  16,000.00
INTEREST 1ST LOAN ...................$  25,745.00
PRINCIPAL 1ST LOAN ..................$   4,368.86
INTEREST 2ND LOAN ...................$       0.00
PRINCIPAL 2ND LOAN ..................$       0.00
TAXABLE INCOME ......................$  73,195.50
STATE TAX PAID ......................$   7,319.55
```

Fig. 11-10. Results of operation for each year (continued on page 118).

```
INVESTMENT TAX CREDIT TAKEN .........$         0.00
FEDERAL TAX PAID ....................$    32,938.00
AFTER TAX CASH FLOW .................$    48,938.00
CONSTANT DOLLAR CASH FLOW ...........$    36,767.80
DISCOUNTED CURRENT YEAR CASH FLOW ...$    34,833.10
DISCOUNTED CONSTANT YR CASH FLOW ....$    26,170.60
SPENDABLE CASH FLOW .................$    44,569.10
 ========================================
                          RESULTS FOR YEAR  4
 ----------------------------------------
GROSS INCOME ........................$ 157,431.00
EXPENSES ............................$  27,672.30
DEPRECIATION ........................$  16,000.00
INTEREST 1ST LOAN ...................$  25,017.60
PRINCIPAL 1ST LOAN ..................$   5,096.27
INTEREST 2ND LOAN ...................$       0.00
PRINCIPAL 2ND LOAN ..................$       0.00
TAXABLE INCOME ......................$  88,740.60
STATE TAX PAID ......................$   8,874.06
INVESTMENT TAX CREDIT TAKEN .........$       0.00
FEDERAL TAX PAID ....................$  39,933.30
AFTER TAX CASH FLOW .................$  55,933.30
CONSTANT DOLLAR CASH FLOW ...........$  38,203.20
DISCOUNTED CURRENT YEAR CASH FLOW ...$  35,546.60
DISCOUNTED CONSTANT YR CASH FLOW ....$  24,278.80
SPENDABLE CASH FLOW .................$  50,837.00
 ========================================
                          RESULTS FOR YEAR  5
 ----------------------------------------
GROSS INCOME ........................$ 176,322.00
EXPENSES ............................$  29,886.10
DEPRECIATION ........................$  16,000.00
INTEREST 1ST LOAN ...................$  24,169.10
```

Fig. 11-10. Continued from page 117).

INVEST2/BAS LISTING

```
 10 CLEAR 200 :REM DELETE TO COMPILE AND FOR MBASIC
 20 REM
*************************************************************
 30 REM PROGRAM INVES2/BAS
 40 REM PROGRAM TO ANALYZE AN INVESTMENT THAT IS EXPECTED
 50 REM TO EARN INCOME AND PAY FOR ITSELF WITH THE INCOME
 60 REM EARNED BY THE INVESTMENT
 70 REM WRITTEN BY L. E. SPARKS VERSION 3.0 NOVEMBER 1981
 80 REM WRITTEN IN TRS-80 DISK BASIC RUNS ON TRS-80
 90 REM MODEL I AND MODEL III REQUIRES 48K RAM. FOR LESS RAM
100 REM REMOVE REMARKS, REDIMENSION ARRAYS, ELIMINATE
SPACES,
```

```
PRINCIPAL 1ST LOAN ..................$    5,944.79
INTEREST 2ND LOAN ...................$        0.00
PRINCIPAL 2ND LOAN ..................$        0.00
TAXABLE INCOME ......................$  106,267.00
STATE TAX PAID ......................$   10,626.70
INVESTMENT TAX CREDIT TAKEN .........$        0.00
FEDERAL TAX PAID ....................$   47,820.10
AFTER TAX CASH FLOW .................$   63,820.10
CONSTANT DOLLAR CASH FLOW ...........$   39,627.30
DISCOUNTED CURRENT YEAR CASH FLOW ...$   36,213.30
DISCOUNTED CONSTANT YR CASH FLOW ....$   22,485.60
SPENDABLE CASH FLOW .................$   57,875.40
 ======================================
                          RESULTS FOR YEAR  6
 --------------------------------------
GROSS INCOME ........................$  197,481.00
EXPENSES ............................$   32,277.00
DEPRECIATION ........................$   16,000.00
INTEREST 1ST LOAN ...................$   23,179.30
PRINCIPAL 1ST LOAN ..................$    6,934.60
INTEREST 2ND LOAN ...................$        0.00
PRINCIPAL 2ND LOAN ..................$        0.00
TAXABLE INCOME ......................$  126,025.00
STATE TAX PAID ......................$   12,602.50
INVESTMENT TAX CREDIT TAKEN .........$        0.00
FEDERAL TAX PAID ....................$   56,711.00
AFTER TAX CASH FLOW .................$   72,711.00
CONSTANT DOLLAR CASH FLOW ...........$   41,043.50
DISCOUNTED CURRENT YEAR CASH FLOW ...$   36,837.70
DISCOUNTED CONSTANT YR CASH FLOW ....$   20,793.90
SPENDABLE CASH FLOW .................$   65,776.40
 ========================================
 ======================================
```

```
110 REM AND USE MULTIPLE STATEMENTS PER LINE.
120 REM IF THE CLS STATEMENT FOR CLEARING THE SCREEN IS
CHANGED
130 REM THE PROGRAM WILL RUN IN MBASIC OR BASIC 80
140 REM FOR CP/M SYSTEMS
150 REM AS WRITTEN REQUIRES 48K RAM FOR LESS RAM REDUCE
DIMENSIONS OF ARRAYS.
160 REM FOR LESS RAM REMOVE REMARK STATEMENTS
170 REM NOTE THAT THE [ IS THE SYMBOL FOR THE UP ARROW.
180 REM
*****************************************************
190 CLS
200 PRINT "================================================"
210 PRINT "  INVESTMENT ANALYSIS PROGRAM INVEST2/BAS"
```

```
220 PRINT "  REFERENCE INVESTMENT ANALYSIS ON MICROCOMPUTER
TAB BOOKS"
230 PRINT "   BY LES VERSION 3.0 NOV 1981"
240 PRINT "=========================================="
250 PRINT "IF YOU WANT INSTRUCTIONS PRESS I ELSE PRESS ANY
KEY TO CONTINUE"
260 Y$=INKEY$: IF Y$="" THEN 260 ELSE IF Y$="I" THEN GOSUB
5690
270 CLS
280 DEFINT K,M,N
290 I=0:J=0:K=0:M=0:N=0 P=0:PV=0 PI=0:SP=0:CS=0:AE=0:AP=0 :
AI = 0 : PN = 0
300 BL = 0 : L=0 : NP = 0
310 REM AE IS ACCUMULATED EQUITY AP IS PRESENT VALUE OF AE
320 D$="$#,######.##"
330 PM = 3 : P1 = 0
340 I9 = 27 : REM MAXIMUM NUMBER OF ITEMS TO BE READ IN
350 IP=0 PP=0:A=0:B=0:V=0:SI=0:F=1:FL=0:TC=0:TX=0:TI=0
360 DIM F$(30),V(30),DP(4,15),D(30),SF(30),PV(4,3),PI(4,3)
370 DIM TU$(6),EX$(9),R1(6),R2(6),EM(9),EY(9)
380 REM D(I) IS DEPRECIATION FOR ITH YEAR, SF IS SPENDABLE
CASH FLOW
390 REM TC IS ALLOWABLE TAX CREDIT TC(I) IS TAX CREDIT
TAKEN IN ITH YEAR.
400 REM DP IS DEPRECIATION FOR NEW 1981 TAX LAW
410 DIM A1(30),A2(30),E1(30),E2(30),EX(30),T1(30),T2(30)
420 REM A1=PRINCIPAL  OF LOAN 1, A1=PRINCIPAL  OF LOAN 2,
E1=INCOME
430 REM E2=INCOME 2, EX=EXPENSES, T1=FEDERAL TAX, T2=STATE
TAX
440 DIM
B1(30),B2(30),CF(30),DF(30),DI(30),DY(30),IP(30),IZ(30),TC(3
0)
450 REM B1=BALANCE ON LOAN 1, B2=BALANCE ON LOAN 2
460 REM CF=CURRENT YEAR CASH FLOW, DF = DISCOUNTED CASH
FLOW
470 REM DI = CONSTANT DOLLAR CASH FLOW DY=DISCOUNTED
CONSTANT
480 REM DOLLAR CASH FLOW
490 REM IP INTEREST PAID LOAN 1, IZ INTEREST PAID LOAN 2
500 GOTO 620
510 REM SUBROUTINE TO DO LOAN CALCULATIONS
520 REM SUBROUTINE IS HERE FOR SPEED
530 FOR J1 = 1 TO NP
```

```
540     IP = I1 * A
550     IP = INT(IP*100)/100
560    SI = SI + IP
570     PP = P - IP
580     A = A - PP
590     B = B + PP
600 NEXT J1
610 RETURN
620 REM TRANSFER TO INITIALIZATION
630 GOSUB 5220
640 GOSUB 6010 : REM GET INCOME AND EXPENSE ESTIMATES
650 PV=0:B=0:SI=0:A=0:DI=0:PI=0:REM INITIALIZE COUNTERS FOR
SUMS
660 TC = 0: F = 0 : FL = 0 : F1 = 1
670 SP = 0 : CS = 0 : AE = 0 : AI = 0: SP = 0 : PN = 0
680 AP = 0
690 REM SP IS TOTAL SPENABLE CASH FLOW LOSS CS IS NUMBER OF
YEARS WITH SPENDABLE LOSS.
700 REM INITIALIZE ALL ARRAYS TO ZERO
710 CLS
720 PRINT "INITIALIZING EVERYTHING"
730 FOR I = 1 TO 30
740     PRINT I;
750      D(I) = 0
760      CF(I) = 0
770      EX(I) = 0
780      E1(I) = 0
790      E2(I) = 0
800      TC(I) = 0
810      T1(I) = 0
820      T2(I) = 0
830     SF(I) = 0
840 NEXT I
850 CLS
860 PRINT "NAME OF INVESTMENT IS ";NI$
870 INPUT" ENTER NEW NAME ";NI$
880 GOSUB 4180 : REM TRANSFER TO DATA INPUT
890 CLS
900 PRINT
"==============================================="
910 PRINT"DO YOU WANT TO TAKE INVESTMENT TAX CREDIT ?"
920 PRINT
"==============================================="
930 Y$=INKEY$:IF Y$="" THEN 930 ELSE IF
INSTR("YN",Y$)=0THEN PRINT "ANSWER Y OR N PLEASE ":GOTO 910
```

```
940 IF Y$="Y" THEN TC = 1 ELSE TC = 0
950 CLS
960 REM NOW READ IN DEPRECIATION TABLE
970 RESTORE
980 CLS
990 PRINT "READING DEPRECIATION TABLE"
1000 GOSUB 4930
1010 GOSUB 1970
1020 REM CALCULATE INVESTMENT TAX CREDIT ALLOWED
1030 REM TAX CREDIT IS ALLOWED ON 100% OF FIVE AND TEN YEAR
PROPERTY
1040 REM TAX CREDIT IS ALLOWED ON 60% OF THREE YEAR
PROPERTY
1050 TC =TC*0.1*(V(22)+V(23)+0.6*V(21))
1060 REM ALL LOANS TAKEN CARE OF NOW LETS DO YEARLY CASH
FLOWS
1070 KD = 0
1080 DT = 0 : REM TOTAL DEPRECIATION TAKEN
1090 CLS
1100 PRINT "NOW WORKING ON YEARLY CASH FLOWS."
1110 REM K IS THE YEAR NUMBER ASSUME THAT INCOME LAGS
EXPENSES
1120 IF V(6) = 0 THEN F = 1 ELSE F = 0
1130 REM THE INVESTMENT MAY NOT EARN INCOME FOR SOME TIME
AFTER
1140 REM THE INITIAL MONEY IS SPENT
1150 FOR K=1 TO V(20)
1160     PRINT K, : REM SHOW USER THAT SOMETHING IS GOING ON
1170    IF (K-V(6))>0 THEN KA =1 ELSE KA =0
1180      IF F = 1 THEN 1240
1190      IF FL = -1 THEN F = 1:F1=F:GOTO 1240
1200      IF V(6) > K THEN F = 0 : GOTO 1240 : REM NO INCOME
YET
1210      F = K - V(6)
1220     F1 = 0
1230      FL = -1
1240     E1(K) = F * TI*(1+V(13)/100)[(K-1)
1250     EX(K) = F * TX*(1+V(14)/100)[(K)
1260    KD = KD + KA
1270    IF KD = 0 THEN 1310
1280     IF KD > 15 THEN 1310 :REM BYPASS DEPRECIATION
1290     D(K) = DP(1,KD)*V(21) + V(22)*DP(2,KD) +
V(23)*DP(3,KD) + V(24)*DP(4,KD) + V(25)/15
1300    DT = DT + D(K)
```

```
1310     E2(K) = E1(K) - D(K) - EX(K) - IP(K) - IZ(K)
1320      IF TL = 0 AND K>1 THEN 1490 :REM CHECK TO SEE IF
HAVE LOSS CARRY FORWARD
1330     IF E2(K)<0 THEN TL = TL + (-1*E2(K)) :
T1(K)=0:T2(K)=0:GOTO 1600
1340     IF E2(K) >TL THEN 1370
1350     TL = TL - (-1*E2(K)) : T1(K)=0:T2(K)=0
1360      GOTO 1600
1370     E2 = E2(K)-TL : TL = 0
1380     T2(K) = V(18)/100 * E2 : REM STATE TAX PAID
1390     T1(K) = V(15)/100*(E2-T2(K)) : REM FED TAX PAID
1400      IF TC = 0 THEN 1600
1410      IF TC < T1(K) THEN 1450 ELSE TC(K) = T1(K)
1420      TC = TC - T1(K)
1430      T1(K) = 0
1440      GOTO 1600
1450      TC(K) = TC
1460      T1(K) = T1(K) - TC
1470      TC = 0
1480     GOTO 1600
1490     IF E2(K) > 0 THEN T2(K) = V(18)/100*E2(K) ELSE
T2(K) = 0
1500     IF E2(K)>=0 THEN T1(K) = (E2(K)-T2(K))*V(15)/100
ELSE T1(K) =0
1510     IF E2(K) < 0 THEN TL = -1*E2(K) :GOTO 1600
1520      IF TC = 0 THEN 1600
1530      IF TC < T1(K) THEN 1570 ELSE TC(K) = T1(K)
1540      TC = TC - T1(K)
1550      T1(K) = 0
1560      GOTO 1600
1570      TC(K) = TC
1580      T1(K) = T1(K) - TC
1590      TC = 0
1600     CF(K) = E2(K)-T1(K)-T2(K)+D(K) : REM CASH FLOW FOR
YR K
1610     DF(K) = CF(K)*(1+V(19)/100)[-K : REM DISCOUNTED
CASH FLOW
1620     DI(K) = CF(K)*(1+V(27)/100)[-K
1630     DY(K) = DI(K)*(1+V(19)/100)[-K
1640     SF(K) =
E1(K)-EX(K)-T1(K)-T2(K)-IP(K)-IZ(K)-A1(K)-A2(K):REM
SPENDABLE CASH FLOW
1650    IF SF(K)<0 THEN SP = SP +(-1)*SF(K): CS = CS + 1
1660 REM KEEP TRACK OF WHEN SPENDABLE CASH FLOW IS NEGATIVE
```

```
AND THE NUMBER OF YEARS WITH NEGATIVE CASH FLOW.
1670     PV = DF(K)+PV
1680     PI = DY(K)+PI
1690    AE = AE +A1(K)+A2(K)
1700    DA = (A1(K)+A2(K))*(1+V(19)/100)[-K
1710    AP = AP + DA
1720    AI = AI + DA*(1+V(27)/100)[-K
1730 NEXT K
1740 BL = V(2)+V(7)-AE : REM BL IS TOTAL LOAN BALANCE
1750 AE = AE + V(1)-V(2)-V(7)
1760 AI = AI + V(1)-V(2)-V(7)
1770 AP = AP + V(1)-V(2) -V(7) : REM ACCUMULATED EQUITY
1780 REM NOW CALCUALTE NEW SELLING PRICE
1790 SZ = V(1) *(1+V(11)/100)[V(20)
1800 CZ = SZ * V(12)/100
1810 REM BASIS FOR PROFIT IS PRICE - DEPRECIATION
1820 BZ = V(1) - DT : REM BASIS FOR TAX COST - DEPRECIATION
1830 REM TAXABLE PROFIT = SELLING PRICE - BASIS - COST
1840 TP = SZ - BZ - CZ
1850 REM CAPITAL GAINS TAX T1
1860 T1 = TP*(V(17)/100) : REM STATE CAPITAL GAINS
1870 T2 = (TP-T1)*V(16)/100
1880 REM NET PROFIT PN
1890 PN = TP - T1 - T2 - DT
1900 PB = PN - BL : REM PROFIT MINUS LOAN BALANCE
1910 REM PRESENT VALUE OF PN PP
1920 PP = PB*(1+V(19)/100)[-V(20)
1930 REM INFLATION CORRECTION
1940 PQ = PP *(1+V(27)/100)[-V(20)
1950 GOSUB 2560 :REM PRINT IT OUT
1960 END
1970 REM NOW TAKE CARE OF LOANS
1980 CLS
1990 PRINT "NOW WORKING ON FIRST LOAN"
2000 REM FIRST LOAN
2010 IF V(2) = 0 THEN 2210 :REM TRANSFER IF NO FIRST LOAN
2020 REM FIRST CALCULATE PAYMENT
2030 I1 = V(3)/100/V(5) : REM INTEREST PER PERIOD
2040 S=0
2050 S2 = 0
2060 A = V(2)
2070 V = (I1+1)[(V(4)*V(5))
2080 P = V(2)*(I1*V)/(V-1)
2090 P = INT(100*P)/100
2100 NP = V(5)
```

```
2110 J2 = 1
2120 GOSUB 510
2130 A1(J2) = B
2140 IP(J2) = SI
2150 IF J2 = V(4) THEN 2270
2160 PRINT J2,
2170 SI=0
2180 B = 0
2190 J2=J2+1
2200 GOTO 2120
2210 REM HERE BECAUSE NO FIRST LOAN V(2)=0
2220 IF IP(1)=0 THEN 2270 : REM CHECK TO SEE IF ARRAYS
ZEROED
2230 FOR JZ = 1 TO 30
2240    IP(JZ)=0
2250   A1(JZ) = 0
2260 NEXT JZ
2270 REM NOW DO SECOND LOAN
2280 CLS
2290 PRINT "NOW WORKING ON SECOND LOAN"
2300 IF V(7) = 0 THEN 2490 : REM TRANSFER IF NO SECOND LOAN
2310 A = V(7)
2320 SI = 0
2330 B = 0
2340 I1 = V(8)/100/V(10)
2350 V = (I1+1)[(V(9)*V(10))
2360 P = V(7)*(I1*V)/(V-1)
2370 P = INT(P*100)/100
2380 NP = V(10)
2390 J2 = 1
2400 PRINT  J2,
2410 GOSUB 510
2420 A2(J2) = B
2430 IZ(J2) = SI
2440 IF J2 = V(9) THEN RETURN
2450 SI = 0
2460 B = 0
2470 J2 = J2 + 1
2480 GOTO 2400
2490 REM HERE BACAUSE NO SECOND LOAN
2500 IF IZ(1) AND A2(1) = 0 THEN RETURN
2510 FOR JZ = 1 TO 30
2520    IZ(JZ) = 0
2530    A2(JZ) = 0
2540 NEXT JZ
```

```
2550 RETURN
2560 REM NOW PRINT OUT THE RESULTS
2570 CLS
2580 PRINT "RESULTS OF CALCULATIONS "
2590 PRINT" SUMMARY"
2600 PRINT "==================================================="
2610 PRINT USING"PRESENT VALUE OF RENT FLOWS
$###,####.##"·PV
2620 PRINT USING"PRESENT VALUE OF PROFIT FORM SALE
$###,#####.##":PP
2630 PRINT USING "PRESENT VALUE OF ALL PROFITS
$###,#####.##"·PP+PV
2640 PRINT USING "PRESENT VALUE RENT CONT YR
$###,####.##";PI
2650 PRINT USING"PRESENT CONSTANT YR PROFIT SALE
$###,####.##";PP*(1+V(27)/100)[-V(20)
2660 PRINT USING"PRESENT CONSTANT YR ALL PROFITS
$###,####.##";PP*(1+V(27)/100)[-V(20)+PI
2670 PRINT USING"ACCUMULATED EQUITY
$###,####.##";AE
2680 PRINT
"================================================="
2690 PRINT "DO YOU WANT TO SEE YEARLY DETAILS Y OR N?"
2700 Y$=INKEY$:IF Y$="" THEN 2700 ELSE IF INSTR("YN",Y$)=0
THEN PRINT"TRY AGAIN":GOTO 2690
2710 IF Y$="N" THEN 2920
2720 FOR K=1 TO V(20)
2730   CLS
2740    PRINT USING"INCOME
$#,######.##";E1(K)
2750    PRINT USING"EXPENSES
$#,######.##";EX(K)
2760    PRINT USING"DEPRECIATION
$#,######.##";D(K)
2770    PRINT USING"INTEREST FIRST LOAN
$#,######.##":IP(K)
2780    PRINT USING"INTEREST SECOND LOAN
$#,######.##";IZ(K)
2790    PRINT USING"PRINCIPAL FIRST LOAN
$#,######.##";A1(K)
2800    PRINT USING"PRINCIPAL SECOND LOAN
$#,######.##";A2(K)
2810    PRINT USING"TAXABLE INCOME
$#,######.##";E1(K)-EX(K)-D(K)-IP(K)-IZ(K)
```

```
2820    PRINT USING"STATE TAXES PAID
$#,######.##";T2(K)
2830   PRINT USING"FEDERAL TAX PAID
$#,######.##";T1(K)
2840    PRINT USING"AFTER TAX CASH FLOW
$#,######.##";CF(K)
2850    PRINT USING"DISCOUNTED CASH FLOW
$#,######.##";DF(K)
2860    PRINT USING"CONSTANT DOLLAR CASH
$#,######.##";DY(K)
2870    PRINT USING"SPENDABLE CASH FLOW
$#,######.##";SF(K)
2880    PRINT"THIS IS YEAR ";K;" PRESS  ANY KEY FOR NEXT
YEAR"
2890    Y$=INKEY$:IF Y$="" THEN 2890
2900 NEXT K
2910 CLS
2920 PRINT"DO YOU WANT HARD COPY Y OR N "
2930 Y$=INKEY$:IF Y$="" THEN 2930 ELSE IF INSTR("YN",Y$)=0
THEN PRINT"TRY AGAIN":GOTO 2920
2940 IF Y$="Y" THEN GOSUB 3020
2950 CLS
2960 PRINT"DO YOU WANT TO RUN ANOTHER CASE Y OR N?"
2970 Y$=INKEY$:IFY$=""THEN 2970 ELSE IF INSTR("YN",Y$)=0
THEN PRINT"TRY AGAIN":GOTO 2400
2980 IF Y$="Y" THEN 640
2990 PRINT"SESSION OVER. PLEASE REMOVE DISKS BEFORE
TURNING"
3000 PRINT"SYSTEM OFF."
3010 END
3020 PRINT"HARD COPY ROUTINE. PLEASE BE SURE PRINTER IS ON"
3030 LPRINT TAB(5);"RESULTS OF INVESTMENT ANALYSIS PROGRAM
V 3.0"
3040 LPRINT TAB(5) ; "NAME OF INVESTMENT ";NI$
3050 LPRINT " "
3060 LPRINT TAB(30);"INPUT DATA SUMMARY"
3070 FOR I = 1 TO I9
3080    LPRINT TAB(8);
3090    LPRINT USING F$(I);V(I)
3100 NEXT I
3110 LPRINT TAB(5);
"============================================================"
3120 LPRINT TAB(20);"INCOME ESTIMATES."
3130 LPRINT TAB(5);
"============================================================"
```

```
3140 LPRINT" "
3150 TR=0
3160 FOR I = 1 TO 6
3170   LPRINT TAB(5);
3180    LPRINT USING TU$(I);NU(I);
3190   LPRINT " ";
3200    LPRINT USING R$(I);R1(I);R2(I)
3210   TR = TR + NU(I)*R2(I)
3220 NEXT I
3230 LPRINT TAB(5);
3240 LPRINT USING "ALLOWANCE FOR VACANCIES ##.##% OR
$####,###.##/YR";VC;VC*TR/100
3250 LPRINT TAB(5);
3260 LPRINT USING "TOTAL YEARLY INCOME
$#####,##.##":TR*(1-VC/100)
3270 LPRINT TAB(5);STRING$(64,"=")
3280 LPRINT TAB(25);"EXPENSES"
3290 FOR I = 1 TO 9
3300    LPRINT TAB(5);
3310    LPRINT USING EX$(I):EM(I):EY(I)
3320 NEXT I
3330 LPRINT TAB(10);
3340 LPRINT USING"TOTAL EXPENSES PER YEAR $#####,##.##";TX
3350 LPRINT " "
3360 PRINT"PRESS ANY KEY WHEN READY FOR NEXT PAGE."
3370 Y$ = INKEY$: IF Y$ = "" THEN 3370
3380 LPRINT TAB(20);"INVESTMENT   ";NI$;"         PAGE 2
OUTPUT"
3390 LPRINT TAB(5);STRING$(73,"=")
3400 LPRINT TAB(30);"*** SUMMARY RESULTS ***"
3410 LPRINT " "
3420   LPRINT TAB(9);
3430 LPRINT USING "CURRENT YEAR DOLLARS PRESENT VALUE OF
RENT PROFIT $#,######.##":PV
3440 LPRINT TAB(9);
3450 LPRINT USING"SELLING PRICE .......... $#####,##.##";SZ
3460 LPRINT TAB(9);
3470 LPRINT USING"COST OF SELLING ........ $#####,##.##";CZ
3480 LPRINT TAB(9);
3490 LPRINT USING"BALANCE DUE ON LOANS ... $#####,##.##";BL
3500 LPRINT TAB(9);
3510 LPRINT USING"BASIS FOR TAX PURPOSE .. $#####,##.##";BZ
3520 LPRINT TAB(9);
3530 LPRINT USING"TAXABLE PROCEEDS ....... $#####,##.##";TP
3540 LPRINT TAB(9);
```

```
3550 LPRINT USING"TOTAL CAPITAL GAINS TAX
$#####,##.##";T1+T2
3560 LPRINT TAB(9);
3570 LPRINT USING"NET PROFIT FROM SALE ... $#####,##.##";PN
3580 LPRINT TAB(9);
3590 LPRINT USING "PRESENT VALUE OF PROFIT FROM SALE -
BALANCE DUE    $#,######.##";PP
3600 LPRINT TAB(9);
3610 LPRINT USING"PRESENT VALUE OF TOTAL PROFITS - BALANCE
DUE        $#,######.##";PP+PV
3620 LPRINT TAB(9);
3630 LPRINT USING"ACCUMULATED EQUITY ...... $####,##.##";AE
3640 LPRINT TAB(9);
3650 LPRINT USING"PRESENT VALUE EQUITY .... $####,##.##";AP
3660 LPRINT TAB(9);
3670 LPRINT USING"CONSTANT YR DOLLAR  .... $####,##.##":AI
3680 LPRINT TAB(9);
3690 LPRINT USING"NET PRESENT VALUE (PROFIT  -EQUITY) =
        $#,######.##";PP + PV - AP
3700 LPRINT TAB(9);
3710  LPRINT USING"CONSTANT YEAR NET PRESENT VALUE ALL
PROFIT-BALANCE $#,######.##";PQ + PI - AI
3720 IF AP>PP+PV THEN LPRINT TAB(10);:LPRINT USING"YOU LOST
$#,######.## IN PRESENT VALUE ";AP-PP-PV
3730 IF AI >PQ +PI THEN  LPRINT TAB(5);:LPRINT
"***";:LPRINT USING "YOU LOST $#,######.## IN PURCHASING
POWER ";AI-PQ-PI
3740 LPRINT TAB(5); STRING$(73,"=")
3750 PRINT "PRESS ANY KEY WHEN READY WITH NEW SHEET OF
PAPER."
3760 Y$=INKEY$:IF Y$="" THEN 3760
3770 LPRINT TAB(30);"RESULTS OF EACH YEARS OPERATION "
3780 FOR I=1 TO V(20)
3790   LPRINT TAB(30);"RESULTS FOR YEAR ";I
3800   LPRINT
TAB(5);"----------------------------------------"
3810    LPRINT USING"    GROSS INCOME
........................$#,######.##";E1(I)
3820    LPRINT USING"    EXPENSES
............................$#,######.##";EX(I)
3830    LPRINT USING"    DEPRECIATION
........................$#,######.##";D(I)
3840    LPRINT USING"    INTEREST 1ST LOAN
...................$#,######.##";IP(I)
3850    LPRINT USING"    PRINCIPAL 1ST LOAN
```

```
..................$#,######.##";A1(I)
3860    LPRINT USING"    INTEREST 2ND LOAN
...................$#,######.##";IZ(I)
3870    LPRINT USING"    PRINCIPAL 2ND LOAN
..................$#,######.##";A2(I)
3880    LPRINT USING"    TAXABLE INCOME
......................$#,######.##";E2(I)
3890    LPRINT USING"    STATE TAX PAID
......................$#,######.##";T2(I)
3900   LPRINT USING"    INVESTMENT TAX CREDIT TAKEN
.........$#,######.##";TC(I)
3910    LPRINT USING"    FEDERAL TAX PAID
....................$#,######.##";T1(I)
3920    LPRINT USING"    AFTER TAX CASH FLOW
.................$#,######.##";CF(I)
3930    LPRINT USING"    CONSTANT DOLLAR CASH FLOW
...........$#,######.##";DI(I)
3940    LPRINT USING"    DISCOUNTED CURRENT YEAR CASH FLOW
...$#,######.##";DF(I)
3950    LPRINT USING"    DISCOUNTED CONSTANT YR CASH FLOW
....$#,######.##";DY(I)
3960    LPRINT USING"    SPENDABLE CASH FLOW
.................$#,######.##";SF(I)
3970    IF SF(I)<0 THEN LPRINT "     NOTE THAT SPENDABLE
CASH IS NEGATIVE. YOU NEED TO BORROW MONEY."
3980   LPRINT
TAB(5);"========================================"
3990   IF INT(I/3)-I/3 = 0 THEN PRINT"PRESS ANY KEY WHEN
READY WITH NEW SHEET OF PAPER IN PRINTER " ELSE 4010
4000   Y$=INKEY$ : IF Y$ = "" THEN 4000
4010 NEXT I
4020   LPRINT
TAB(5);"======================================"
4030 RETURN
4040 REM ERROR SUBROUTINE
4050 CLS
4060 PRINT "*****************************"
4070 PRINT "INPUT DATA ERROR!!!"
4080 IF V(1) < V(21)+V(22)+V(23)+V(24)+V(25) THEN 4130
4090 IF V(20) >30 THEN PRINT "MAXIMUM LIFE ALLOWED IS 30
YEARS"
4100 PRINT "PLEASE CORRECT DATA ENTRY "
4110 FOR KO = 1 TO 400
4120 NEXT KQ
```

```
4130 PRINT"VALUE OF DEPRECIATED PROPERTY EXCEEDS
INVESTMENT."
4140 FOR K1 =  1 TO 500
4150 NEXT K1
4160 RETURN
4170 RETURN
4180 REM DATA ENTRY SUBROUTINE
4190 P1=1
4200 IZ=1: IX=9
4210 I=IZ:IQ=1
4220 CLS
4230 PRINT"INVESTMENT ANALYSIS DATA INPUT PAGE ";P1
4240 PRINT"PROVIDE DATA ASKED FOR. CURRENT VALUE SHOWN IN
()"
4250 PRINT"IF YOU WISH TO CORRECT A PREVIOUS ENTRY ENTER C"
4260 PRINT"TO GO TO NEXT PAGE ENTER >"
4270 PRINT STRING$(63,"=")
4280 IF I = IZ THEN 4300 ELSE FOR IQ=IZ TO I-1:PRINT USING
F$(IQ);V(IQ):NEXT IQ
4290 IF I > I9 THEN 4420
4300    PRINT USING F$(I);V(I);
4310 V$=""
4320    INPUT V$
4330   IF V$="" THEN 4400
4340    IF V$=">" THEN 4560 ELSE IF V$="C" THEN 4690
4350   IF V$="<" THEN 4630
4360   V(I)=VAL(V$):V$=""
4370   IF V(1) <V(21)+V(22)+V(23)+V(24)+V(25) THEN GOSUB
4040 : GOTO 4220
4380   IF V(20)>30 THEN GOSUB 4040 : GOTO 4220
4390  IF I = I9 THEN 4420
4400 I=I+1:IF I<=IX THEN 4220
4410  GOTO 4510
4420 PRINT STRING$(63,"=")
4430 PRINT"END OF DATA ENTRY. PLEASE CHECK DATA ON THIS
PAGE."
4440 PRINT"TO CORRECT DATA ENTER C. TO REVIEW PREVIOUS PAGE
ENTER <"
4450 PRINT"TO REVIEW ALL DATA ENTER R. TO START
CALCULATIONS ENTER G.";
4460 Y$=""
4470 INPUT Y$
4480 IF Y$="G" THEN RETURN ELSE IF Y$="C" THEN 4520 ELSE IF
Y$="<" THEN 4630
```

```
4490 IF Y$ <> "R" THEN PRINT "PLEASE ENTER C,<,R,OR
G.":GOTO 4430
4500 CLS
4510 PRINT "END OF PAGE ":P1;" REVIEW DATA ENTER > TO GO TO
NEXT PAGE"
4520 PRINT"ENTER C TO CORRECT ENTRY AND ENTER R TO RETURN
TO MAIN PROGRAM";
4530 Y$="":INPUT Y$
4540 IF Y$ = "<" THEN 4630
4550 IF Y$=">" THEN 4560 ELSE IF Y$="C" THEN 4690 ELSE IF
Y$<>"R" THEN PRINT"PLEASE ANSWER >,C,OR R":GOTO 4510
4560 REM
4570 IF P1 = PM THEN 4420
4580 P1=P1+1
4590 IZ=IZ+9
4600 IX =IZ+8
4610 I=IZ:IQ=IZ
4620 GOTO 4220
4630 IF P1>1 THEN P1=P1-1 ELSE GOTO 4220
4640 IF P1 =1 THEN IZ = 1 : IX =8
4650 IF P1 = 2 THEN IZ = 9 : IX = 16
4660 IF P1 = 3 THEN IZ = 17 : IX = 24
4670 IF I > IX THEN I = IX
4680 GOTO 4220
4690 REM CORRECTION PAGE
4700 CLS
4710 V$=""
4720 PRINT "ROUTINE TO CORRECT ENTRY ON PAGE ";P1
4730 PRINT STRING$(63,"=")
4740 IF IX > I9 THEN IX = I9
4750 FOR J=IZ TO IX
4760   PRINT J;
4770     PRINT USING F$(J);V(J)
4780 NEXT J
4790 PRINT STRING$(63,"=")
4800 PRINT "IF YOU WANT TO CORRECT ALL ENTRIES ENTER A
ELSE"
4810 INPUT "ENTER ITEM NUMBER TO CORRECT R TO RETURN ";YI$
4820 IF YI$="A" THEN GOTO 4180
4830 IF YI$="R" THEN 4900 ELSE J=VAL(YI$)
4840 IF J>IX THEN PRINT "NOT ON THIS PAGE ":GOTO 4810
4850 IF J<=0 THEN J = IX
4860 PRINT USING F$(J);V(J):INPUT"ENTER CORRECT VALUE C IF
OK ";C$
```

```
4870 IF C$="C" THEN GOTO 4690 ELSE V(J)=VAL(C$)
4880 GOTO 4690
4890 END
4900 REM
4910 GOTO 4220
4920 IF V(24)<1982 THEN V(24)=1982
4930 REM READ IN NEW DEPRECIATION
4940 FOR I=1 TO 4
4950   IF I = 1 THEN JM = 3 ELSE IF I = 2 THEN JM = 5 ELSE
IF I = 3 THEN JM = 10 ELSE JM = 15
4960    FOR J = 1 TO JM
4970            READ DP(I,J)
4980           DP(I,J)=DP(I,J)/100 : REM CONVERT TO DECIMAL
FRACTION
4990    NEXT J
5000 NEXT I
5010 IF V(24) <1985 THEN RETURN
5020 JZ = JZ +1
5030 IF V(24) = 1985 AND JZ = 1 THEN 4940 ELSE IF V(24) =
1985 THEN RETURN
5040 IF JZ <= 2 THEN 4940 ELSE RETURN
5050 REM DEPRECIATION FOR 3  YEAR
5060 DATA 25,38,37
5070 REM DEPRECIATION FOR 5 YEAR
5080 DATA 15,22,21,21,21
5090 REM DEPRECIATION DATA FOR 10 YEAR
5100 DATA 8,14,12,10,10,10,9,9,9,9
5110 REM FOR 15 YEAR
5120 DATA 5,10,9,8,7,7,6,6,6,6,6,6,6,6,6
5130 REM DATA FOR 1985
5140 DATA 29,47,24,18,33,25,16,8
5150 DATA 9,19,16,14,12,10,8,6,4,2
5160 DATA 6,12,12,11,10,9,8,7,6,5,4,4,3,2,1
5170 REM DATA FOR 1986
5180 DATA 33,45,22,20,32,24,16,8
5190 DATA 10,18,16,14,12,10,8,6,4,2
5200 DATA 7,12,12,11,10,9,8,7,6,5,4,3,3,2,1
5210 END
5220 REM INITIALIZATION SUBROUTINE
5230 F$(1)="TOTAL AMOUNT OF INVESTMENT
$#,#####.##"
5240 F$(2)="AMOUNT OF FIRST LOAN
$#,#####.##"
5250 F$(3)="YEARLY INTEREST RATE FOR 1ST LOAN
##.##%
```

```
5260 F$(4)="LIFE OF FIRST LOAN YEARS
##.##  YRS"
5270 F$(5)="NUMBER OF LOAN PAYMENTS PER YEAR
##"
5280 F$(6)="TIME AFTER INVESTING BEFORE REC. INCOME
#.## YRS"
5290 F$(7)="AMOUNT OF SECOND LOAN
$#,######.##
5300 F$(8)="YEARLY INTEREST RATE FOR 2ND LOAN
##.##%"
5310 F$(9)="LIFE OF SECOND LOAN YEARS
## YRS"
5320 F$(10) ="NUMBER OF PAYMENTS PER YEAR  2ND LOAN
##"
5330 F$(11)="ESCLATION FOR VALUE OF PROPERTY
##.##%"
5340 F$(12)="COST OF SELLING AS % OF PRICE
##.##%"
5350 F$(13)="ESCALATION FOR RENTS
##.##%"
5360 F$(14)="ESCALATION FOR EXPENSES
##.##%"
5370 F$(15)="FEDERAL INCOME TAX RATE
##.##%"
5380 F$(16)="FEDERAL CAPITAL GAINS TAX RATE
##.##%"
5390 F$(17)="STATE CAPITAL GAINS TAX RATE
##.##%"
5400 F$(18)="STATE INCOME TAX RATE
##.##%"
5410 F$(19)="DISCOUNT RATE
##.## %"
5420 F$(20)="LIFE OF INVESTMENT
## YRS"
5430 F$(21) = "VALUE OF 3 YEAR PROPERTY
$#,######.##"
5440 F$(22) = "VALUE OF 5 YEAR PROPERTY
$#,######.##"
5450 F$(23) = "VALUE OF 10 YEAR PROPERTY
$#,######.##"
5460 F$(24) = "VALUE OF 15 YEAR PU PROP
$#,######.##"
5470 F$(25) = "VALUE OF ST LINE REAL ESTATE
$#,######.##"
```

```
5480 F$(26) = "YEAR PROPERY PLACED IN SVC
 ####"
5490 F$(27) = "INFLATION RATE
  ##.##%"
5500 TU$(1)="NUMBER OF 1 BED ROOM UNFUR ###"
5510 TU$(2)="NUMBER OF 1 BED ROOM FUR   ###"
5520 TU$(3)="NUMBER OF 2 BED ROOM UNFUR ###"
5530 TU$(4)="NUMBER OF 2 BED ROOM FUR   ###"
5540 TU$(5)="NUMBER OF 3 BED ROOM UNFUR ###"
5550 TU$(6)="NUMBER OF 3 BED ROOM FUR   ###"
5560 FOR J=1 TO 6
5570    R$(J)="RENT $##,###.##/MO   $####,###.##/YR"
5580 NEXT J
5590 EX$(1) = "INSURANCE  $###,#.##/MO   $####,#.##/YR"
5600 EX$(2) = "LICENSES   $###,#.##/MO   $####,#.##/YR"
5610 EX$(3) = "PROP TAX   $###,#,##/MO   $####,#.##/YR"
5620 EX$(4) = "UTILITIES  $###,#.##/MO   $####,#.##/YR"
5630 EX$(5) = "MANAGEMENT $###,#.##/MO   $####,#.##/YR"
5640 EX$(6) = "JANITOR    $###,#.##/MO   $####,#.##/YR"
5650 EX$(7) = "ADVERTIS   $###,#.##/MO   $####,#.##/YR"
5660 EX$(8) = "MAINT EXP  $###,#.##/MO   $####,#.##/YR"
5670 EX$(9) = "MISC EXP   $###,#.##/MO   $####,#.##/YR"
5680 RETURN
5690 CLS
5700 PRINT
"================================================="
5710 PRINT "INSTRUCTIONS "
5720 PRINT "THIS PROGRAM CALCULATES THE PRESENT VALUE OF
THE"
5730 PRINT "CASH FLOWS FROM AN INVESTMENT. IN ORDER TO USE"
5740 PRINT "THE PROGRAM, YOU MUST SUPPLY THE INPUT
INFORMATION."
5750 PRINT " FIRST DATA TO ENTER ARE INCOME ESTIMATES. THEN
ENTER"
5760 PRINT "THE EXPENSES. THESE TWO TYPES OF INFORMATION
ARE ENTERED"
5770 PRINT "ON A TWO PAGE FORM - 1 PAGE FOR INCOME AND 1
FOR EXPENSES."
5780 PRINT"FINALLY DATA ON COST ETC ARE ENTERED USING A 3
PAGE FORM"
5790 PRINT "FOR THESE PAGES YOU CAN MOVE  WITH THE < AND >
KEYS."
5800 PRINT "YOU CAN CORRECT A WRONG ENTRY BY ENTERING C
AND"
5810 PRINT "THEN FOLLOWING THE INSTRUCTIONS."
```

```
5820 PRINT "WHEN ALL THE DATA ARE CORRECT, YOU CAN START
THE"
5830 PRINT "CALCULATIONS BY ENTERING G."
5840 PRINT "YOU MUST ENTER ALL THE DATA BEFORE YOU CAN RUN
THE PROGRAM."
5850 PRINT "PRESS ANY KEY TO CONTINUE"
5860 Y$=INKEY$:IF Y$="" THEN 5860
5870 CLS
5880 PRINT "INSTRUCTIONS PAGE 2"
5890 PRINT "ALL DATA ASKED FOR IS SELF EXPLANATORY, WITH
THE
5900 PRINT "POSSIBLE EXCEPTION OF YEARS AFTER INVEST BEFORE
REC
5910 PRINT "INCOME. THIS QUESTION IS BASED ON THE FACT THAT
MANY
5920 PRINT "INVESTMENTS DO NOT START PAYING UNITIL SOME
TIME
5930 PRINT "AFTER THE MONEY IS SPENT. YOU ENTER THE NUMBER
OF"
5940 PRINT "YEARS YOU ESTIMATE IT WILL TAKE FOR INCOME TO
START"
5950 PRINT "COMING AFTER THE INVESTMENT IS MADE. FOR
EXAMPLE IF"
5960 PRINT "YOU KNOW IT WILL TAKE ONE YEAR ENTER 1. IF IT
WILL
5970 PRINT "TAKE HALF A YEAR, ENTER 0.5."
5980 PRINT "PRESS ANY KEY TO CONTINUE"
5990 Y$=INKEY$:IF Y$="" THEN 5990
6000 RETURN
6010 FOR I = 1 TO 6
6020      CLS
6030 PRINT"INCOME ESTIMATES FOR RENTAL PROPERTY"
6040 PRINT "ENTER DATA ASKED FOR. DO NOT WORRY IF YOU
6050 PRINT "MAKE AN ERROR. YOU WILL HAVE A CHANCE TO
CORRECT"
6060 PRINT "IT LATER. TO ENTER MONTHLY EXPENSES PRECEED
AMOUNT"
6070 PRINT "WITH <M> AND FOR YEARLY PRECEED WITH <Y>. "
6080 PRINT "EG M100 IS $100 PER MONTH Y2000 IS $2000 PER
YR"
6090    PRINT USING TU$(I);NU(I);
6100   NU$ = ""
6110    INPUT NU$
6120   IF NU$ = "" THEN 6140
6130   NU(I) = VAL(NU$)
```

```
6140    IF NU(I) = 0 THEN 6230
6150     PRINT USING R$(I);R1(I);R2(I)
6160     R$=""
6170     INPUT R$
6180     IF R$ = "" THEN 6230
6190    IF INSTR("MY",LEFT$(R$,1)) = 0 THEN PRINT "WRONG
FORMAT. TRY AGAIN.":GOTO 6160
6200     GOSUB 6640
6210     R1(I) = RM
6220     R2(I) = RY
6230 NEXT I
6240 PRINT USING "ALLOWANCE FOR VACANCIES AS % OF RENTS
(##.##%)";VC;
6250 R$ = ""
6260 INPUT R$
6270 IF R$ = "" THEN 6280 ELSE VC = VAL(R$)
6280 CLS
6290 TI = 0
6300 PRINT "CHECK DATA TO BE SURE THEY ARE CORRECT."
6310 FOR I=1 TO 6
6320     PRINT USING TU$(I);NU(I)
6330     PRINT USING R$(I);R1(I);R2(I)
6340    TI = TI + NU(I)*R2(I)
6350 NEXT I
6360 PRINT USING "ALLOWANCE FOR VACENCIES ##.##%";VC
6370 TI = TI*(1-VC/100)
6380 PRINT USING "TOTAL YEARLY INCOME $#####,##.##";TI
6390 PRINT "ARE THESE CORRECT Y OR N?"
6400 Y$ = INKEY$ : IF Y$ = "" THEN 6400 ELSE IF
INSTR("YN",Y$)=0 THEN PRINT "TRY AGAIN PLEASE.":GOTO 6390
6410 IF Y$ = "N" THEN 6010
6420 CLS
6430 PRINT "ENTER EXPENSES. PRECEED BY M FOR MONTHLY Y FOR
YEARLY"
6440 FOR I = 1 TO 9
6450     PRINT USING EX$(I);EM(I);EY(I);
6460     R$=""
6470     INPUT R$
6480    IF R$="" THEN 6530
6490    IF INSTR("MY",LEFT$(R$,1)) = 0 THEN PRINT "WRONG
FORMAT. TRY AGAIN." : GOTO 6460
6500     GOSUB 6640
6510     EM(I) = RM
6520     EY(I) = RY
```

```
6530 NEXT I
6540 CLS
6550 PRINT "CHECK DATA TO BE SURE THAT THEY ARE CORRECT."
6560 TX = 0
6570 FOR I=1 TO 9
6580    PRINT USING EX$(I);EM(I);EY(I)
6590   TX = TX + EY(I)
6600 NEXT I
6610 PRINT "ARE THESE CORRECT Y OR N?"
6620 Y$ = INKEY$ : IF Y$ = "" THEN 6620 ELSE IF
INSTR("YN",Y$)=0 THEN PRINT"TRY AGAIN.":GOTO 6610
6630 IF Y$ = "Y" THEN RETURN ELSE GOTO 6420
6640 IF LEFT$(R$,1)="M" THEN 6680
6650 RY = VAL(RIGHT$(R$,LEN(R$)-1))
6660 RM = RY/12
6670 RETURN
6680 RM = VAL(RIGHT$(R$,LEN(R$)-1))
6690 RY = 12*RM
6700 RETURN
6710 END
```

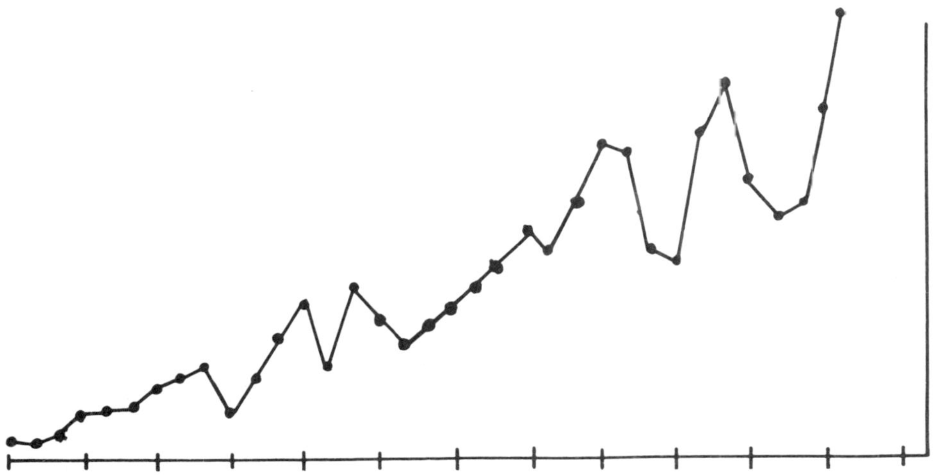

Chapter 12

INVEST3 Program

How can you estimate the risk in an investment such as the real estate investment examined in the previous chapter? One way is to vary the input assumptions and then see what happens. The sensitivity analysis used in INVEST1 is an example where one variable is changed at a time.

MONTE CARLO SIMULATION

Another way to examine the risk is to use the computer to simulate the investment under various conditions in which several variables are allowed to vary at a time. If this is done properly, you can then estimate the average or excepted return from the investment and can say something about the probability of making a given return on the investment. This type of simulation is called *Monte Carlo simulation*.

To use Monte Carlo simulation you must replace the absolute values of important variables by probability functions. If your probability functions represent the real world, you can have a great deal of faith in the results of the simulation.

The problem is, of course, that you don't really have a good idea of what probability distribution to use. If you are playing craps, you know the exact probability distribution to use. However, the choice of probability distribution for real estate investments is not at all clear.

Even if you don't know an exact probability distribution, you can still obtain useful qualitative results if you assume reasonable probability distributions.

The easiest way to go about providing the computer with the required information is to assume that all important input variables follow a given type of distribution. Then all you require as input information are the data needed to quantify the assumed distribution.

If there is no way for you to estimate the required information, you still haven't been helped.

Fortunately, there is a fair body of empirical work on investment analysis that can help. This work shows that you can make good estimates of the most likely, best possible, and worst possible values of the factors that affect an investment. These three values can then be used to estimate the important parameters of the probability distribution used in the Monte Carlo simulation.

This still leaves the problem of choosing the exact distribution. Different authors suggest different distributions. The two most likely candidates are distribution and *normal distribution*. There is no clear criterion for selecting one distribution. Program INVEST3 uses normal distribution.

The program for conducting a Monte Carlo simulation of a real estate investment is a modification of the INVEST2 program. The modification consists of adding a module for the Monte Carlo simulation. The module includes all code for obtaining the necessary input information. Because you already have the best estimate as part of the data entered for INVEST2, you need the best case and worst case estimates to conduct the Monte Carlo simulation, and you need a routine to generate the values used in the program calculations.

The number of times to run the simulation must be carefully chosen. You want to run the program enough times to get a good statistical picture of the investment, yet you don't want to run so many trials that computing time becomes excessive. By trial and error I have found that between 20 and 30 runs seems to work well.

INPUT DATA

All initial input data for INVEST3 is the same as the input data for INVEST2. The same worksheets can be used. The only difference is that best case and worst case estimates are required for the following data:

- Escalation rate for increase in value of property.
- Inflation rate.
- Escalation rate for increase in rents.
- Escalation rate for increase in expenses.

All remaining input data are the same as for INVEST2.

OUTPUT DATA

The output information for the Monte Carlo simulation shows the average value of the present value of all profits (after tax) and the standard deviation of the profits from the investment. The standard deviation gives us some measure of the risk involved in the investment.

If you assume that the calculated results of the Monte Carlo simulation follow a normal distribution, then 95.45 percent of all values are within plus or minus 2 standard deviations of the mean. And 99.73 percent of all values are within plus or minus 3 standard deviations of the mean. These statistical statements, although exact in theory, should not be taken too quantitatively. The answers you get depend on the assumption that the normal distribution best describes the distribution of the likely input data. If this assumption is not valid, then the mean and standard deviation will be somewhat different.

There is also another problem. The statistics are based on the assumption that you can make the same investment several times. (Shooting craps is a good example.) So while an investment may sometimes make money and lose money other times, on the average it will give the average profit. You only have one chance at the investment, so you only see one of the possible outcomes. If it lost money, then no matter what the chances of obtaining that one single outcome, you lost money.

But this does not distract from the usefulness of the results. An investment with a large standard deviation is more risky than an investment with a small standard deviation. The investment with the large standard deviation may make more money or it may lose more money.

For example, assume that you have two investments; both have an average profit of $100,000; investment A has a standard deviation of $10,000 and investment B has a standard deviation of $50,000. There is only a 5 percent that investment A will generate more than $120,000 in profits or less than $80,000. The same range of profits for investment B (all but 5 percent of the total possible profits are covered) is $200,000 and $0.00, and the chance of getting zero is the same as the chance of getting $200,000.

Because investments with large standard deviations are more risky than investments with small standard deviations, the average profit should be high. In the example above, most investors would select investment B only if the cost of buying the investment were much less than the cost of buying investment A.

USER INSTRUCTIONS

An abbreviated set of user instructions for INVEST3 is included as part of the program. You can see these instructions by pressing <I> when you are asked if you want instructions. You do not have to press <ENTER>. The first two pages of user instructions are the same as the user instructions for INVEST2. The third page explains the Monte Carlo simulation.

User instructions for INVEST3 as displayed on the crt are given in Fig. 12-1.

The initial data entry for INVEST3 is the same as the data entry for INVEST2. All data is the same and the manner of entering the data is also the same. If you have any questions, see the previous chapter.

After the program makes its initial calculations, you are asked if you want to run a risk analysis. This question must be answered by pressing <Y> or <N>. If you press any other key, you will get an error message. If you press <N>, the program returns control to BASIC and displays a message to remove disks before shutting down the system.

If you press <Y> you are transferred to the data entry module for the Monte Carlo simulation. The data required for this part of the program are:

- Most likely value of inflation rate (already entered and displayed)
- Best case estimate of inflation rate (you enter this)
- Worst case estimate of inflation rate (you enter this)
- Most likely escalation rate for income (already entered and displayed)
- Best case escalation rate for income (you enter this)
- Worst case escalation rate for income (you enter this)
- Best estimate of escalation for expenses (already entered and displayed)
- Best estimate of escalation for expenses (you enter this)
- Worst case estimate of escalation for expenses (you enter this)
- Best estimate of escalation rate for increase in property value (already entered and displayed)
- Best case estimate of escalation rate for increase in property value (you enter this)
- Worst case estimate of escalation rate for increases in property value (you enter this)

Your best case estimate should be based on the assumption that everything goes fine. It should be a case that can happen and not a case that could never happen. The worst case estimate should be based on the assumption that everything that can go wrong will go wrong. But don't include flood, and other really bad things (unless your investment is located in a place where flood is not unlikely).

The best and worst case estimates should reflect your thinking about how good things could be and how bad things could be. How well this method of risk analysis works for you depends on how well your best and worst case estimates reflect reality. So if you use this program, spend time to assure that

```
INSTRUCTIONS
THIS PROGRAM CALCULATES THE PRESENT VALUE OF THE
CASH FLOWS FROM A INVESTMENT IN REAL ESATATE.  IN ORDER TO USE
THE PROGRAM, YOU MUST SUPPLY THE INPUT INFORMATION.
 FIRST DATA TO ENTER ARE INCOME ESTIMATES. THEN ENTER
THE EXPENSES. THESE TWO TYPES OF INFORMATION ARE ENTERED
ON A TWO PAGE FORM - 1 PAGE FOR INCOME AND 1 FOR EXPENSES.
FINALLY DATA ON COST ETC ARE ENTERED USING A 3 PAGE FORM
FOR THESE PAGES YOU CAN MOVE  WITH THE < AND > KEYS.
YOU CAN CORRECT A WRONG ENTRY BY ENTERING C AND
THEN FOLLOWING THE INSTRUCTIONS.
WHEN ALL THE DATA ARE CORRECT, YOU CAN START THE
CALCULATIONS BY ENTERING G.
YOU MUST ENTER ALL THE DATA BEFORE YOU CAN RUN THE PROGRAM.
PRESS ANY KEY TO CONTINUE


INSTRUCTIONS PAGE 2
ALL DATA ASKED FOR IS SELF EXPLANATORY, WITH THE
POSSIBLE EXCEPTION OF YEARS AFTER INVEST BEFORE REC
INCOME. THIS QUESTION IS BASED ON THE FACT THAT MANY
INVESTMENTS DO NOT START PAYING UNITIL SOME TIME
AFTER THE MONEY IS SPENT. YOU ENTER THE NUMBER OF
YEARS YOU ESTIMATE IT WILL TAKE FOR INCOME TO START
COMING AFTER THE INVESTMENT IS MADE. FOR EXAMPLE IF
YOU KNOW IT WILL TAKE ONE YEAR ENTER 1. IF IT WILL
TAKE HALF A YEAR, ENTER 0.5.
PRESS ANY KEY TO CONTINUE


INSTRUCTIONS PAGE 3.

AFTER THE INITIAL CALCULATIONS ARE COMPLETED, YOU
WILL BE ASKED IF YOU WANT TO RUN A RISK ANALYSIS.
THIS QUESTION MUST BE ANSWERED BY PRESSING <Y> OR <N>.
IF YOU PRESS <Y>, YOU ARE THEN PASSED TO THE DATA ENTRY
MODULE OF THE MONTE CARLO SIMULATION. THERE IS ONE PAGE
OF DATA FOR THE MONTE CARLO SIMULATION. DATA ENTRY IS
A MATTER OF PROVIDING THE DATA ASKED FOR. YOU HAVE A
CHANCE TO CORRECT DATA ERRORS BEFORE CALCULATIONS BEGIN.
PRESS ANY KEY TO CONTINUE AND RETURN TO THE PROGRAM.
```

Fig. 12-1. Crt display of instructions for calculation of present value of cash flows from investment in real estate.

your estimates are reasonable. A sample run of the program is given later in this chapter.

As an example of how to use INVEST3, look at the same investment that was used in INVEST2. All initial data and printout are the same as for the example in INVEST 2. When all data is printed, you are asked if you want to run the risk analysis. Press <Y>.

The data for the risk analysis is given below:

- Best case estimate for inflation rate is six percent
- Worst case estimate for inflation rate is 18 percent
- Best estimate (most likely inflation rate is 10 percent (from original data)
- Best case estimate of escalation for rental income is 16 percent
- Worst case estimate of escalation for rental income is six percent
- Most likely estimate of escalation for rental income is 12 percent (from original data)
- Best case estimate of escalation for expenses is five percent
- Worst case estimate for escalation for expenses is 14 percent
- Most likely estimate of escalation for expenses is eight percent (from original data)
- Best case estimate of escalation for value of property is 20 percent
- Worst case estimate of escalation for value of property is 10 percent
- Most likely estimate of escalation for value of property is 16 percent (from original data)

Most of the hard copy for the sample run of INVEST3 is shown in Figs. 12-2 and 12-3. The program does provide for hard copy of the detailed results for the original data (not the risk analysis). However, since these detailed results are the same as the detailed (yearly) results of the INVEST2 example, they are not shown.

The results of the risk analysis are on the last page of the hard copy output. The mean present value of the profits from the investment is $266,438 with a standard deviation of $27,960. This means that the minimum likely profit is $266,438 − 3 × $27,960 = $182,558, and the maximum likely profit is $266,438 + 3 × $27,960 = $350,318.

Thus there is less than 1 percent probability that the profit will exceed $350,000 or be less than $182,558. Since the present value of your equity is $132,239, there is virtually no chance you will lose money on this investment (given that, all of your assumptions about distribution of the variables are correct).

```
                VARIABLES FOR RISK ANALYSIS
MOST LIKELY VALUE OF INFLATION 10.00, HIGHEST LIKELY 18.00, LOWEST LIKELY  6.00%
MOST LIKELY VALUE OF ESCALTION FOR INCOME 12.00, HIGHEST LIKELY 16.00 AND LOWEST  6.00%
MOST LIKELY VALUE OF ESCALATION FOR EXPENSES  8.00, HIGHEST LIKELY 14.00, AND LOWEST  5.00%
MOST LIKELY VALUE OF APPRECIATION OF PROPERTY 16.00, HIGHEST 20.00 LOWEST 10.00%
============================================================
    THE MEAN PRESENT VALUE OF ALL PROFITS - LOAN BALANCE IS $ 266,438.00
    WITH A STANDARD DEVIATION OF $27,960.40

    THE MEAN CONSTANT YEAR $ PRESENT VALUE OF ALL PROFIT IS $ 172,757.00
    WITH STANDARD DEVIATION OF $12,722.70
    THE PRESENT VALUE OF YOUR EQUITY IS $132,239.00
```

Fig. 12-2. Using INVEST3 in risk analysis of investment, example 1.

```
                VARIABLES FOR RISK ANALYSIS
MOST LIKELY VALUE OF INFLATION 10.00, HIGHEST LIKELY 20.00, LOWEST LIKELY  4.00%
MOST LIKELY VALUE OF ESCALTION FOR INCOME 12.00, HIGHEST LIKELY 18.00 AND LOWEST  4.00%
MOST LIKELY VALUE OF ESCALATION FOR EXPENSES  8.00, HIGHEST LIKELY 20.00, AND LOWEST  6.00%
MOST LIKELY VALUE OF APPRECIATION OF PROPERTY 16.00, HIGHEST 22.00 LOWEST  4.00%
================================================================
    THE MEAN PRESENT VALUE OF ALL PROFITS - LOAN BALANCE IS $ 253,628.00
    WITH A STANDARD DEVIATION OF $46,200.70

    THE MEAN CONSTANT YEAR $ PRESENT VALUE OF ALL PROFIT IS $ 163,179.00
    WITH STANDARD DEVIATION OF $22,127.60
    THE PRESENT VALUE OF YOUR EOUITY IS $132,239.00
```

Fig. 12-3. Using INVEST3 in risk analysis of investment, example 2.

Even if your assumptions about the statistical distribution of the variables are wrong, you still have covered a wide range of possible values. And in most, if not all, cases the investment was fine. So in this case risk analysis adds confidence to the idea that the investment is a good one. Even in the worst case you get your money back. And the risk is low.

Now rerun the example and allow wider variation in the possible input variables. The results are shown below. The input data allowed is:

- Best case inflation rate is four percent
- Worst case inflation rate is 20 percent
- Best case escalation for income is 18 percent
- Worst case escalation for income is four percent
- Best case escalation for expenses is six percent
- Worst case escalation for expenses is 20 percent
- Best case escalation for property is 22 percent
- Worst case escalation for property is four percent

The most likely values of the variables are the same as before. The possible range of the variables is much wider than in the previous example.

In this case the mean present value of all profits is $253,628 with a standard deviation of $46,200. Because the standard deviation of the present value of all profits is much greater in this case, both the possible gains and losses in the investment are greater than in the previous example. The maximum likely profit is $392,228 compared with $350,000 for the first case. However, the minimum likely profit is $115,028 compared with $182,558. In other words, this is a riskier investment and should be selected only if the expected profit is large enough to compensate for the risk. The expected profit is actually lower than in the first example, so this appears to be a risky investment with too little return compared to the return from the previous example.

INVEST3/BAS LISTING

```
10 CLEAR 200
20 REM
*****************************************************
30 REM PROGRAM INVEST3/BAS
40 REM PROGRAM TO ANALYZE AN INVESTMENT THAT IS EXPECTED
```

```
50 REM TO EARN INCOME AND PAY FOR ITSELF WITH THE INCOME
60 REM EARNED BY THE INVESTMENT
70 REM WRITTEN BY L. E. SPARKS VERSION 1.0 FEB 1982
80 REM WRITTEN IN TRS-80 DISK BASIC RUNS ON TRS-80
90 REM MODEL I AND MODEL III REQUIRES 48K RAM. FOR LESS RAM
100 REM REMOVE REMARKS, REDIMENSION ARRAYS, ELIMINATE
SPACES,
110 REM AND USE MULTIPLE STATEMENTS PER LINE.
120 REM IF THE CLS STATEMENT FOR CLEARING THE SCREEN IS
CHANGED
130 REM THE PROGRAM WILL RUN IN MBASIC OR BASIC 80
140 REM FOR CP/M SYSTEMS
150 REM AS WRITTEN REQUIRES 48K RAM FOR LESS RAM REDUCE
DIMENSIONS OF ARRAYS.
160 REM FOR LESS RAM REMOVE REMARK STATEMENTS
170 REM NOTE THAT THE [ IS THE SYMBOL FOR THE UP ARROW.
180 REM
***********************************************
190 CLS
200 PRINT "=========================================="
210 PRINT "  INVESTMENT ANALYSIS PROGRAM INVEST3/BAS"
220 PRINT "  REFERENCE INVESTMENT ANALYSIS ON MICROCOMPUTER
TAB BOOKS"
230 PRINT "   BY LES VERSION 3.0 NOV 1981"
240 PRINT "==========================================="
250 PRINT "IF YOU WANT INSTRUCTIONS PRESS I ELSE PRESS ANY
KEY TO CONTINUE"
260 Y$=INKEY$: IF Y$="" THEN 260  ELSE IF Y$="I" THEN GOSUB
5250
270 CLS
280 DEFINT K,N
290 I=0:J=0:K=0:N=0:P=0:PV=0:PI=0:SP=0:CS=0:AE=0:AP=0 : AI
= 0 : PN = 0
300 BL = 0 : L=0 : NP = 0 :
SZ1=0:Z2=0:Z3=0:Z4=0:M1=0:M2=0:M3=0:M4=0:M5=0:
310
H1=0:H2=0:H3=0:H4=0:L1=0:L2=0:L3=0:L4=0:EX=0:VX=0:X=0:SX=0-R
=0:X1=0:X2=0:X3=0:X4=0:
320 REM AE IS ACCUMULATED EQUITY AP IS PRESENT VALUE OF AE
330 D$="$#,######.##"
340 PM = 3 : P1 = 0
350 I9 = 27 : REM MAXIMUM NUMBER OF ITEMS TO BE READ IN
360 IP=0:PP=0:A=0:B=0:V=0:SI=0:F=1:FL=0:TC=0:TX=0:TI=0
370 DIM D(30),SF(30),PV(20),PI(20),DP(4,15),F$(30),V(30)
380 DIM TU$(6),EX$(9),R1(6),R2(6),EM(9),EY(9)
```

```
390 REM D(I) IS DEPRECIATION FOR ITH YEAR, SF IS SPENDABLE
CASH FLOW
400 REM TC IS ALLOWABLE TAX CREDIT TC(I) IS TAX CREDIT
TAKEN IN ITH YEAR.
410 REM DP IS DEPRECIATION FOR NEW 1981 TAX LAW
420 DIM A1(30),A2(30),E1(30),E2(30),EX(30),T1(30),T2(30)
430 REM A1=PRINCIPAL  OF LOAN 1, A1=PRINCIPAL  OF LOAN 2,
E1=INCOME
440 REM E2=INCOME 2, EX=EXPENSES, T1=FEDERAL TAX, T2=STATE
TAX
450 DIM
B1(30),B2(30),CF(30),DF(30),DI(30),DY(30),IP(30),IZ(30),TC(3
0)
460 REM B1=BALANCE ON LOAN 1, B2=BALANCE ON LOAN 2
470 REM CF=CURRENT YEAR CASH FLOW, DF = DISCOUNTED CASH
FLOW
480 REM DI = CONSTANT DOLLAR CASH FLOW DY=DISCOUNTED
CONSTANT
490 REM DOLLAR CASH FLOW
500 REM IP INTEREST PAID LOAN 1, IZ INTEREST PAID LOAN 2
510 GOTO 6630
520 REM SUBROUTINE TO DO LOAN CALCULATIONS
530 REM SUBROUTINE IS HERE FOR SPEED
540 FOR J1 = 1 TO NP
550     IP = I1 * A
560     IP = INT(IP*100)/100
570    SI = SI + IP
580     PP = P - IP
590     A = A - PP
600     B = B + PP
610 NEXT J1
620 RETURN
630 REM CALCULATE INVESTMENT TAX CREDIT ALLOWED
640 REM TAX CREDIT IS ALLOWED ON 100% OF FIVE AND TEN YEAR
PROPERTY
650 REM TAX CREDIT IS ALLOWED ON 60% OF THREE YEAR PROPERTY
660 TC =TC*0.1*(V(22)+V(23)+0.6*V(21))
670 REM ALL LOANS TAKEN CARE OF NOW LETS DO YEARLY CASH
FLOWS
680 KD = 0
690 DT = 0 : REM TOTAL DEPRECIATION TAKEN
700 RETURN
710 CLS
720 PRINT "NOW WORKING ON YEARLY CASH FLOWS."
```

```
730 REM K IS THE YEAR NUMBER ASSUME THAT INCOME LAGS
EXPENSES
740 IF V(6) = 0 THEN F = 1 ELSE F = 0
750 REM THE INVESTMENT MAY NOT EARN INCOME FOR SOME TIME
AFTER
760 REM THE INITIAL MONEY IS SPENT
770 FOR K=1 TO V(20)
780    PRINT K, : REM SHOW USER THAT SOMETHING IS GOING ON
790   IF (K-V(6))>0 THEN KA =1 ELSE KA =0
800     IF F = 1 THEN 860
810     IF FL = -1 THEN F = 1:F1=F:GOTO 860
820     IF V(6) > K THEN F = 0 : GOTO 860  : REM NO INCOME
YET
830     F = K - V(6)
840    F1 = 0
850     FL = -1
860    E1(K) = F * TI*(1+V(13)/100)[(K-1)
870    EX(K) = F * TX*(1+V(14)/100)[(K)
880   KD = KD + KA
890   IF KD = 0 THEN 930
900    IF KD > 15 THEN 930  :REM BYPASS DEPRECIATION
910    D(K) = DP(1,KD)*V(21) + V(22)*DP(2,KD) +
V(23)*DP(3,KD) + V(24)*DP(4,KD) + V(25)/15
920   DT = DT + D(K)
930    E2(K) = E1(K) - D(K) - EX(K) - IP(K) - IZ(K)
940     IF TL = 0 AND K>1 THEN 1110 :REM CHECK TO SEE IF
HAVE LOSS CARRY FORWARD
950    IF E2(K)<0 THEN TL = TL + (-1*E2(K)) :
T1(K)=0:T2(K)=0:GOTO 1220
960    IF E2(K) >TL THEN 990
970    TL = TL - (-1*E2(K)) : T1(K)=0:T2(K)=0
980     GOTO 1220
990    E2 = E2(K)-TL : TL = 0
1000    T2(K) = V(18)/100 * E2 : REM STATE TAX PAID
1010    T1(K) = V(15)/100*(E2-T2(K)) : REM FED TAX PAID
1020     IF TC = 0 THEN 1220
1030     IF TC < T1(K) THEN 1070 ELSE TC(K) = T1(K)
1040     TC = TC - T1(K)
1050     T1(K) = 0
1060     GOTO 1220
1070     TC(K) = TC
1080     T1(K) = T1(K) - TC
1090     TC = 0
1100    GOTO 1220
```

```
1110    IF E2(K) > 0 THEN T2(K) = V(18)/100*E2(K) ELSE
T2(K) = 0
1120    IF E2(K)>=0 THEN T1(K) = (E2(K)-T2(K))*V(15)/100
ELSE T1(K) =0
1130    IF E2(K) < 0 THEN TL = -1*E2(K) :GOTO 1220
1140     IF TC = 0 THEN 1220
1150     IF TC < T1(K) THEN 1190 ELSE TC(K) = T1(K)
1160     TC = TC - T1(K)
1170     T1(K) = 0
1180     GOTO 1220
1190     TC(K) = TC
1200     T1(K) = T1(K) - TC
1210     TC = 0
1220    CF(K) = E2(K)-T1(K)-T2(K)+D(K) : REM CASH FLOW FOR
YR K
1230    DF(K) = CF(K)*(1+V(19)/100)[-K : REM DISCOUNTED
CASH FLOW
1240    DI(K) = CF(K)*(1+V(27)/100)[-K
1250    DY(K) = DI(K)*(1+V(19)/100)[-K
1260    SF(K) =
E1(K)-EX(K)-T1(K)-T2(K)-IP(K)-IZ(K)-A1(K)-A2(K):REM
SPENDABLE CASH FLOW
1270   IF SF(K)<0 THEN SP = SP +(-1)*SF(K): CS = CS + 1
1280 REM KEEP TRACK OF WHEN SPENDABLE CASH FLOW IS NEGATIVE
AND THE NUMBER OF YEARS WITH NEGATIVE CASH FLOW.
1290    PV = DF(K)+PV
1300    PI = DY(K)+PI
1310   AE = AE +A1(K)+A2(K)
1320   DA = (A1(K)+A2(K))*(1+V(19)/100)[-K
1330   AP = AP + DA
1340   AI = AI + DA*(1+V(27)/100)[-K
1350 NEXT K
1360  RETURN
1370 CLS
1380 PRINT "WORKING ON SELLING PRICE "
1390 BL = V(2)+V(7)-AE : REM BL IS TOTAL LOAN BALANCE
1400 AE = AE + V(1)-V(2)-V(7)
1410 AI = AI + V(1)-V(2)-V(7)
1420 AP = AP + V(1)-V(2) -V(7) : REM ACCUMULATED EQUITY
1430 REM NOW CALCUALTE NEW SELLING PRICE
1440 SZ = V(1) *(1+V(11)/100)[V(20)
1450 CZ = SZ * V(12)/100
1460 REM BASIS FOR PROFIT IS PRICE - DEPRECIATION
1470 BZ = V(1) - DT : REM BASIS FOR TAX COST - DEPRECIATION
1480 REM TAXABLE PROFIT = SELLING PRICE - BASIS - COST
```

```
1490 TP = SZ - BZ - CZ
1500 REM CAPITAL GAINS TAX T1
1510 T1 = TP*(V(17)/100) : REM STATE CAPITAL GAINS
1520 T2 = (TP-T1)*V(16)/100
1530 REM NET PROFIT PN
1540 PN = TP - T1 - T2 - DT
1550 PB = PN - BL : REM PROFIT MINUS LOAN BALANCE
1560 REM PRESENT VALUE OF PN PP
1570 PP = PB*(1+V(19)/100)[-V(20)
1580 REM INFLATION CORRECTION
1590 PQ = PP *(1+V(27)/100)[-V(20)
1600 RETURN
1610 GOSUB 2220 :REM PRINT IT OUT
1620 END
1630 REM NOW TAKE CARE OF LOANS
1640 CLS
1650 PRINT "NOW WORKING ON FIRST LOAN"
1660 REM FIRST LOAN
1670 IF V(2) = 0 THEN 1870 :REM TRANSFER IF NO FIRST LOAN
1680 REM FIRST CALCULATE PAYMENT
1690 I1 = V(3)/100/V(5) : REM INTEREST PER PERIOD
1700 S=0
1710 S2 = 0
1720 A = V(2)
1730 V = (I1+1)[(V(4)*V(5))
1740 P = V(2)*(I1*V)/(V-1)
1750 P = INT(100*P)/100
1760 NP = V(5)
1770 J2 = 1
1780 GOSUB 520
1790 A1(J2) = B
1800 IP(J2) = SI
1810 IF J2 = V(4) THEN 1930
1820 PRINT J2,
1830 SI=0
1840 B = 0
1850 J2=J2+1
1860 GOTO 1780
1870 REM HERE BECAUSE NO FIRST LOAN V(2)=0
1880 IF IP(1)=0 THEN 1930 : REM CHECK TO SEE IF ARRAYS
ZEROED
1890 FOR JZ = 1 TO 30
1900     IP(JZ)=0
1910   A1(JZ) = 0
1920 NEXT JZ
```

```
1930 REM NOW DO SECOND LOAN
1940 CLS
1950 PRINT "NOW WORKING ON SECOND LOAN"
1960 IF V(7) = 0 THEN 2150 : REM TRANSFER IF NO SECOND LOAN
1970 A = V(7)
1980 SI = 0
1990 B = 0
2000 I1 = V(8)/100/V(10)
2010 V = (I1+1)[(V(9)*V(10))
2020 P = V(7)*(I1*V)/(V-1)
2030 P = INT(P*100)/100
2040 NP = V(10)
2050 J2 = 1
2060 PRINT  J2,
2070 GOSUB 520
2080 A2(J2) = B
2090 IZ(J2) = SI
2100 IF J2 = V(9) THEN RETURN
2110 SI = 0
2120 B = 0
2130 J2 = J2 + 1
2140 GOTO 2060
2150 REM HERE BACAUSE NO SECOND LOAN
2160 IF IZ(1) AND A2(1) = 0 THEN RETURN
2170 FOR JZ = 1 TO 30
2180    IZ(JZ) = 0
2190    A2(JZ) = 0
2200 NEXT JZ
2210 RETURN
2220 REM NOW PRINT OUT THE RESULTS
2230 CLS
2240 PRINT "RESULTS OF CALCULATIONS "
2250 PRINT" SUMMARY"
2260 PRINT "================================================"
2270 PRINT USING"PRESENT VALUE OF RENT FLOWS
$###,####.##" PV
2280 PRINT USING"PRESENT VALUE OF PROFIT FORM SALE
$###,#####.##":PP
2290 PRINT USING "PRESENT VALUE OF ALL PROFITS
$###,#####.##";PP+PV
2300 PRINT USING "PRESENT VALUE RENT CONT YR
$###,####.##";PI
2310 PRINT USING"PRESENT CONSTANT YR PROFIT SALE
$###,####.##";PP*(1+V(27)/100)[-V(20)
2320 PRINT USING"PRESENT CONSTANT YR ALL PROFITS
```

```
$###,####.##";PP*(1+V(27)/100)[-V(20)+PI
2330 PRINT USING"ACCUMULATED EQUITY
$###,####.##";AE
2340 PRINT
"=============================================="
2350 PRINT "DO YOU WANT TO SEE YEARLY DETAILS Y OR N?"
2360 Y$=INKEY$:IF Y$="" THEN 2360 ELSE IF INSTR("YN",Y$)=0
THEN PRINT"TRY AGAIN":GOTO 2350
2370 IF Y$="N" THEN RETURN
2380 FOR K=1 TO V(20)
2390   CLS
2400     PRINT USING"INCOME
$#,######.##";E1(K)
2410     PRINT USING"EXPENSES
$#,######.##";EX(K)
2420     PRINT USING"DEPRECIATION
$#,######.##";D(K)
2430     PRINT USING"INTEREST FIRST LOAN
$#,######.##";IP(K)
2440     PRINT USING"INTEREST SECOND LOAN
$#,######.##";IZ(K)
2450     PRINT USING"PRINCIPAL FIRST LOAN
$#,######.##";A1(K)
2460     PRINT USING"PRINCIPAL SECOND LOAN
$#,######.##";A2(K)
2470     PRINT USING"TAXABLE INCOME
$#,######.##";E1(K)-EX(K)-D(K)-IP(K)-IZ(K)
2480     PRINT USING"STATE TAXES PAID
$#,######.##";T2(K)
2490    PRINT USING"FEDERAL TAX PAID
$#,######.##";T1(K)
2500     PRINT USING"AFTER TAX CASH FLOW
$#,######.##";CF(K)
2510     PRINT USING"DISCOUNTED CASH FLOW
$#,######.##";DF(K)
2520     PRINT USING"CONSTANT DOLLAR CASH
$#,######.##";DY(K)

2530     PRINT USING"SPENDABLE CASH FLOW
$#,######.##";SF(K)
2540     PRINT"THIS IS YEAR ";K;" PRESS  ANY KEY FOR NEXT
YEAR"
2550     Y$=INKEY$:IF Y$="" THEN 2550
2560 NEXT K
2570 RETURN
```

```
2580 PRINT"HARD COPY ROUTINE. PLEASE BE SURE PRINTER IS ON"
2590 LPRINT TAB(5);"RESULTS OF INVESTMENT ANALYSIS PROGRAM
V 3.0"
2600 LPRINT TAB(5) ; "NAME OF INVESTMENT ";NI$
2610 LPRINT " "
2620 LPRINT TAB(30);"INPUT DATA SUMMARY"
2630 FOR I = 1 TO I9
2640    LPRINT TAB(8);
2650    LPRINT USING F$(I);V(I)
2660 NEXT I
2670 LPRINT TAB(5);
"========================================================="
2680 LPRINT TAB(20);"INCOME ESTIMATES."
2690 LPRINT TAB(5);
"=========================================================="
2700 LPRINT" "
2710 TR=0
2720 FOR I = 1 TO 6
2730   LPRINT TAB(5);
2740    LPRINT USING TU$(I);NU(I);
2750   LPRINT " ";
2760    LPRINT USING R$(I);R1(I);R2(I)
2770   TR = TR + NU(I)*R2(I)
2780 NEXT I
2790 LPRINT TAB(5);
2800 LPRINT USING "ALLOWANCE FOR VACANCIES ##.##% OR
$####,###.##/YR";VC;VC*TR/100
2810 LPRINT TAB(5);
2820 LPRINT USING "TOTAL YEARLY INCOME
$#####,##.##";TR*(1-VC/100)
2830 LPRINT TAB(5);STRING$(64,"=")
2840 LPRINT TAB(25);"EXPENSES"
2850 FOR I = 1 TO 9
2860    LPRINT TAB(5);
2870    LPRINT USING EX$(I);EM(I);EY(I)
2880 NEXT I
2890 LPRINT TAB(10);
2900 LPRINT USING"TOTAL EXPENSES PER YEAR $#####,##.##";TX
2910 LPRINT " "
2920 PRINT"PRESS ANY KEY WHEN READY FOR NEXT PAGE."
2930 Y$ = INKEY$: IF Y$ = "" THEN 2930
2940 LPRINT TAB(5);"INVESTMENT   ";NI$;"        PAGE 2
OUTPUT"
2950 LPRINT TAB(5);STRING$(73,"=")
2960 LPRINT TAB(30);"*** SUMMARY RESULTS ***"
```

```
2970 LPRINT " "
2980   LPRINT TAB(9);
2990 LPRINT USING "CURRENT YEAR DOLLARS PRESENT VALUE OF
RENT PROFIT $#,######.##":PV
3000 LPRINT TAB(9);
3010 LPRINT USING"SELLING PRICE .......... $#####,##.##";SZ
3020 LPRINT TAB(9);
3030 LPRINT USING"COST OF SELLING ........ $#####,##.##":CZ
3040 LPRINT TAB(9);
3050 LPRINT USING"BALANCE DUE ON LOANS ... $#####,##.##";BL
3060 LPRINT TAB(9);
3070 LPRINT USING"BASIS FOR TAX PURPOSE .. $#####,##.##";BZ
3080 LPRINT TAB(9);
3090 LPRINT USING"TAXABLE PROCEEDS ....... $#####,##.##";TP
3100 LPRINT TAB(9);
3110 LPRINT USING"TOTAL CAPITAL GAINS TAX
$#####,##.##";T1+T2
3120 LPRINT TAB(9);
3130 LPRINT USING"NET PROFIT FROM SALE ... $#####,##.##";PN
3140 LPRINT TAB(9);
3150 LPRINT USING "PRESENT VALUE OF PROFIT FROM SALE -
BALANCE DUE   $#,######.##";PP
3160 LPRINT TAB(9);
3170 LPRINT USING"PRESENT VALUE OF TOTAL PROFITS - BALANCE
DUE      $#,######.##";PP+PV
3180 LPRINT TAB(9);
3190 LPRINT USING"ACCUMULATED EQUITY ...... $####,##.##";AE
3200 LPRINT TAB(9);
3210 LPRINT USING"PRESENT VALUE EQUITY .... $####,##.##";AP
3220 LPRINT TAB(9);
3230 LPRINT USING"CONSTANT YR DOLLAR  .... $####,##.##";AI
3240 LPRINT TAB(9);
3250 LPRINT USING"NET PRESENT VALUE (PROFIT  -EQUITY) =
       $#,######.##":PP + PV - AP
3260 LPRINT TAB(9);
3270  LPRINT USING"CONSTANT YEAR NET PRESENT VALUE ALL
PROFIT-BALANCE $#,######.##";PQ + PI - AI
3280 IF AP>PP+PV THEN LPRINT TAB(10);:LPRINT USING"YOU LOST
$#,######.## IN PRESENT VALUE ";AP-PP-PV
3290 IF AI >PQ +PI THEN  LPRINT TAB(5);:LPRINT
"***";:LPRINT USING "YOU LOST $#,######.## IN PURCHASING
POWER ";AI-PQ-PI
3300 LPRINT TAB(5); STRING$(73,"=")
3310 PRINT "PRESS ANY KEY WHEN READY WITH NEW SHEET OF
PAPER."
```

```
3320 Y$=INKEY$:IF Y$="" THEN 3320
3330 LPRINT TAB(30);"RESULTS OF EACH YEARS OPERATION "
3340 FOR I=1 TO V(20)
3350   LPRINT TAB(30);"RESULTS FOR YEAR ";I
3360   LPRINT
TAB(5);"---------------------------------------------"
3370    LPRINT USING"    GROSS INCOME
........................$#,######.##";E1(I)
3380    LPRINT USING"    EXPENSES
............................$#,######.##";EX(I)
3390    LPRINT USING"    DEPRECIATION
........................$#,######.##";D(I)
3400    LPRINT USING"    INTEREST 1ST LOAN
...................$#,######.##";IP(I)
3410    LPRINT USING"    PRINCIPAL 1ST LOAN
..................$#,######.##";A1(I)
3420    LPRINT USING"    INTEREST 2ND LOAN
...................$#,######.##";IZ(I)
3430    LPRINT USING"    PRINCIPAL 2ND LOAN
..................$#,######.##";A2(I)
3440    LPRINT USING"    TAXABLE INCOME
......................$#,######.##";E2(I)
3450    LPRINT USING"    STATE TAX PAID
......................$#,######.##";T2(I)
3460   LPRINT USING"    INVESTMENT TAX CREDIT TAKEN
..........$#,######.##";TC(I)
3470    LPRINT USING"    FEDERAL TAX PAID
....................$#,######.##";T1(I)
3480    LPRINT USING"    AFTER TAX CASH FLOW
.................$#,######.##";CF(I)
3490    LPRINT USING"    CONSTANT DOLLAR CASH FLOW
...........$#,######.##";DI(I)
3500    LPRINT USING"    DISCOUNTED CURRENT YEAR CASH FLOW
...$#,######.##";DF(I)
3510    LPRINT USING"    DISCOUNTED CONSTANT YR CASH FLOW
....$#,######.##";DY(I)
3520    LPRINT USING"    SPENDABLE CASH FLOW
.................$#,######.##";SF(I)
3530    IF SF(I)<0 THEN LPRINT "     NOTE THAT SPENDABLE
CASH IS NEGATIVE. YOU NEED TO BORROW MONEY."
3540   LPRINT
TAB(5);"============================================="
3550   IF INT(I/3)-I/3 = 0 THEN PRINT"PRESS ANY KEY WHEN
READY WITH NEW SHEET OF PAPER IN PRINTER " ELSE 3570
```

```
3560   Y$=INKEY$ : IF Y$ = "" THEN 3560
3570 NEXT I
3580   LPRINT
TAB(5);"======================================="
3590 RETURN
3600 REM ERROR SUBROUTINE
3610 CLS
3620 PRINT "*****************************"
3630 PRINT "INPUT DATA ERROR!!!"
3640 IF V(1) < V(21)+V(22)+V(23)+V(24)+V(25) THEN 3690
3650 IF V(20) >30 THEN PRINT "MAXIMUM LIFE ALLOWED IS 30
YEARS"
3660 PRINT "PLEASE CORRECT DATA ENTRY "
3670 FOR KQ = 1 TO 400
3680 NEXT KQ
3690 PRINT"VALUE OF DEPRECIATED PROPERTY EXCEEDS
INVESTMENT."
3700 FOR K1 =  1 TO 500
3710 NEXT K1
3720 RETURN
3730 RETURN
3740 REM DATA ENTRY SUBROUTINE
3750 P1=1
3760 IZ=1: IX=9
3770 I=IZ:IQ=1
3780 CLS
3790 PRINT"INVESTMENT ANALYSIS DATA INPUT PAGE ";P1
3800 PRINT"PROVIDE DATA ASKED FOR. CURRENT VALUE SHOWN IN
()"
3810 PRINT"IF YOU WISH TO CORRECT A PREVIOUS ENTRY ENTER C"
3820 PRINT"TO GO TO NEXT PAGE ENTER >"
3830 PRINT STRING$(63,"=")
3840 IF I = IZ THEN 3860 ELSE FOR IQ=IZ TO I-1:PRINT USING
F$(IQ);V(IQ):NEXT IQ
3850 IF I > I9 THEN 3980
3860    PRINT USING F$(I);V(I);
3870 V$=""
3880    INPUT V$
3890   IF V$="" THEN 3960
3900    IF V$=">" THEN 4120 ELSE IF V$="C" THEN 4250
3910   IF V$="<" THEN 4190
3920   V(I)=VAL(V$):V$=""
3930   IF V(1) <V(21)+V(22)+V(23)+V(24)+V(25) THEN GOSUB
3600 : GOTO 3780
3940   IF V(20)>30 THEN GOSUB 3600 : GOTO 3780
```

```
3950  IF I = I9 THEN 3980
3960 I=I+1:IF I<=IX THEN 3780
3970  GOTO 4070
3980 PRINT STRING$(63,"=")
3990 PRINT"END OF DATA ENTRY. PLEASE CHECK DATA ON THIS
PAGE."
4000 PRINT"TO CORRECT DATA ENTER C. TO REVIEW PREVIOUS PAGE
ENTER <"
4010 PRINT"TO REVIEW ALL DATA ENTER R. TO START
CALCULATIONS ENTER G.";
4020 Y$=""
4030 INPUT Y$
4040 IF Y$="G" THEN RETURN ELSE IF Y$="C" THEN 4080 ELSE IF
Y$="<" THEN 4190
4050 IF Y$ <> "R" THEN PRINT "PLEAS  ENTER C,<,R,OR
G.":GOTO 3990
4060 CLS
4070 PRINT "END OF PAGE ";P1;" REVIEW DATA ENTER > TO GO TO
NEXT PAGE"
4080 PRINT"ENTER C TO CORRECT ENTRY AND ENTER R TO RETURN
TO MAIN PROGRAM";
4090 Y$="":INPUT Y$
4100 IF Y$ = "<" THEN 4190
4110 IF Y$=">" THEN 4120 ELSE IF Y$="C" THEN 4250 ELSE IF
Y$<>"R" THEN PRINT"PLEASE ANSWER >,C,OR R":GOTO 4070
4120 REM
4130 IF P1 = PM THEN 3980
4140 P1=P1+1
4150 IZ=IZ+9
4160 IX =IZ+8
4170 I=IZ:IQ=IZ
4180 GOTO 3780
4190 IF P1>1 THEN P1=P1-1 ELSE GOTO 3780
4200 IF P1 =1 THEN IZ = 1 : IX =8
4210 IF P1 = 2 THEN IZ = 9 : IX = 16
4220 IF P1 = 3 THEN IZ = 17 : IX = 24
4230 IF I > IX THEN I = IX
4240 GOTO 3780
4250 REM CORRECTION PAGE
4260 CLS
4270 V$=""
4280 PRINT "ROUTINE TO CORRECT ENTRY ON PAGE ";P1
4290 PRINT STRING$(63,"=")
4300 IF IX > I9 THEN IX = I9
```

```
4310 FOR J=IZ TO IX
4320   PRINT J;
4330    PRINT USING F$(J);V(J)
4340 NEXT J
4350 PRINT STRING$(63,"=")
4360 PRINT "IF YOU WANT TO CORRECT ALL ENTRIES ENTER A
ELSE"
4370 INPUT "ENTER ITEM NUMBER TO CORRECT R TO RETURN ";YI$
4380 IF YI$="A" THEN GOTO 3740
4390 IF YI$="R" THEN 4460 ELSE J=VAL(YI$)
4400 IF J>IX THEN PRINT "NOT ON THIS PAGE ":GOTO 4370
4410 IF J<=0 THEN J = IX
4420 PRINT USING F$(J);V(J):INPUT"ENTER CORRECT VALUE C IF
OK ";C$
4430 IF C$="C" THEN GOTO 4250 ELSE V(J)=VAL(C$)
4440 GOTO 4250
4450 END
4460 REM
4470 GOTO 3780
4480 IF V(24)<1982 THEN V(24)=1982
4490 REM READ IN NEW DEPRECIATION
4500 FOR I=1 TO 4
4510   IF I = 1 THEN JM = 3 ELSE IF I = 2 THEN JM = 5 ELSE
IF I = 3 THEN JM = 10 ELSE JM = 15
4520    FOR J = 1 TO JM
4530           READ DP(I,J)
4540          DP(I,J)=DP(I,J)/100 : REM CONVERT TO DECIMAL
FRACTION
4550    NEXT J
4560 NEXT I
4570 IF V(24) <1985 THEN RETURN
4580 JZ = JZ +1
4590 IF V(24) = 1985 AND JZ = 1 THEN 4500 ELSE IF V(24) =
1985 THEN RETURN
4600 IF JZ <= 2 THEN 4500 ELSE RETURN
4610 REM DEPRECIATION FOR 3  YEAR
4620 DATA 25,38,37
4630 REM DEPRECIATION FOR 5 YEAR
4640 DATA 15,22,21,21,21
4650 REM DEPRECIATION DATA FOR 10 YEAR
4660 DATA 8,14,12,10,10,10,9,9,9,9
4670 REM FOR 15 YEAR
4680 DATA 5,10,9,8,7,7,6,6,6,6,6,6,6,6,6
4690 REM DATA FOR 1985
4700 DATA 29,47,24,18,33.25,16,8
```

```
4710 DATA 9,19,16,14,12,10,8,6,4,2
4720 DATA 6,12,12,11,10,9,8,7,6,5,4,4,3,2,1
4730 REM DATA FOR 1986
4740 DATA 33,45,22,20,32,24,16,8
4750 DATA 10,18,16,14,12,10,8,6,4,2
4760 DATA 7,12,12,11,10,9,8,7,6,5,4,3,3,2,1
4770 END
4780 REM INITIALIZATION SUBROUTINE
4790 F$(1)="TOTAL AMOUNT OF INVESTMENT
$#,######.##"
4800 F$(2)="AMOUNT OF FIRST LOAN
$#,######.##"
4810 F$(3)="YEARLY INTEREST RATE FOR 1ST LOAN
##.##%
4820 F$(4)="LIFE OF FIRST LOAN YEARS
##.##  YRS"
4830 F$(5)="NUMBER OF LOAN PAYMENTS PER YEAR
##"
4840 F$(6)="TIME AFTER INVESTING BEFORE REC. INCOME
#.## YRS"
4850 F$(7)="AMOUNT OF SECOND LOAN
$#,######.##
4860 F$(8)="YEARLY INTEREST RATE FOR 2ND LOAN
##.##%"
4870 F$(9)="LIFE OF SECOND LOAN YEARS
## YRS"
4880 F$(10) ="NUMBER OF PAYMENTS PER YEAR  2ND LOAN
##"
4890 F$(11)="ESCLATION FOR VALUE OF PROPERTY
##.##%"
4900 F$(12)="COST OF SELLING AS % OF PRICE
##.##%"
4910 F$(13)="ESCALATION FOR RENTS
##.##%"
4920 F$(14)="ESCALATION FOR EXPENSES
##.##%"
4930 F$(15)="FEDERAL INCOME TAX RATE
##.##%"
4940 F$(16)="FEDERAL CAPITAL GAINS TAX RATE
##.##%"
4950 F$(17)="STATE CAPITAL GAINS TAX RATE
##.##%"
4960 F$(18)="STATE INCOME TAX RATE
##.##%"
```

```
4970 F$(19)="DISCOUNT RATE
##.## %"
4980 F$(20)="LIFE OF INVESTMENT
## YRS"
4990 F$(21) = "VALUE OF 3 YEAR PROPERTY
$#,######.##"
5000 F$(22) = "VALUE OF 5 YEAR PROPERTY
$#,######.##"
5010 F$(23) = "VALUE OF 10 YEAR PROPERTY
$#,######.##"
5020 F$(24) = "VALUE OF 15 YEAR PU PROP
$#,######.##"
5030 F$(25) = "VALUE OF ST LINE REAL ESTATE
$#,######.##"
5040 F$(26) = "YEAR PROPERY PLACED IN SVC
 ####"
5050 F$(27) = "INFLATION RATE
  ##.##%"
5060 TU$(1)="NUMBER OF 1 BED ROOM UNFUR ###"
5070 TU$(2)="NUMBER OF 1 BED ROOM FUR   ###"
5080 TU$(3)="NUMBER OF 2 BED ROOM UNFUR ###"
5090 TU$(4)="NUMBER OF 2 BED ROOM FUR   ###"
5100 TU$(5)="NUMBER OF 3 BED ROOM UNFUR ###"
5110 TU$(6)="NUMBER OF 3 BED ROOM FUR   ###"
5120 FOR J=1 TO 6
5130    R$(J)="RENT $##,###.##/MO   $####,###.##/YR"
5140 NEXT J
5150 EX$(1) = "INSURANCE  $###,#.##/MO   $####,#.##/YR"
5160 EX$(2) = "LICENSES   $###,#.##/MO   $####,#.##/YR"
5170 EX$(3) = "PROP TAX   $###,#.##/MO   $####,#.##/YR"
5180 EX$(4) = "UTILITIES  $###,#.##/MO   $####,#.##/YR"
5190 EX$(5) = "MANAGEMENT $###,#.##/MO   $####,#.##/YR"
5200 EX$(6) = "JANITOR    $###,#.##/MO   $####,#.##/YR"
5210 EX$(7) = "ADVERTIS   $###,#.##/MO   $####,#.##/YR"
5220 EX$(8) = "MAINT EXP  $###,#.##/MO   $####,#.##/YR"
5230 EX$(9) = "MISC EXP   $###,#.##/MO   $####,#.##/YR"
5240 RETURN
5250 CLS
5260 PRINT
"================================================"
5270 PRINT "INSTRUCTIONS "
5280 PRINT "THIS PROGRAM CALCULATES THE PRESENT VALUE OF
THE"
5290 PRINT "CASH FLOWS FROM A INVESTMENT IN REAL ESATATE.
IN ORDER TO USE"
```

```
5300 PRINT "THE PROGRAM, YOU MUST SUPPLY THE INPUT
INFORMATION."
5310 PRINT " FIRST DATA TO ENTER ARE INCOME ESTIMATES. THEN
ENTER"
5320 PRINT "THE EXPENSES. THESE TWO TYPES OF INFORMATION
ARE ENTERED"
5330 PRINT "ON A TWO PAGE FORM - 1 PAGE FOR INCOME AND 1
FOR EXPENSES."
5340 PRINT"FINALLY DATA ON COST ETC ARE ENTERED USING A 3
PAGE FORM"
5350 PRINT "FOR THESE PAGES YOU CAN MOVE  WITH THE < AND >
KEYS."
5360 PRINT "YOU CAN CORRECT A WRONG ENTRY BY ENTERING C
AND"
5370 PRINT "THEN FOLLOWING THE INSTRUCTIONS."
5380 PRINT "WHEN ALL THE DATA ARE CORRECT, YOU CAN START
THE"
5390 PRINT "CALCULATIONS BY ENTERING G."
5400 PRINT "YOU MUST ENTER ALL THE DATA BEFORE YOU CAN RUN
THE PROGRAM."
5410 PRINT "PRESS ANY KEY TO CONTINUE"
5420 Y$=INKEY$:IF Y$="" THEN 5420
5430 CLS
5440 PRINT "INSTRUCTIONS PAGE 2"
5450 PRINT "ALL DATA ASKED FOR IS SELF EXPLANATORY, WITH
THE
5460 PRINT "POSSIBLE EXCEPTION OF YEARS AFTER INVEST BEFORE
REC
5470 PRINT "INCOME. THIS QUESTION IS BASED ON THE FACT THAT
MANY
5480 PRINT "INVESTMENTS DO NOT START PAYING UNITIL SOME
TIME
5490 PRINT "AFTER THE MONEY IS SPENT. YOU ENTER THE NUMBER
OF"
5500 PRINT "YEARS YOU ESTIMATE IT WILL TAKE FOR INCOME TO
START"
5510 PRINT "COMING AFTER THE INVESTMENT IS MADE. FOR
EXAMPLE IF"
5520 PRINT "YOU KNOW IT WILL TAKE ONE YEAR ENTER 1. IF IT
WILL
5530 PRINT "TAKE HALF A YEAR, ENTER 0.5."
5540 PRINT "PRESS ANY KEY TO CONTINUE"
5550 Y$ = INKEY$ : IF Y$ = "" THEN 5550
5560 CLS
5570 PRINT "INSTRUCTIONS PAGE 3."
```

```
5580 PRINT
5590 PRINT"AFTER THE INITIAL CALCULATIONS ARE COMPLETED,
YOU"
5600 PRINT"WILL BE ASKED IF YOU WANT TO RUN A RISK
ANALYSIS."
5610 PRINT "THIS QUESTION MUST BE ANSWERED BY PRESSING <Y>
OR <N>."
5620 PRINT "IF YOU PRESS <Y>, YOU ARE THEN PASSED TO THE
DATA ENTRY"
5630 PRINT "MODULE OF THE MONTE CARLO SIMULATION. THERE IS
ONE PAGE"
5640 PRINT "OF DATA FOR THE MONTE CARLO SIMULATION. DATA
ENTRY IS"
5650 PRINT "A MATTER OF PROVIDING THE DATA ASKED FOR. YOU
HAVE A"
5660 PRINT "CHANCE TO CORRECT DATA ERRORS BEFORE
CALCULATIONS BEGIN."
5670 PRINT "PRESS ANY KEY TO CONTINUE AND RETURN TO THE
PROGRAM."
5680 Y$ = INKEY$ : IF Y$ = "" THEN 5680
5690 RETURN
5700 FOR I = 1 TO 6
5710      CLS
5720 PRINT"INCOME ESTIMATES FOR RENTAL PROPERTY"
5730 PRINT "ENTER DATA ASKED FOR. DO NOT WORRY IF YOU
5740 PRINT "MAKE AN ERROR. YOU WILL HAVE A CHANCE TO
CORRECT"
5750 PRINT "IT LATER. TO ENTER MONTHLY EXPENSES PRECEED
AMOUNT"
5760 PRINT "WITH <M> AND FOR YEARLY PRECEED WITH <Y>. "
5770 PRINT "EG M100 IS $100 PER MONTH Y2000 IS $2000 PER
YR"
5780    PRINT USING TU$(I);NU(I);
5790   NU$ = ""
5800    INPUT NU$
5810   IF NU$ = "" THEN 5830
5820   NU(I) = VAL(NU$)
5830   IF NU(I) = 0 THEN 5920
5840    PRINT USING R$(I);R1(I);R2(I)
5850    R$=""
5860    INPUT R$
5870    IF R$ = "" THEN 5920
5880   IF INSTR("MY",LEFT$(R$,1)) = 0 THEN PRINT"WRONG
FORMAT. TRY AGAIN.":GOTO 5850
5890    GOSUB 6330
```

```
5900    R1(I) = RM
5910    R2(I) = RY
5920 NEXT I
5930 PRINT USING "ALLOWANCE FOR VACANCIES AS % OF RENTS
(##.##%)";VC;
5940 R$ = ""
5950 INPUT R$
5960 IF R$ = "" THEN 5970 ELSE VC = VAL(R$)
5970 CLS
5980 TI = 0
5990 PRINT "CHECK DATA TO BE SURE THEY ARE CORRECT."
6000 FOR I=1 TO 6
6010    PRINT USING TU$(I);NU(I)
6020    PRINT USING R$(I);R1(I);R2(I)
6030   TI = TI + NU(I)*R2(I)
6040 NEXT I
6050 PRINT USING "ALLOWANCE FOR VACENCIES ##.##%";VC
6060 TI = TI*(1-VC/100)
6070 PRINT USING "TOTAL YEARLY INCOME $#####,##.##":TI
6080 PRINT "ARE THESE CORRECT Y OR N?"
6090 Y$ = INKEY$ : IF Y$ = "" THEN 6090 ELSE IF
INSTR("YN",Y$)=0 THEN PRINT "TRY AGAIN PLEASE.":GOTO 6080
6100 IF Y$ = "N" THEN 5700
6110 CLS
6120 PRINT "ENTER EXPENSES. PRECEED BY M FOR MONTHLY Y FOR
YEARLY"
6130 FOR I = 1 TO 9
6140    PRINT USING EX$(I);EM(I);EY(I);
6150    R$=""
6160    INPUT R$
6170   IF R$="" THEN 6220
6180   IF INSTR("MY",LEFT$(R$,1)) = 0 THEN PRINT "WRONG
FORMAT. TRY AGAIN." : GOTO 6150
6190    GOSUB 6330
6200    EM(I) = RM
6210    EY(I) = RY
6220 NEXT I
6230 CLS
6240 PRINT "CHECK DATA TO BE SURE THAT THEY ARE CORRECT."
6250 TX = 0
6260 FOR I=1 TO 9
6270    PRINT USING EX$(I);EM(I);EY(I)
6280   TX = TX + EY(I)
6290 NEXT I
```

```
6300 PRINT "ARE THESE CORRECT Y OR N?"
6310 Y$ = INKEY$ : IF Y$ = "" THEN 6310 ELSE IF
INSTR("YN",Y$)=0 THEN PRINT"TRY AGAIN.":GOTO 6300
6320 IF Y$ = "Y" THEN RETURN ELSE GOTO 6110
6330 IF LEFT$(R$,1)="M" THEN 6370
6340 RY = VAL(RIGHT$(R$,LEN(R$)-1))
6350 RM = RY/12
6360 RETURN
6370 RM = VAL(RIGHT$(R$,LEN(R$)-1))
6380 RY = 12*RM
6390 RETURN
6400 END
6410 PV=0:B=0:SI=0:A=0:DI=0:PI=0:REM INITIALIZE COUNTERS
FOR SUMS
6420 TC = 0: F = 0 : FL = 0 : F1 = 1
6430 SP = 0 : CS = 0 : AE = 0 : AI = 0: SP = 0 : PN = 0
6440 AP = 0
6450 REM SP IS TOTAL SPENABLE CASH FLOW LOSS CS IS NUMBER
OF YEARS WITH SPENDABLE LOSS.
6460 REM INITIALIZE ALL ARRAYS TO ZERO
6470 CLS
6480 PRINT "INITIALIZING EVERYTHING"
6490 FOR I = 1 TO 30
6500    PRINT I;
6510     D(I) = 0
6520     CF(I) = 0
6530     EX(I) = 0
6540     E1(I) = 0
6550     E2(I) = 0
6560     TC(I) = 0
6570     T1(I) = 0
6580     T2(I) = 0
6590    SF(I) = 0
6600 NEXT I
6610 CLS
6620 RETURN
6630 REM TRANSFER TO INITIALIZATION
6640 GOSUB 4780
6650 GOSUB 5700 : REM GET INCOME AND EXPENSE ESTIMATES
6660 PRINT "NAME OF INVESTMENT IS ";NI$
6670 INPUT" ENTER NEW NAME ";NI$
6680 GOSUB 3740 : REM TRANSFER TO DATA INPUT
6690 CLS
6700 PRINT
"=================================================="
```

```
6710 PRINT"DO YOU WANT TO TAKE INVESTMENT TAX CREDIT ?"
6720 PRINT
"================================================"
6730 Y$=INKEY$:IF Y$="" THEN 6730 ELSE IF
INSTR("YN",Y$)=0THEN PRINT "ANSWER Y OR N PLEASE ":GOTO
6710
6740 IF Y$="Y" THEN TC = 1 ELSE TC = 0
6750 GOSUB 6410
6760 CLS
6770 REM NOW READ IN DEPRECIATION TABLE
6780 RESTORE
6790 CLS
6800 PRINT "READING DEPRECIATION TABLE"
6810 GOSUB 4490
6820 GOSUB 1630
6830 GOSUB 630
6840 GOSUB 710
6850 GOSUB 1370
6860 GOSUB 2220
6870 CLS
6880 PRINT"DO YOU WANT HARD COPY Y OR N "
6890 Y$=INKEY$:IF Y$="" THEN 6890 ELSE IF INSTR("YN",Y$)=0
THEN PRINT"TRY AGAIN":GOTO 6880
6900 IF Y$="Y" THEN GOSUB 2580
6910 CLS
6920 PRINT "DO YOU WANT TO RUN A RISK ANALYSIS Y OR N?"
6930 Y$ = INKEY$: IF Y$ = "" THEN 6930 ELSE IF
INSTR("YN",Y$)=0 THEN PRINT "TRY AGAIN"GOTO6920
6940 IF Y$="Y" THEN GOSUB 7020
6950 CLS
6960 PRINT"DO YOU WANT TO RUN ANOTHER CASE Y OR N?"
6970 Y$=INKEY$:IFY$=""THEN 6970 ELSE IF INSTR("YN",Y$)=0
THEN PRINT"TRY AGAIN":GOTO 2060
6980 IF Y$="Y" THEN 6650
6990 PRINT"SESSION OVER. PLEASE REMOVE DISKS BEFORE
TURNING"
7000 PRINT"SYSTEM OFF."
7010 END
7020 REM RISK ANALYSIS SUBROUTINE
7030 CLS
7040 PRINT "RISK ANALYSIS. PLEASE ENTER THE DATA ASKED
FOR."
7050 PRINT USING "THE BEST ESTIMATE OF THE INFLATION RATE
IS ##.##%";V(27)
```

```
7060 X1 = V(27) : X2 = V(13) : X3 = V(14) : X4 = V(11)
7070 PRINT USING "ENTER THE HIGHEST LIKELY INFLATION RATE
(##.##%)";H1;
7080 INPUT H1 :REM NOTE THIS IS H1 (ONE)
7090 PRINT USING "ENTER THE LOWEST LIKELY INFLATION RATE
(##.##%)";L1;
7100 INPUT L1
7110 PRINT USING "THE BEST ESTIMATE OF THE ESCLATION RATE
FOR INCOME IS ##.##%";V(13)
7120 PRINT USING "ENTER THE HIGHEST LIKELY RATE
(##.##%)";H2;
7130 INPUT H2
7140 PRINT USING "ENTER THE LOWEST LIKELY RATE
(##.##%)";L2;
7150 INPUT L2
7160 PRINT USING "THE BEST ESTIMATE OF EXPENSE ESCALATION
IS ##.##%";X3
7170 PRINT USING "ENTER THE HIGHEST LIKELY RATE
(##.##%)";H3;
7180 INPUT H3
7190 PRINT USING "ENTER THE LOWEST LIKELY RATE
(##.##%)";L3;
7200 INPUT L3
7210 PRINT USING "THE BEST ESTIMATE OF INCREASE IN VALUE IS
##.##%";X4
7220 PRINT USING "ENTER HIGHEST LIKELY RATE (##.##%)";H4;
7230 INPUT H4
7240 PRINT USING "ENTER LOWEST LIKELY RATE (##.##%)";L4;
7250 INPUT L4
7260 CLS: PRINT "REVIEW THE DATA TO BE SURE THEY ARE
CORRECT."
7270 PRINT USING "INFLATION RATE -- ##.##% MOST LIKELY
##.## BEST CASE ##.## WORST CASE";V(27);H1;L1
7280 PRINT USING "ESCAL INCOME -- ##.##% MOST LIKELY  ##.##
BEST CASE ##.## WORST CASE";X2;H2;L2
7290 PRINT USING "ESCAL EXP  ---  ##.##% MOST LIKEY   ##.##
BEST ##.## WORST";X3;H3;L3
7300 PRINT USING "ESCAL VALUE -- ##.##% MOST LIKELY   ##.##
BEST ##.## WORST";X4;H4;L4
7310 PRINT "ARE THESE CORRECT Y OR N?"
7320 Y$ = INKEY$ : IF Y$ = "" THEN 7320 ELSE IF
INSTR("YN",Y$)=0 THEN PRINT "PLEASE ANSWER Y OR N": GOTO
7320
7330 IF Y$ = "N" THEN 7020
```

```
7340 REM NOW ESTIMATE MEAN AND STANDARD DEVIATION
7350 M1 = (H1+L1+4*V(27))/6
7360 V1 = (H1-L1)/6
7370 M2 = (H2 + L2 +4* X2)/6
7380 V2 = (H2-L2)/6
7390 M3 = (H3+L3+4*X3 )/6
7400 V3 = (H3-L3)/6
7410 M4 = (H4+L4 + 4*X4)/6
7420 V4 = (H4-L4)/6
7430 CLS
7440 PRINT "NOW WORKING ON MONTE CARLO SIMULATION
7450 Z1=0:Z2=0:Z3=0:Z4=0:Z5=0:Z6=0:Z7=0
7460 FOR KZ = 1 TO 20
7470 EX = M1
7480 VX = V1
7490    GOSUB 8040
7500    V(27) = X
7510    EX = M2
7520    VX = V2
7530    V(13) = X
7540    EX = M3
7550    VX = V3
7560    GOSUB 8040
7570    V(14) = X
7580    EX = M4
7590    VX = V4
7600    GOSUB 8040
7610    V(11) = X
7620 REM NOW HAVE NEW VALUES OF INPUT SO NOW REDO ALL OF
CASH FLOWS
7630    GOSUB 6410
7640    GOSUB 630
7650    GOSUB 710
7660    GOSUB 1370
7670    PV(KZ) = PV+PP
7680    PI(KZ) = PI+PQ
7690   Z2 = Z2 + PI(KZ)
7700   Z1 = Z1 + PV(KZ)
7710 NEXT KZ
7720 MM = Z1/20
7730 MN = Z2/20
7740 FOR I = 1 TO 20
7750    Z3 = Z3 +(PV(I)-MM)[2
7760    Z4 = Z4 + (PI(I)-MN)[2
```

```
7770 NEXT
7780 S1 = SQR(Z3/19)
7790 S2 = SQR(Z4/19)
7800 CLS
7810 PRINT USING "THE MEAN PRESENT VALUE OF ALL PROFITS -
BALANCE $####,##.##";MM
7820 PRINT "THE STANDARD DEVIATION OF PRESENT VALUE IS ";S1
7830 PRINT USING"THE MEAN INFLATION CORRECTED PRESENT VALUE
IS $###,#####.##";MN
7840 PRINT USING "THE STANDARD DEVIATION OF INFLATION
CORRECTED IS $####,#.##";S2
7850 PRINT "PRESS <H> FOR HARD COPY."
7860 Y$ = INKEY$: IF Y$="" THEN 7860 ELSE IF Y$<>"H" THEN
8020
7870 LPRINT TAB(5);"RISK ANALYSIS FOR INVESTMENT ";NI$
7880 LPRINT " "
7890 LPRINT TAB(20);"VARIABLES FOR RISK ANALYSIS "
7900 LPRINT TAB(9);
7910 LPRINT USING "MOST LIKELY VALUE OF INFLATION ##.##,
HIGHEST LIKELY ##.##, LOWEST LIKELY ##.##%";X1;H1;L1
7920 LPRINT TAB(9);:LPRINT USING "MOST LIKELY VALUE OF
ESCALTION FOR INCOME ##.##, HIGHEST LIKELY ##.## AND LOWEST
##.##%";X2;H2;L2
7930 LPRINT TAB(9);:LPRINT USING"MOST LIKELY VALUE OF
ESCALATION FOR EXPENSES ##.##, HIGHEST LIKELY ##.##, AND
LOWEST ##.##%";X3;H3;L3
7940 LPRINT TAB(9);:LPRINT USING "MOST LIKELY VALUE OF
APPRECIATION OF PROPERTY ##.##, HIGHEST ##.## LOWEST
##.##%";X4;H4;L4
7950 LPRINT TAB(5);STRING$(64,"=")
7960 LPRINT USING "THE MEAN PRESENT VALUE OF ALL PROFITS -
LOAN BALANCE IS $#####,##.##";MM
7970 LPRINT USING "WITH A STANDARD DEVIATION OF
$####,#.##";S1
7980 LPRINT " "
7990 LPRINT USING "THE MEAN CONSTANT YEAR $ PRESENT VALUE
OF ALL PROFIT IS $#####,##.##";MN
8000 LPRINT USING "WITH STANDARD DEVIATION OF
$####,#.##";S2
8010 LPRINT USING "THE PRESENT VALUE OF YOUR EQUITY IS
$####,##.##";AP
8020 V(11) = X4 : V(27) = X1 : V(13) = X2 :V(14) = X3
8030 RETURN
8040 REM NORMAL DISTRIBUTION
```

```
8050 SX = 0
8060 FOR KX = 1 TO 12
8070    SX = SX +RND(0)
8080 NEXT KX
8090 X = VX*(SX-6)+EX
8100 RETURN
```

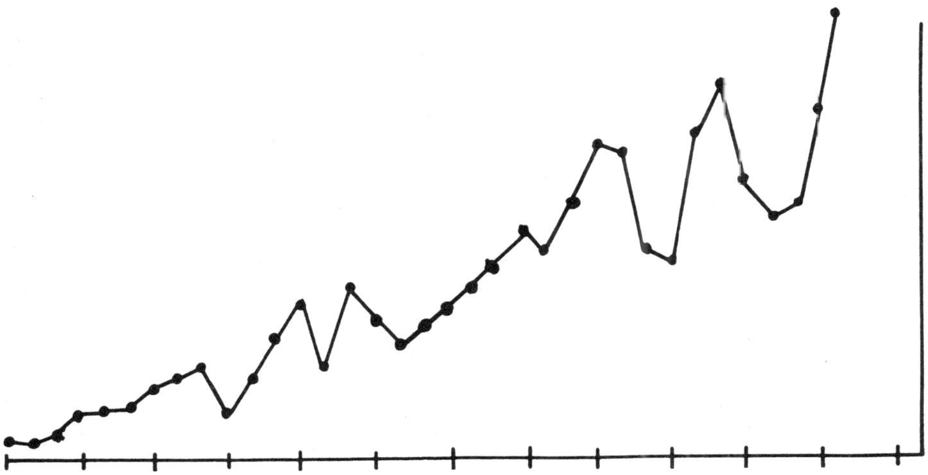

Chapter 13

Other Uses of the Program

Although the programs are set up to analyze fairly specific investments, they can also be used to analyze a broad range of investments if the input data is correctly interpreted. This chapter shows you how to use INVEST1 to determine whether a new, more efficient piece of equipment should be purchased to replace an old piece of equipment that still has useful life and how to use INVEST2 to determine the value of a common stock investment.

OLD EQUIPMENT REPLACEMENT

Now that energy prices are high, many of you are facing the issue of whether old energy-inefficient equipment should be replaced by new more efficient equipment. For example, should you replace your old furnace with a new one or should you install a solar hot water heater? You can use INVEST1 to help answer the economic portion of these questions.

You want to compare the present value of keeping old equipment with its high operating cost, with the present value of obtaining new equipment with its high capital cost and low operating costs. The easiest way is to run INVEST1 and treat the difference between the old and new operating costs as the income from the investment.

Example: Equipment Replacement

Your friend Sam is offering you a chance to purchase a new water heater that will cost $1,000. Operating costs of the new unit are $150/year. You are currently paying $600 per year, and Sam says you will get your money back in slightly more than two years. Moreover, you know that you have to replace your old water heater in five years anyway. What are the economics of the proposal?

Run program INVEST1 and compare the option of keeping your old water heater for 5 years with buying a new unit from Sam. Run the program for the water heater. The income is the difference between the present cost of operating the water heater and the new cost. Assume there is no expense. Sam's offer is a good one if the present value of the savings for five years exceeds the $1,000 cost. Use a discount rate of 15 percent. The program run shows that the present value of the savings is $1,508, so you make $508 in present value by buying the new water heater from Sam.

COMMON STOCK INVESTMENT

As a final example let's see how to use INVEST2 to evaluate a stock investment. Your friend Sam has a hot tip to invest in a new company. The company's stock is paying an eight percent dividend and you can buy $10,000 worth of stock right now. Sam says that the stock is going up at an annual rate of 12 percent. He won't charge a commission if you buy the stock, and will charge four percent when you want to sell it. You can run INVEST2 to examine whether this is as good an offer as the last one Sam offered.

Use the yearly rental income from the one bedroom unfurnished apartment to take care of the $800 dividend (eight percent of $10,000). There are no expenses so enter 0. The amount of the investment is $10,000 with no loans. The escalation for increase in value is 12 percent and there is no escalation for income. Your tax is 50 percent for federal income, 25 percent for capital gains, and 10 percent for state income. The discount rate will be 10 percent. The life of the investment is 10 years and there is no property to depreciate.

Enter G, and the program starts calculating. After a few seconds you can see that the present value of all profits is about $8,000, so it wasn't a good investment. It would be better to put your money in the investment represented by the discount rate (the capital gains tax is what did you in).

This should provide some idea of how to extend the programs by changing the meaning of the input information. I'm sure you can find additional uses for the program. Good luck!

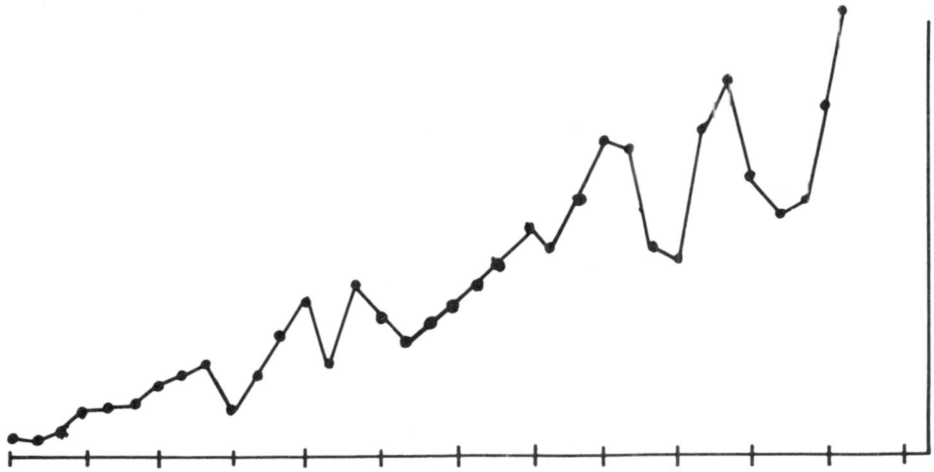

Chapter 14

Forecasting

Forecasting is the art of determining what the future holds. Because investments deal with the future, estimates of what the future holds are a necessary part of investment decision making. Thus, forecasting is an important tool for investment analysis. There are many ways, ranging from simple guesswork or wishful thinking to huge computer models of the entire economy, to make the necessary estimates of the future. In this chapter you will look at forecasting techniques in general and then examine some of the more useful forecasting methods, most of which can be used for computer assisted forecasting.

Quite often forecasting is confused with investment analysis. It is sometimes assumed that once a good forecast is made, the chore of investment analysis is over. Actually, quite the opposite is true. Investment analysis begins once good forecasts are made. Remember that a forecast only tells you what the future holds for a particular investment. The forecast does not tell you whether or not a particular investment is good or bad.

Perhaps an example will demonstrate the difference between forecasting and investment analysis. Suppose you plan to purchase stock and a complete analysis of the future prospects of the stock in question shows that a $1,000 purchase of the stock now will be worth $1,100 in 10 months. The question you still have to answer is, "Is this a good investment or should I look else-where?" Most of this book is devoted to helping you answer such questions. The forecast future of the stock provides you with the information needed to do a present value analysis of the future payback. It is the present value analysis that really tells you if the stock is a good buy.

GENERAL COMMENTS

During the past twenty years, several techniques have been developed for forecasting. The different techniques can be divided into two main groups: quantitative techniques and qualitative techniques. The main distinction between the two groups is that quantitative techniques are based on examining historical data and then following various calculation rules extrapolating the historical data into the future. Qualitative techniques, on the other hand, are generally based more on expert interpretation of past and present situations than on simple mechanical extrapolation of past trends. Another difference between the two techniques is that quantitative techniques generally assume that the future patterns of the data will be similar to those of the past, whereas qualitative techniques assume that the basic patterns of future data will be different from those of the past. Generally this difference means that quantitative techniques are applied to develop near and medium term forecasts and qualitative techniques are applied to develop long term forecasts.

During the past twenty years, quantitative techniques have been accepted as useful tools for decision making. One reason is that quantitative techniques have had a record of reasonably accurate forecasts; thus people have developed confidence in quantitative forecasts. Another reason is the availability of computers. Computers make both storage and analysis of historical data fairly easy. Finally, quantitative forecasts are generally cheaper than qualitative forecasts.

Qualitative forecasting is often referred to as technological forecasting, primarily because the techniques are often applied to forecasting changes in technology. However, the techniques can be applied to many other situations. In general, qualitative forecasts are used when you want to forecast major changes in the way things are. For example, you might want to forecast a change in living patterns from single homes to multiunit apartments. In general qualitative forecasts deal with the long term. And because of the expense involved in making them, qualitative forecasts are limited to issues that are of major importance to the long term future of the investor.

Because qualitative forecasts often attempt to predict a major change in the pattern of the historical data, the historical data are generally not sufficient to allow a forecast. (This does not mean however that the historical data are not used in making the forecast.) The general approach is to have a group of experts review the historical data and other factors, both past and present that may affect the pattern. Then these experts make predictions based on their interpretation of all the factors plus their own personal feelings about the future. Because some of the predictions are based on personal feeling about the future, the quality of the forecast strongly depends on who makes the forecast. Some individuals have good records for making forecasts and others have poor records.

The techniques for qualitative forecasting are not as well developed as the techniques of quantitative forecasting, and the computer is not as useful for qualitative forecasting as it is for quantitative forecasting. For these reasons, the bulk of the discussion in this chapter deals with quantitative forecasting.

SELECTION OF TECHNIQUE

Selection of the forecasting technique depends on several factors. Some of the more important are:

- The use of the forecast. If you want to play "what if" games, for example, you need a casual forecast. Time series forecasts do not provide the possibility of looking at "what if."
- Time horizon for the forecast. Some methods are well suited for short term forecasts; other methods are well suited for medium and long term forecasts. A long term forecast based on a short term technique could prove worse than no forecast at all.
- The underlying pattern of the data. Most forecasting methods assume there is some underlying pattern to the data. Various techniques are de-

signed to find specific patterns. If the actual pattern is not the same as that assumed by the techniques, then poor forecasts can result. Care must be taken to insure that the techniques being used is appropriate for the data.

- The type of model for the forecast. Most forecasts are based on some mathematical model. While it is not too important to understand the mathematics of the model used to make the forecast, it is important to understand the underlying assumptions of the model.
- Cost of the forecast. The cost of the forecast, especially the cost relative to the investment decision situation, must be kept in mind. For example, it doesn't make sense to spend $1,000 on forecasting for an investment decision that involves $500. If the investment involves several million dollars, considerable expense in forecasting is justified.
- Accuracy of the forecast. The accuracy required of the forecast is an important consideration. The accuracy required must be considered in the context of the particular investment decision that must be made.
- Availability of data for the forecast. The data available for the forecast must be considered in selecting a technique. A technique that requires data that is not available is of no value, no matter what its other virtues might be. Some techniques require a large amount of data before forecasts can be made; others require only a limited amount of data.

The remainder of this chapter discusses various forecasting techniques. A short section is devoted to qualitative forecasting, but most of the discussion focuses on quantitative techniques. The discussion of the various techniques is rather brief. If you need additional detail, you should consult some of the references on forecasting given in the Bibliography.

QUALITATIVE FORECASTING

Qualitative forecasting is generally concerned with the very long term, say the next ten years or even longer. You have all seen the results of qualitative forecasting methods in articles such as "The US in the year 2000" or "The shape of Education in 1990." Many of these forecasts assume major changes in many factors of society, such as drastic changes in technology.

The basis for qualitative forecasts is the use of experts to help prepare the forecasts. The techniques of qualitative forecasting are generally designed to help these experts express their views and to focus their discussions. Finally, the techniques are designed to consolidate expert opinion into some type of forecast that can be used for decision making.

The fact that qualitative forecasting depends on opinion makes qualitative forecasts somewhat fuzzy. Considerable judgment is required to interpret the forecast and then to determine appropriate action.

Qualitative forecasts are also expensive, mainly because a number of experts must be employed to make the forecast. This expense has generally limited application of qualitative forecasting techniques to long term situations. The large expense has limited the use to government and large companies, where, despite the cost and the fuzzy nature of qualitative forecasts, they are being widely used with some success.

In general the individual investor does not have the time, money, or expertise to make qualitative forecasts. Best for the individual is to keep up with the forecasts of the experts as published. Newspapers and business magazines are good sources for expert opinion.

One of the main problems with expert forecasts is that quite often two leading experts will forecast opposite futures. To prove this, look at the various long term economic forecasts. No two experts seem to agree on anything, which does not help those of us who are trying to decide how to invest our funds.

QUANTITATIVE FORECASTING

Quantitative forecasting can be divided into two broad groupings, causal or explanatory and time series. Causal methods are based on the assumption that the behavior of the forecast variable depends on other factors, and that if one can estimate these other factors, one can predict the forecast variable. Large econometric models are an example of causal forecast techniques.

Time series methods are based on the assumption that the forecast variable depends on its past time history. Thus all the information needed to forecast the variable is contained in its past history. Time series methods do not assume a casual relationship between the variables. Technical analysis of the stock market is an example of a time series forecasting technique.

The basic problem with time series forecasting is determining the pattern in the data. It is generally assumed that the pattern is made up of a trend, a cycle, and random noise. The analysis is usually aimed at extracting the trend from the pattern. However, in some cases the cycle portion of the pattern is of interest.

Which of the two broad methods of forecasting is best is still an open question. Since 1960 econometric modeling has been popular. Forecasts from the models were good and became widely accepted. Unfortunately, the accuracy of the econometric models has not been as good recently. It is still an open question as to whether causal models, which are generally more complicated and expensive, provide better forecasts that do simpler, less expensive time series methods.

One advantage of causal methods is that they allow you to forecast the effects of your decisions. This is especially true if you can construct simple models using data already collected. For example, if you have a model that predicts the vacancy rate of your apartment complex as a function of advertising, you can estimate the impact of increasing or reducing your advertising. Such a simple model should not be expensive nor difficult to prepare, and uses data that should be available.

An additional advantage of causal methods is that they tend to keep things tied together, thus usually avoiding predictions that are inconsistent with past experience, such as predicting high inflation rates and low interest rates. Such a relationship is inconsistent with past experience, yet time series could lead to such a forecast.

The simplest forecast is that the future will be the same as the present. For the near term this simple forecast is probably as accurate as any, and many investment decisions are based on forecasts derived from this simple method. When all else fails you can use this forecast. The next section discusses one way to apply the causal method.

LINEAR REGRESSION

The simplest way to apply a causal method is to plot the behavior of the forecast variable versus the causal factor. For example, if you are interested in the effects of advertising on sales, you can plot sales versus advertising (see Fig. 14-1). Then a straight line can be drawn through the data. This

Advertising $	Sales $
100	1100
90	920
80	760
110	1009
200	2100
300	2999
320	3300
400	4090
155	1620
124	1300

Fig. 14-1. Data used in linear regression example.

line is then used to predict the impact of any level of advertising on sales. You can use the line to interpolate between values or to extrapolate to values of advertising not previously considered.

One of the problems with drawing a straight line through the data points is determining where to draw the line. This problem has been studied in considerable detail and a technique called *linear regression analysis* has been developed to draw the "best" line through the data. The best straight line through the data is well defined in mathematical terms and a set of equations can be written to find this line. The calculations can be done by hand, although a computer can be written to do the calculations involved in linear regression analysis. The future values of the dependent variables are plugged into the equation and the computer calculates the future values of the forecast variables.

LINREG/BAS PROGRAM

Following is a program for simple linear regression.

LINREG/BAS Listing

```
10 REM ************************************************
20 REM SIMPLE LINEAR REGRESSION PROGRAM VERSION 1.0
30 REM BY LES FEB 1982
40 REM NAME LINREG/BAS
50 REM WRITTEN IN TRS-80 DISK BASIC FOR THE
60 REM TRS-80 MODEL I AND III
70 REM CAN BE USED WITH MINIMUM CHANGE ON ANY COMPUTER
80 REM USING MICROSOFT BASIC
90 REM ************************************************
100 CLS : REM WILL HAVE TO BE CHANGED FOR OTHER COMPUTERS
110 CLEAR 1000 : REM CLEAR STRING SPACE
120 DEFINT I,J,K,N
130 DEFSTR T : REM ALL VARIABLES STARTING WITH T ARE
STRINGS
140 DIM T(4),X(100),Y(100),F(100)
150 REM X IS THE TIME PERIOD AND Y IS THE FORECAST VARIABLE
160 REM T(1) AND T(2) ARE REMARKS AND T(3) IS THE NAME OF
THE
170 REM X VARIABLE AND T(4) IS THE NAME OF THE Y VARIABLE
180 REM ************************************************
190 CLS
200 PRINT "SIMPLE LINEAR REGRESSION PROGRAM"
210 PRINT "BY LES VERSION 1.1"
220 PRINT STRING$(63,"=")
230 INPUT "ENTER TITLE OF FORECAST ";T(1)
240 INPUT "ENTER REMARKS (ONE LINE LIMIT)"; T(2)
250 INPUT "NAME OF X VARIABLE ";T(3)
260 INPUT "NAME OF Y VARIABLE ";T(4)
270 CLS
280 PRINT T(1)
```

```
290 PRINT T(2)
300 PRINT T(3)
310 PRINT T(4)
320 PRINT
330 PRINT "ARE THESE CORRECT Y OR N ?"
340 Y$ = INKEY$ : IF Y$ = "" THEN 340
350 IF Y$="Y"  THEN 370
360 IF Y$ = "N" THEN 210 ELSE PRINT "PLEASE ANSWERY OR N "
: GOTO 270
370 CLS
380 PRINT "ENTER DATA ASKED FOR"
390 I=1
400 PRINT "ENTER VALUE OF X(" I;") -99 TO QUIT (";X(I);")";
410 INPUT X(I)
420 IF X(I) = -99 THEN 470
430 PRINT "ENTER VALUE OF Y(";I;") (";Y(I);")";
440 INPUT Y(I)
450 I=I+1
460 GOTO 400
470 CLS
480 PRINT "REVIEW DATA"
490 N= I-1
500 FOR J=1 TO N
510      PRINT "X(";J;") = ";X(J);"  Y(";J;") = "·Y(J)
520     IF J = N THEN 540
530      IF INT(J/12)-12 <> 0 THEN 660
540      PRINT "ARE THESE CORRECT Y OR N "
550      Y$ = INKEY$: IF Y$ ="" THEN 550
560      IF Y$ = "Y"  THEN 660
570     IF Y$ <>"N" THEN PRINT "ANSWER Y OR N":GOTO550
580      INPUT "ENTER INDEX OF DATUM TO BE CHANGED ";J1
590      PRINT "ENTER CORRECT VALUE OF X(;"J1;")";
600      INPUT X(J1)
610      PRINT "ENTER CORRECT VALUE OF Y(";J1;")";
620      INPUT Y(J1)
630      CLS
640      GOTO 470
650     CLS
660 NEXT J
670 REM NOW READY TO DO THE CALCULATIONS
680 A1=0
690 A2=0
700 B1=0
710 B2=0
```

```
720 FOR J=1 TO N
730      A1 = A1 +X(J)
740      A2 = A2 + X(J)*X(J)
750      B1 = B1 + Y(J)
760      B2 = B2 + Y(J)*X(J)
770 NEXT J
780 A1 = A1/N
790 A2 = A2/N
800 B1 = B1/N
810 B2 = B2/N
820 C = A1*A1-A2
830 A = (A1*B2 - A2*B1)/C
840 B = A1*B1-B2
850 B = B/C
860 REM CALCULATE THE STANDARD DEVIATON
870 SUM = 0
880 FOR J=1 TO N-1
890      S1 = Y(J)-A-B*X(J)
900      SUM = SUM +S1*S1
910 NEXT J
920 SD = SQR(SUM/(N-2))
930 CLS
940 PRINT "RESULTS OF LINEAR LEAST SQUARES FIT"
950 PRINT
960 PRINT "THE EQUATION IS Y = ";A ;" + ";B;"* X"
970 PRINT
980 PRINT "THE STANDARD DEVIATION IS ";SD
990 PRINT
1000 PRINT "DO YOU WISH TO MAKE A FORECAST Y OR N "
1010 Y$ = INKEY$: IF Y$="" THEN 1010
1020 IF Y$="Y" THEN GOSUB 1420
1030 IF Y$ ="N" THEN 1040  ELSE PRINT "PLEASE ANSWER Y OR
N":GOTO1000
1040 PRINT "PRESS H FOR HARD COPY ANY OTHER KEY TO
CONTINUE"
1050 Y$=INKEY$: IF Y$ = "" THEN 1050
1060 IF Y$="H" THEN GOSUB 1130
1070 PRINT "DO YOU WANT TO RUN ANOTHER CASE Y OR N?"
1080 Y$= INKEY$: IF Y$ = "" THEN 1080
1090 IF Y$ = "Y" THEN 190
1100 IF Y$ = "N" THEN END
1110 PRINT "PLEASE ANSWER Y OR N"
1120 GOTO 1070
1130 REM HARDCOPY ROUTINE
```

```
1140 PRINT
1150 CLS
1160 PRINT
1170 PRINT"HARD COPY ROUTINE"
1180 PRINT "PRESS ANY KEY WHEN PRINTER IS READY "
1190 Y$ = INKEY$: IF Y$ = "" THEN 1190
1200 LPRINT
1210 LPRINT TAB(10);"LINEAR REGRESSION ANALYSIS"
1220 LPRINT TAB(10);T(1)
1230 LPRINT TAB(10);T(2)
1240 LPRINT
1250 LPRINT TAB(10);" INPUT DATA "
1260 LPRINT TAB(10);T(3);TAB(20)T(4)
1270 FOR J1 = 1 TO N
1280    LPRINT TAB(10);X(J1) TAB(20):Y(J1)
1290 NEXT J1
1300 LPRINT
1310 LPRINT TAB(10);"THE EQUATION IS Y = ";A;" + ";B;"* X"
1320 LPRINT TAB(10);"THE STANDARD DEVIATION IS ";SD
1330 LPRINT
1340 LPRINT TAB(10);"RESULTS OF FORECASTS "
1350 LPRINT TAB(10);T(3);TAB(20);"FORECAST VALUE OF ";T(4)
1360 FOR J1 = 1 TO J
1370    LPRINT TAB(10);X(J1);TAB(25);F(J1)
1380 NEXT J1
1390 LPRINT
1400 RETURN
1410 END
1420 REM SUBROUTINE FOR FORECASTING
1430 J=0
1440 CLS
1450 PRINT "FORECASTING SUBROUTINE"
1460 PRINT
1470 J=J+1
1480 PRINT"ENTER VALUE OF ";T(3);" THAT FORECAST IS DESIRED
FOR";
1490 INPUT X
1500 F(J) = A + B*X
1510 PRINT "VALUE OF ";T(4);" IS ";F(J)
1520 PRINT "DO YOU WISH ANOTHER FORECAST "
1530 Y$ = INKEY$: IF Y$ ="" THEN 1530
1540 IF Y$ = "Y" THEN 1470 ELSE IF Y$="N" THEN RETURN
1550 PRINT "PLEASE ANSWER Y OR N"
1560 GOTO 1520
```

Example

Suppose you own a business. During the past several weeks you have collected data on the dollars spent on advertising and the dollars received from sales. You would like to estimate the impact on sales if you spend various amounts on advertising. The data (Fig. 14-1) collected is plotted in Fig. 14-2.

The data is entered into the computer according to the instructions contained in the program. The results of the calculations are shown in Fig. 14-3.

A problem with simple linear regression analysis is that it assumes the forecast variable is a linear function of only one factor. In many cases the forecast variable is a function of several factors. This problem can be solved using a technique called *multiple linear regression.* Several major econometric models are based on multilinear regression analysis, where the variable of interest is assumed to be a linear function of the factors being studied. One of the best multilinear regression programs for the TRS-80 is FLURP (Flynn Laboratory's Ulti-

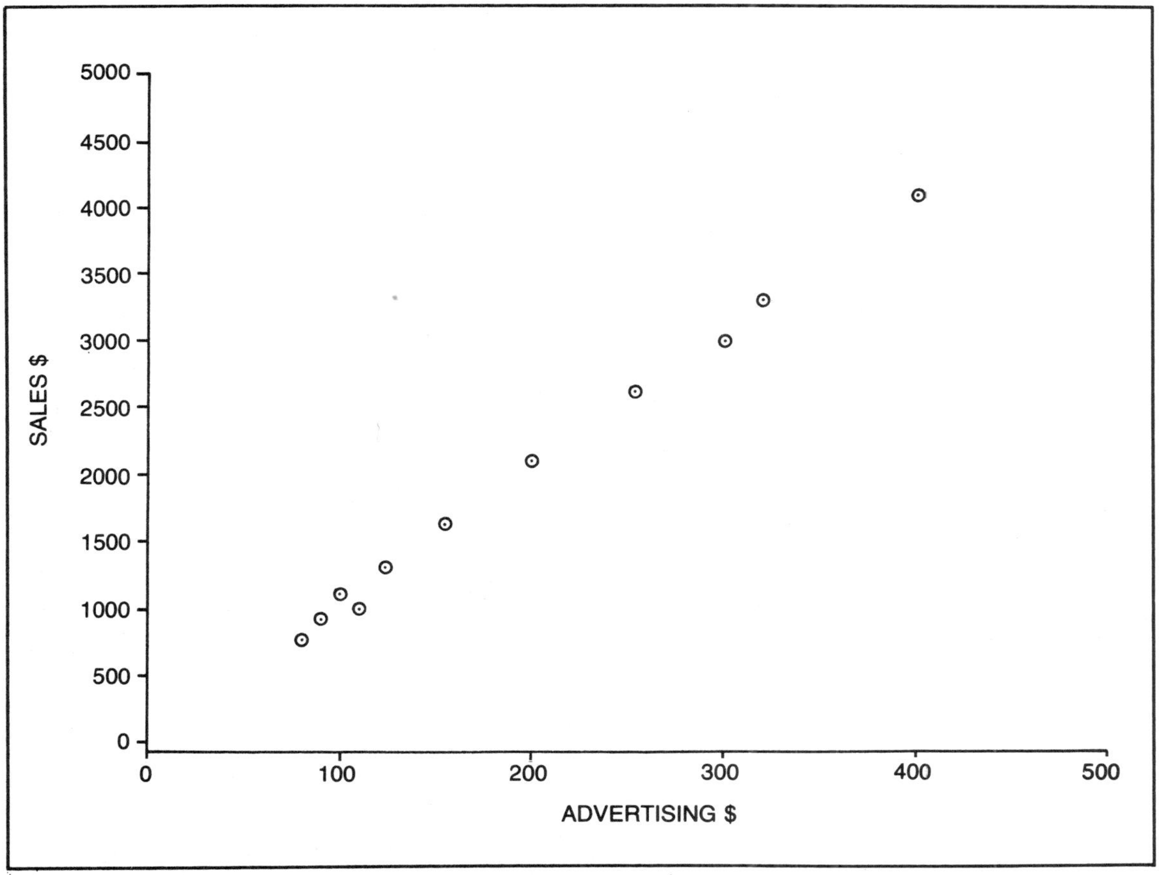

Fig. 14-2. Plot of dollars spent for advertising and sales generated for linear regression example.

```
INPUT DATA
ADVERTISING $SALES $
 100          1100
 90           920
 80           760
 110          1009
 200          2100
 300          2999
 320          3300
 400          4090
 155          1620
 124          1300
 254          2600

THE EQUATION IS Y = -4.70208  +  10.2437  * X
THE STANDARD DEVIATION IS  60.9914

RESULTS OF FORECASTS
ADVERTISING $FORECAST VALUE OF SALES $
 100              917.227
 90               1255.27
 80               1531.85
 110              2556.21
 200              8190.22
 300              763.572
 320              7678.04
```

Fig. 14-3. Results of linear regression example.

mate Regression Program), available from LEDS Publishing Co., Inc., P.O. Box 12847 Research Triangle Park, NC 27709. The programs are discussed in *ACCESS,* Volume 1, issues 1, 2, 3, and 4.

Development of multilinear regression programs is beyond the scope of this book, but an example showing the possibilities of the technique is useful. Consider the problem of forecasting future interest rates as represented by the rate for three month Treasury Bills (T-Bills). A plot of past T-Bill rates is shown in Fig. 14-4. Note that the rate fluctuates. The result of multilinear regression analysis of T-Bill rates as a function of the inflation rate [change in the Consumer Price Index (CPI) and economic growth (change in the Gross National Product (GNP)] gives the equation below (See "Multilinear Regression Analysis on a Microcomputer" by Brian Flynn in *ACCESS*, Volume 1, number 1, page 17 for additional details.).

$$TBILL = 0.9 + 0.7 \times INF + 0.2 \times GNP$$

where TBILL is the three month Treasury Bill rate,

INF is the percent change in the consumer price index (the rate of inflation), and GNP is the change in Gross National Product. All of these factors are usually available. Both the inflation rate and the change in GNP are predicted by the government and many private organizations. These projections are often widely published, so you can use this equation and the projections of various groups to predict the future Treasury Bill rate. (This equation explains about 90 percent of the variation in interest rates during 1933-1980. Remember, though, that just because an equation worked in the past is no guarantee it will work in the future.)

The use of the equation is demonstrated below. Assume that the projected inflation rate is 12 percent and the economy is projected to grow at a rate of three percent per year. What is the projected Treasury Bill rate? The forecast Treasury Bill rate is 9.9 percent. Now if economic growth is projected to be 5 percent and the inflation rate is projected to be 13 percent, the Treasury Bill rate is forecast to be 11 percent.

The above equation can be combined with another result from multilinear regression to form a simple econometric model. The second equation relates the inflation rate to the price of oil and the money supply. The equation is:

$$CPI = 0.27 + 0.17\ OIL + 0.00052\ MONEY$$

where CPI is the consumer price index (1976 =1), OIL is the oil price index (1976 = 1), and MONEY is the money stock (M2) in billions of dollars. These two equations can be used together to help you forecast the future of the economy.

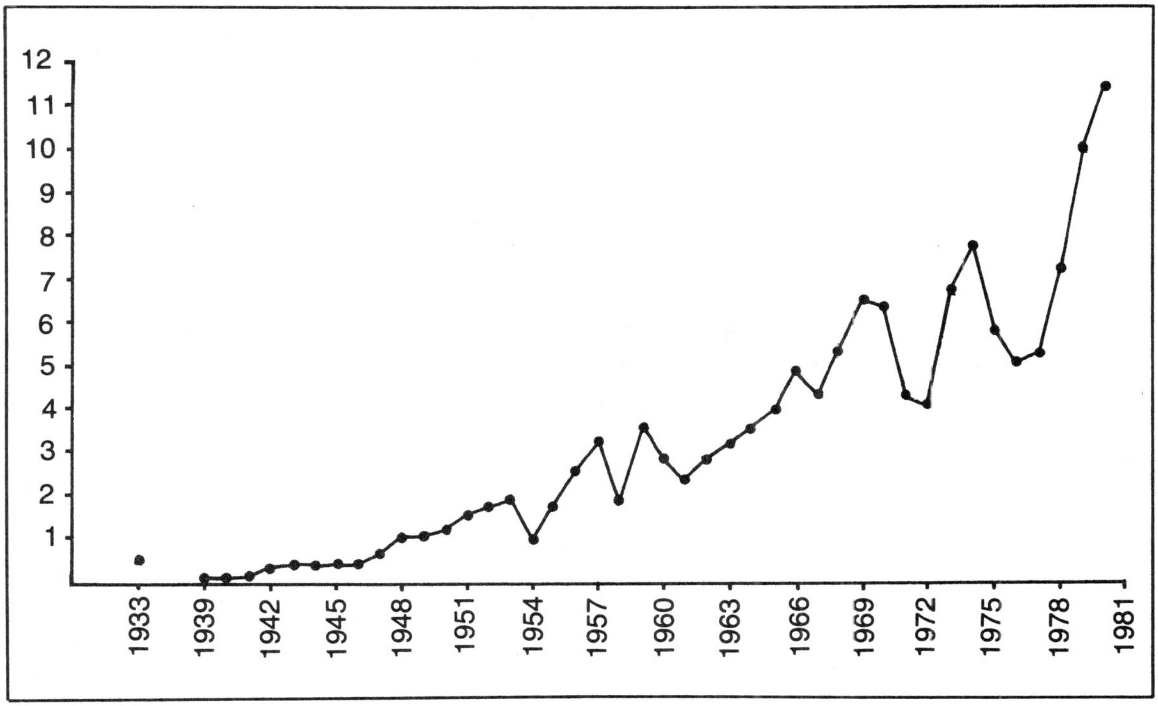

Fig. 14-4. Plot of past T-Bill rates from 1933 to 1981.

TIME SERIES METHODS

Time series methods are the most popular methods of forecasting. Examples of time series methods include technical analysis of the stock market, analysis of monthly retail sales, and analysis of unemployment rates.

In general, time series methods are used for short-term forecasting, such as next week, next month, or perhaps even next year. One reason for the short time horizon of time series forecasting is that the forecast variable is generally assumed to change by relatively small amounts from one time period to another.

Time series forecasting techniques are often referred to as *smoothing techniques,* because one of the objectives of time series methods is to remove random noise from the data to leave a smooth curve. The most common of these methods are moving averages and exponential smoothing. The basic idea of moving averages and exponential smoothing, (and most quantitative methods) is that there is some pattern in the historical data. This pattern is hidden by random fluctuations or noise in the data. The noise is removed by smoothing the data. The smoothed data is then used to forecast the future.

MOVING AVERAGE

The moving average technique is the simplest of the smoothing techniques. The method removes the noise from the historical data by replacing the data by the average of a given fixed number of observations. The forecast for the next period is the average of the last set of observations. The number of observations included in the average is set by the user and is held constant during the analysis. The more observations included in the average, the smoother the analysis will be.

MOVAVE/BAS PROGRAM

A program for calculating simple moving average follows.

MOVAVE/BAS Listing

```
10 REM MOVING AVERAGE PROGRAM VERSION 1.1
20 REM BY LES FEB 1982
30 REM NAME MOVAVE/BAS
40 REM WRITTEN IN TRS-80 DISK BASIC FOR THE
50 REM TRS-80 MODEL I AND III
60 REM CAN BE USED WITH MINIMUM CHANGE ON ANY COMPUTER
70 REM USING MICROSOFT BASIC
80 REM *************************************************
90 CLS : REM WILL HAVE TO BE CHANGED FOR OTHER COMPUTERS
100 CLEAR 1000 : REM CLEAR STRING SPACE
110 DEFINT I,J,K,N
120  DEFSTR T  :  REM  ALL VARIABLES  STARTING  WITH  T  ARE
STRINGS
130 DIM T(3),X(100),Y(100),F(100)
140 REM X IS THE TIME PERIOD AND Y IS THE FORECAST VARIABLE
150 REM T(1)  AND T(2) ARE REMARKS  AND  T(3) IS THE NAME OF
THE
160 REM Y VARIABLE
170 REM ***********************************************
```

```
180 CLS
190 PRINT "SIMPLE MOVING AVERAGE PROGRAM"
200 PRINT "BY LES VERSION 1.1"
210 PRINT STRING$(63,"=")
220 INPUT "ENTER TITLE OF FORECAST ";T(1)
230 INPUT "ENTER REMARKS (ONE LINE LIMIT)"; T(2)
240 INPUT "NAME OF Y VARIABLE ";T(3)
250 CLS
260 PRINT T(1)
270 PRINT T(2)
280 PRINT T(3)
290 PRINT
300 PRINT "ARE THESE CORRECT Y OR N ?"
310 Y$ = INKEY$ : IF Y$ = "" THEN 310
320 IF Y$="Y"  THEN 340
330 IF Y$ = "N" THEN 200 ELSE PRINT "PLEASE  ANSWERY OR  N "
: GOTO 250
340 CLS
350 PRINT "ENTER DATA ASKED FOR"
360 I=1
370 PRINT "ENTER VALUE OF X(";I;") -99 TO QUIT (";X(I);")";
380 INPUT X(I)
390 IF X(I) = -99 THEN 440
400 PRINT "ENTER VALUE OF Y(";I;") (";Y(I);")";
410 INPUT Y(I)
420 I=I+1
430 GOTO 370
440 INPUT "ENTER VALUE OF X FOR FINAL FORECAST ";X(I)
450 CLS
460 PRINT "REVIEW DATA"
470 N = I
480 FOR J=1 TO N
490      PRINT "X(";J;") = ";X(J);"  Y(";J;") = ";Y(J)
500     IF J = N THEN 520
510      IF INT(J/12)-12 <> 0 THEN 640
520      PRINT "ARE THESE CORRECT Y OR N "
530      Y$ = INKEY$: IF Y$ ="" THEN 530
540      IF Y$ = "Y"  THEN 640
550     IF Y$ <>"N" THEN PRINT "ANSWER Y OR N":GOTO530
560      INPUT "ENTER INDEX OF DATUM TO BE CHANGED ";J1
570      PRINT "ENTER CORRECT VALUE OF X(;"J1;")";
580      INPUT X(J1)
590      PRINT "ENTER CORRECT VALUE OF Y(";J1;")";
600      INPUT Y(J1)
```

```
610       CLS
620       GOTO 440
630      CLS
640 NEXT J
650 INPUT "ENTER NUMBER OF  VALUES TO BE INCLUDED IN AVERAGE
";NA
660 PRINT "NOW CALCULATING MOVING AVERAGE "
670 FOR J=1 TO N
680       IF J <= NA THEN 750
690      F(J) = 0
700       J1 = 1
710       F(J) = F(J)+ Y(J-J1)
720       J1 = J1+1
730       IF J1 > NA THEN 740 ELSE 710
740      F(J) = F(J)/NA
750 NEXT J
760 CLS
770 PRINT "RESULTS "
780 PRINT "X(I)","Y(I)","FORECAST"
790 FOR J=1 TO N
800       PRINT X(J),Y(J),F(J)
810       IF INT(J/12)-J/12 <> 0 THEN 840
820       PRINT "PRESS ANY KEY TO CONTINUE "
830       Y$ = INKEY$:IFY$ = "" THEN 830
840 NEXT J
850 PRINT "PRESS H FOR HARDCOPY"
860 Y$ = INKEY$: IF Y$ = "" THEN 860
870 IF Y$ = "H" THEN GOSUB 930
880 PRINT "DO YOU WANT TO RUN ANOTHER CASE "
890 Y$ = INKEY$ : IF Y$ = "" THEN 890
900 IF Y$ = "Y" THEN 180
910 IF Y$ = "N" THEN END ELSE PRINT "PLEASE ANSWER Y OR N"
920 GOTO 860
930 CLS
940 PRINT "HARD COPY PLEASE BE SURE THAT PRINTER IS ON"
950 LPRINT
960 LPRINT  TAB(10) "RESULTS OF  MOVING  AVERAGE FOR  ";NA;"
PERIODS IN AVERAGE"
970 LPRINT
980 LPRINT T(1)
990 LPRINT T(2)
1000 LPRINT
1010 LPRINT
1020 LPRINT "RESULTS"
1030                LPRINT                TAB(10);"PERIOD
```

```
";TAB(20);T(3);TAB(40);"FORECAST"TAB(50)"ABS.      VALUE      OF
ERROR"
1040 FOR J=1 TO N-1
1050                                                     LPRINT
TAB(10);X(J);TAB(25);Y(J);TAB(40);F(J);TAB(52)
ABS(F(J)-Y(J))
1060 NEXT J
1070 LPRINT TAB(10)X(N);TAB(40);F(N)
1080 RETURN
```

Example: Moving Average Program

You want to forecast the price of the stock of Sam's Inc. The historical data for the stock is given in Fig. 14-5 and plotted in Fig. 14-6.

To use MOVAVE, first enter the data requested. Then you have to choose the number of observations to be included in the average; three will be used for this problem. The program prints the original data and the moving average for the data.

Period	Price
1970	20
1971	14
1972	20
1973	19.80
1974	32
1975	18
1976	15
1977	12
1978	20
1979	25
1980	28
1981	25

Fig. 14-5. Data used in moving average example.

Results

The results for the moving average forecast for two values are given in Fig. 14-7 and plotted in Fig. 14-8. In this case the error in the forecasts is higher when the number of terms is five. The forecast for three terms is that the stock will increase from $25 to $26, and the forecast for five terms is that the stock will decrease from $25 to $22. None of the results indicates whether this will be a good investment. In real stock forecasts, weekly data would probably be used and the forecast made on a 30 week moving average. The exact moving average to use depends on the judgment of the particular person doing the forecasting.

EXPONENTIAL SMOOTHING

For two reasons, most forecasters use exponential smoothing instead of moving averages for most forecasts. First, you must have at least N data points (N is the number of terms to be averaged) before you can use the moving average method and you must always store at least the last N observations. Second, moving averages gives equal weight to all of the last N observations. What you would really like is a method that gives more weight to the most recent observations and less weight to the more distant observations. Exponential smoothing meets this requirement and also eliminates the need to store most of the historical data. Only two pieces of historical data are needed.

The basic idea behind exponential smoothing is that the noise can be removed from the data.

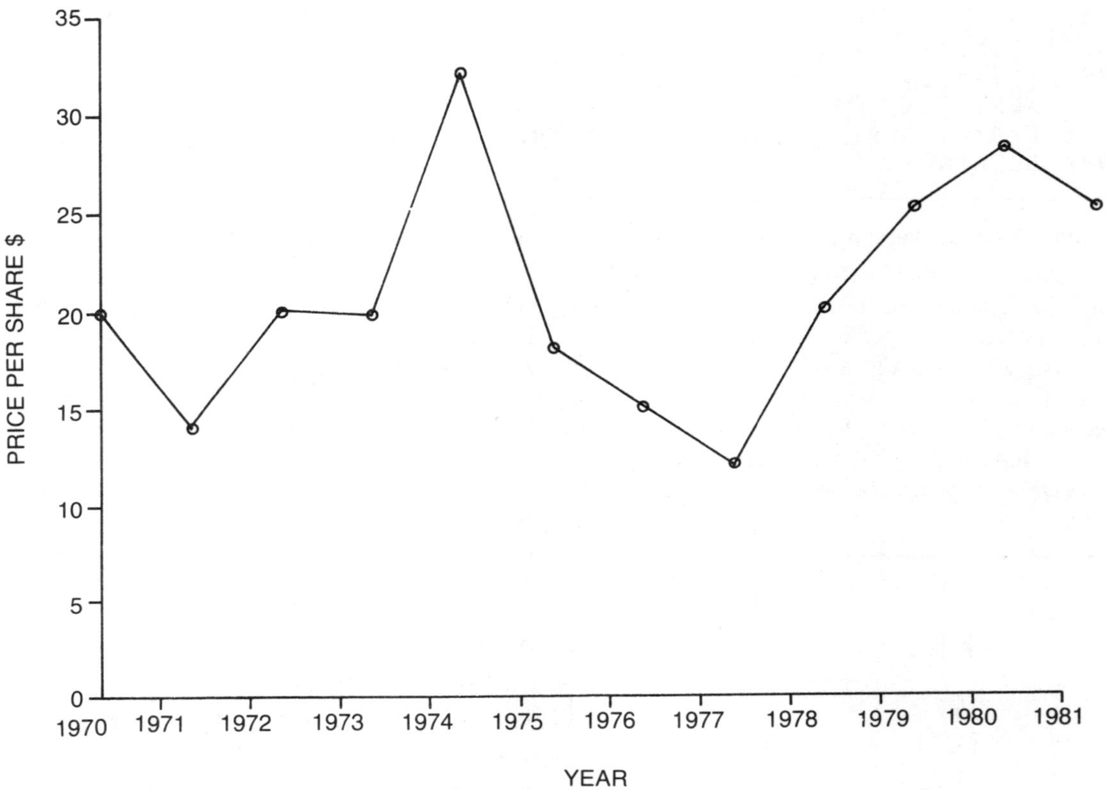

Fig. 14-6. Plot of data used in moving average example.

$$F(t) = F(t-1) + A \times [Y(t-1) - F(t-1)]$$

where F(t) is the forecast for time t, F(t−1) is the forecast for time t-1 (the previous time period), A is the parameter, and Y(t−1) is the actual value of Y during the previous period.

The value of the smoothing parameter must be determined by the forecaster. There is no single good way to determine the value of the parameter A. In general the best approach to determining A is to try different values of A, and then use the one that seems to give the best results (best in the sense that the forecasts agree well with past trends of the data).

EXPSMO/BAS PROGRAM

A Microsoft BASIC program, EXPSMO/BAS, for exponential smoothing begins on page 188.

```
          RESULTS OF MOVING AVERAGE FOR  3  PERIODS IN AVERAGE

EXAMPLE
PROJECTIONS FOR PRICE OF SAMS INC. FOR 1982


RESULTS
          PERIOD     PRICE OF SAMS INC.   FORECAST   ABS. VALUE OF ERROR
           1970           20               0           20
           1971           14               0           14
           1972           20               0           20
           1973           19.8             18          1.8
           1974           32               17.9333     14.0667
           1975           18               23 9333     5.93333
           1976           15               23.2667     8.26667
           1977           12               21.6667     9.66667
           1978           20               15          5
           1979           25               15.6667     9.33333
           1980           28               19          9
           1981           25               24.3333     .666666
           1982                            26

          RESULTS OF MOVING AVERAGE FOR  5  PERIODS IN AVERAGE

EXAMPLE
PROJECTIONS FOR PRICE OF SAMS INC. FOR 1982


RESULTS
          PERIOD     PRICE OF SAMS INC.   FORECAST   ABS. VALUE OF ERROR
           1970           20               0           20
           1971           14               0           14
           1972           20               0           20
           1973           19.8             18          1.8
           1974           32               17.9333     14.0667
           1975           18               21.16       3.16
           1976           15               20.76       5.76
           1977           12               20.96       8.96
           1978           20               19 36       .639999
           1979           25               19.4        5.6
           1980           28               18          10
           1981           25               20          5
           1982                            22
```

Fig. 14-7. Moving average results.

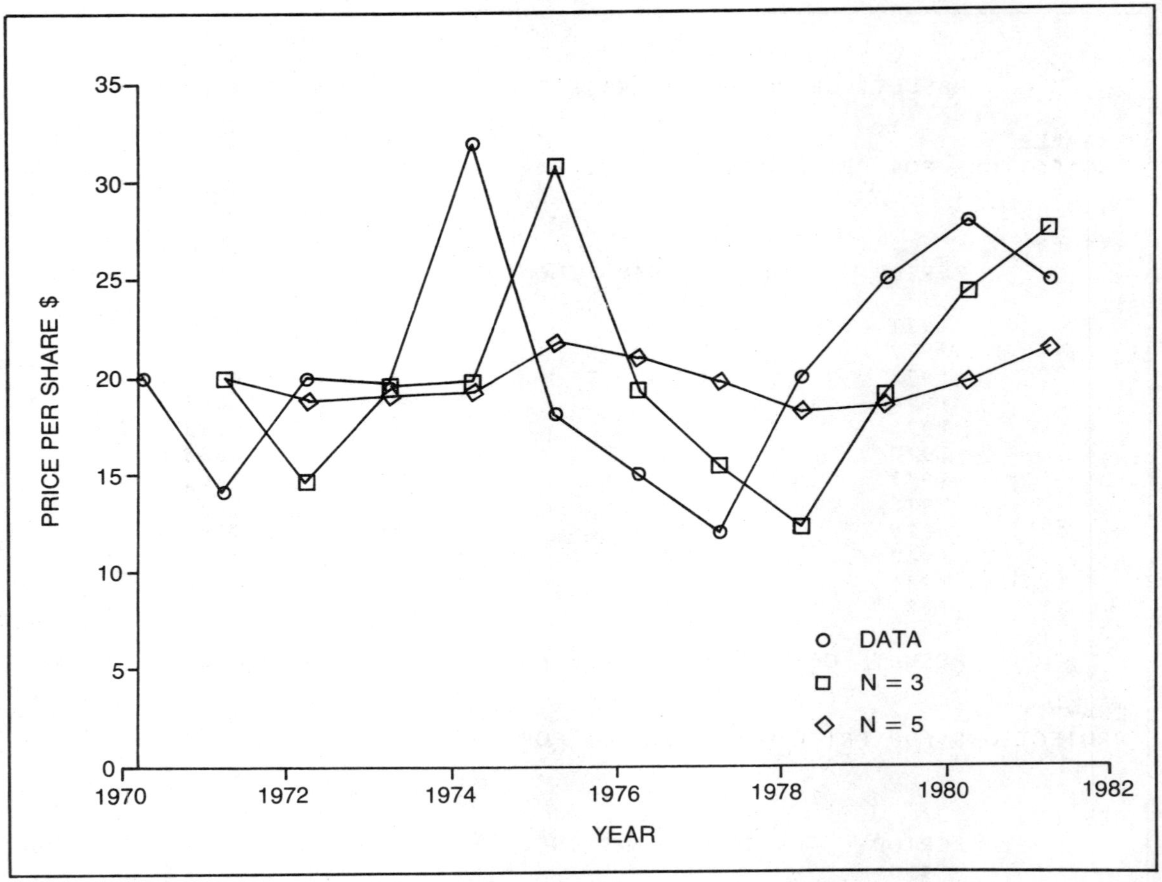

Fig. 14-8. Plot of moving average results.

EXPSMO/BAS Listing

```
10 REM EXPONENTIAL SMOOTHING PROGRAM VERSION 1
20 REM BY LES FEB 1982
30 REM NAME EXPSMO/BAS
40 REM WRITTEN IN TRS-80 DISK BASIC FOR THE
50 REM TRS-80 MODEL I AND III
60 REM CAN BE USED WITH MINIMUM CHANGE ON ANY COMPUTER
70 REM USING MICROSOFT BASIC
80 REM ********************************************
90 CLS : REM WILL HAVE TO BE CHANGED FOR OTHER COMPUTERS
100 CLEAR 1000 : REM CLEAR STRING SPACE
110 DEFINT I,J,K,N
```

```
120 DEFSTR T : REM ALL VARIABLES STARTING WITH T ARE
STRINGS
130 DIM T(3),X(100),Y(100),F(100)
140 REM X IS THE TIME PERIOD AND Y IS THE FORECAST VARIABLE
150 REM T(1) AND T(2) ARE REMARKS AND T(3) IS THE NAME OF
THE
160 REM Y VARIABLE
170 REM ***********************************************
180 CLS
190 PRINT "EXPONENTIAL SMOOTHING PROGRAM"
200 PRINT "BY LES VERSION 1"
210 PRINT STRING$(63,"=")
220 INPUT "ENTER TITLE OF FORECAST ";T(1)
230 INPUT "ENTER REMARKS (ONE LINE LIMIT)"; T(2)
240 INPUT "NAME OF Y VARIABLE ";T(3)
250 CLS
260 PRINT T(1)
270 PRINT T(2)
280 PRINT T(3)
290 PRINT
300 PRINT "ARE THESE CORRECT Y OR N ?"
310 Y$ = INKEY$ : IF Y$ = "" THEN 310
320 IF Y$="Y"  THEN 340
330 IF Y$ = "N" THEN 200 ELSE PRINT "PLEASE ANSWERY OR N "
: GOTO 250
340 CLS
350 PRINT "ENTER DATA ASKED FOR"
360 I=1
370 PRINT "ENTER VALUE OF X(";I;") -99 TO QUIT (";X(I);")";
380 INPUT X(I)
390 IF X(I) = -99 THEN 440
400 PRINT "ENTER VALUE OF Y(";I;") (";Y(I);")";
410 INPUT Y(I)
420 I=I+1
430 GOTO 370
440 INPUT "ENTER VALUE OF X FOR FINAL FORECAST ";X(I)
450 CLS
460 PRINT "REVIEW DATA"
470 N = I
480 FOR J=1 TO N
490      PRINT "X(";J;") = ";X(J);"  Y(";J;") = ";Y(J)
500     IF J = N THEN 520
510      IF INT(J/12)-12 <> 0 THEN 640
520      PRINT "ARE THESE CORRECT Y OR N "
```

```
530      Y$ = INKEY$:  IF Y$ ="" THEN 530
540      IF Y$ = "Y"  THEN 630
550     IF Y$ <>"N" THEN PRINT "ANSWER Y OR N":GOTO530
560      INPUT "ENTER INDEX OF DATUM TO BE CHANGED ";J1
570      PRINT "ENTER CORRECT VALUE OF X(;"J1;")";
580      INPUT X(J1)
590      PRINT "ENTER CORRECT VALUE OF Y(";J1;")";
600      INPUT Y(J1)
610      CLS
620      GOTO 440
630     CLS
640 NEXT J
650 INPUT "ENTER VALUE OF SMOOTHING COEFFICIENT ";A
660 PRINT "NOW CALCULATING"
670 F(2) = Y(1)
680 FOR J=3 TO N
690     F(J) = F(J-1) + (Y(J-1)-F(J-1))*A
700 NEXT J
710 CLS
720 PRINT "RESULTS "
730 PRINT "X(I)","Y(I)","FORECAST"
740 FOR J=1 TO N
750      PRINT X(J),Y(J),F(J)
760      IF INT(J/12)-J/12 <> 0 THEN 790
770      PRINT "PRESS ANY KEY TO CONTINUE "
780      Y$ = INKEY$:IFY$ = "" THEN 780
790 NEXT J
800 PRINT "PRESS H FOR HARDCOPY"
810 Y$ = INKEY$:  IF Y$ = "" THEN 810
820 IF Y$ = "H" THEN GOSUB 880
830 PRINT "DO YOU WANT TO RUN ANOTHER CASE "
840 Y$ = INKEY$ : IF Y$ = "" THEN 840
850 IF Y$ = "Y" THEN 180
860 IF Y$ = "N" THEN END ELSE PRINT "PLEASE ANSWER Y OR N"
870 GOTO 810
880 CLS
890 PRINT "HARD COPY PLEASE BE SURE THAT PRINTER IS ON"
900 LPRINT
910 LPRINT TAB(10);"RESULTS OF EXPONENTIAL SMOOTHING WITH A
= ";A
920 LPRINT
930 LPRINT T(1)
940 LPRINT T(2)
950 LPRINT
960 LPRINT
```

```
970 LPRINT "RESULTS"
980 LPRINT TAB(10);"PERIOD
";TAB(20);T(3);TAB(40);"FORECAST"TAB(50)"ABS. VALUE OF
ERROR"
990 FOR J=1 TO N-1
1000      LPRINT
TAB(10);X(J);TAB(25);Y(J);TAB(40);F(J);TAB(52)
ABS(F(J)-Y(J))
1010 NEXT J
1020 LPRINT TAB(10)X(N);TAB(40);F(N)
1030 RETURN
```

Example: EXPSMO/BAS in Action

Run EXPSMO/BAS on the same data used for the moving average example (see Fig. 14-5). The hard copy output of the program is given in Fig. 14-9 for two values of A. The forecasts for A = 0.9 appear to be somewhat better than the forecasts for N = 0.2. This does not generalize, which is one of the major problems with exponential smoothing.

Example: Moving Average Versus Exponential Smoothing

Let's use the same data with the moving average technique and then with exponential smoothing program to show how smoothing can be used to forecast Dow Jones averages. The data is given in Fig. 14-10.

The results from the moving average program are given in Figs. 14-11 through 14-15. The results for the exponential smoothing program are given in Figs. 14-16 through 14-18 for the smoothing coefficients. You'll have to make up your own mind as to which value of the averaging time and the smoothing coefficient gives the best results.

The results are also plotted in Figs. 14-19 and 14-20 to show how the various methods follow the data. The long averaging time moving averages and the exponential smoothing with A = .1 show the trend of the data but miss the fine structure. The short averaging time moving average and the exponential smoothing with A = 0.9 follow the fluctuations in the data but are not very useful for finding trends. This behavior is general and not a function of the particular data set.

HIGHER ORDERS OF SMOOTHING

The preceding discussion covered the two simplest methods of smoothing. These methods have been found to work well and inexpensively in many situations. However, the methods are not useful if the underlying pattern of data is complex. Higher forms of smoothing have to be used in such cases. These have many of the same advantages as the simple smoothing methods, and have the advantage of being amenable to more complex data patterns. Higher order smoothing methods can be used effectively with data that exhibit a trend. Unfortunately, the methods are nonstatistical and are difficult to evaluate in exact terms. The two simplest higher order techniques are double moving average and double exponential smoothing, discussed below.

DOUBLE MOVING AVERAGE

The first step in using double moving average is to compute the single moving average for the data. The next step is to compute a second moving average of the moving average. The forecast is made by taking the difference between the single and double moving average and then using this difference to adjust the single moving average to improve the forecast.

```
RESULTS
              PERIOD      PRICE OF SAMS INC.   FORECAST   ABS. VALUE OF ERROR
               1970            20              0             20
               1971            14              20            6
               1972            20              18.8          1.2
               1973            19.8            19.04         .76
               1974            32              19.192        12.808
               1975            18              21.7536       3.7536
               1976            15              21.0029       6.00288
               1977            12              19.8023       7.8023
               1978            20              18.2418       1.75816
               1979            25              18.5935       6.40653
               2980            28              19.8748       8.12522
               1981            25              21.4998       3.50018
               1982                            22.1999


              RESULTS OF EXPONENTIAL SMOOTHING WITH A =   .9


EXAMPLE OF EXPONENTIAL SMOOTHING
PROJECTION OF PRICE OF SAMS INC TO 1982


RESULTS
              PERIOD      PRICE OF SAMS INC.   FORECAST   ABS. VALUE OF ERROR
               1970            20              0             20
               1971            14              20            6
               1972            20              14.6          5.4
               1973            19.8            19.46         .339998
               1974            32              19.766        12.234
               1975            18              30.7766       12.7766
               1976            15              19.2777       4.27766
               1977            12              15.4278       3.42777
               1978            20              12.3428       7.65722
               1979            25              19.2343       5.76572
               2980            28              24.4234       3.57657
               1981            25              27.6423       2.64234
               1982                            25.2642
```

Fig. 14-9. Exponential smoothing example results for two values of A.

YEAR	DJI CLOSING AVERAGE	YEAR	DJI CLOSING AVERAGE	YEAR	DJI CLOSING AVERAGE	YEAR	DJI CLOSING AVERAGE
1981	875.00	1973	850.86	1965	840.36	1957	419.79
1980	963.99	1972	1020.02	1964	766.08	1956	462.35
1979	838.74	1971	890.20	1963	646.79	1955	388.2
1978	805.01	1970	838.92	1962	535.76	1954	279.87
1977	831.17	1969	800.36	1961	610.25	1953	255.49
1976	1004.65	1968	943.75	1960	566.05	1952	256.35
1975	852.41	1967	905.11	1959	574.46	1951	238.9
1974	616.24	1966	744.32	1958	436.84		

Fig. 14-10. Dow Jones Industrial closing averages from 1951 through 1981 (courtesy *Barron's*, July 26, 1981).

RESULTS

PERIOD	DJI CLOSE	FORECAST	ABS. VALUE OF ERROR
1951	238.99	0	238.99
1952	256.35	0	256.35
1953	255.49	247.67	7.81999
1954	279.87	255.92	23.95
1955	388.2	267.68	120.52
1956	462.35	334.035	128.315
1957	419.79	425.275	5.48505
1958	436.89	441.07	4.18002
1959	574.46	428.34	146.12
1960	566.05	505.675	60.375
1961	610.25	570.255	39.995
1962	535.76	588.15	52.39
1963	646.79	573.005	73.785
1964	766.08	591.275	174.805
1965	840.59	706.435	134.155
1966	744.32	803.335	59.015
1967	905.11	792.455	112.655
1968	943.75	824.715	119.035
1969	800.36	924.43	124.07
1970	838.92	872.055	33.135
1971	890.2	819.64	70.56
1972	1020.02	864.56	155.46
1973	850.86	955.11	104.25
1974	616.24	935.44	319.2
1975	852.41	733.55	118.86
1976	1004.65	734.325	270.325
1977	831.17	928.53	97.36
1978	805.01	917.91	112.9
1979	838.74	818.09	20.65
1980	963.99	821.875	142.115
1981	875	901.365	26.3651
1982		919.495	

Fig. 14-11. Moving average results for Dow Jones Industrial for 2 periods.

RESULTS

PERIOD	DJI CLOSE	FORECAST	ABS. VALUE OF ERROR
1951	238.99	0	238.99
1952	256.35	0	256.35
1953	255.49	0	255.49
1954	279.87	250.277	29.5933
1955	388.2	263.903	124.297
1956	462.35	307.853	154.497
1957	419.79	376.807	42.9833
1958	436.89	423.447	13.4433
1959	574.46	439.677	134.783
1960	566.05	477.047	89.0033
1961	610.25	525.8	84.45
1962	535.76	583.587	47.8267
1963	646.79	570.687	76.1033
1964	766.08	597.6	168.48
1965	840.59	649.543	191.047
1966	744.32	751.153	6.83331
1967	905.11	783.663	121.447
1968	943.75	830.007	113.743
1969	800.36	864.393	64.0333
1970	838.92	883.073	44.1533
1971	890.2	861.01	29.19
1972	1020.02	843.16	176.86
1973	850.86	916.38	65.5201
1974	616.24	920.36	304.12
1975	852.41	829.04	23.3699
1976	1004.65	773.17	231.48
1977	831.17	824.433	6.73669
1978	805.01	896.077	91.0667
1979	838.74	880.277	41.5366
1980	963.99	824.973	139.017
1981	875	869.247	5.75324
1982		892.577	

Fig. 14-12. Moving average results for Dow Jones Industrial for 3 periods.

RESULTS

PERIOD	DJI CLOSE	FORECAST	ABS. VALUE OF ERROR
1951	238.99	0	238.99
1952	256.35	0	256.35
1953	255.49	0	255.49
1954	279.87	0	279.87
1955	388.2	0	388.2
1956	462.35	283.78	178.57
1957	419.79	328.452	91.338

Fig. 14-13. Moving average results for Dow Jones Industrial for 5 periods (continued on page 195).

RESULTS

PERIOD	DJI CLOSE	FORECAST	ABS. VALUE OF ERROR
1958	436.89	361.14	75.75
1959	574.46	397.42	177.04
1960	566.05	456.338	109.712
1961	610.25	491.908	118.342
1962	535.76	521.488	14.272
1963	646.79	544.682	102.108
1964	766.08	586.662	179.418
1965	840.59	624.986	215.604
1966	744.32	679.894	64.426
1967	905.11	706.708	198.402
1968	943.75	780.578	163.172
1969	800.36	839.97	39.61
1970	838.92	846.826	7.90594
1971	890.2	846.492	43.708
1972	1020.02	875.668	144.352
1973	850.86	898.65	47.7901
1974	616.24	880.072	263.832
1975	852.41	843.248	9.16193
1976	1004.65	845.946	158.704
1977	831.17	868.836	37.666
1978	805.01	831.066	26.056
1979	838.74	821.896	16.8441
1980	963.99	866.396	97.5939
1981	875.	888.712	13.7121
1982		862.782	

Fig. 14-13. Continued from page 194.

RESULTS

PERIOD	DJI	FORECAST	ABS. VALUE OF ERROR
1951	238.99	0	238.99
1952	256.35	0	256.35
1953	255.49	0	255.49
1954	279.87	0	279.87
1955	388.2	0	388.2
1956	462.35	0	462.35
1957	419.79	0	419.79
1958	436.89	0	436.89
1959	574.46	0	574.46
1960	566.05	368.043	198.007
1961	610.25	404.383	205.867
1962	535.76	443.706	92.0544
1963	646.79	474.847	171.943

Fig. 14-14. Moving average results for Dow Jones Industrial for 9 periods (continued on page 196).

RESULTS

PERIOD	DJI	FORECAST	ABS. VALUE OF ERROR
1964	766.08	515.616	250.464
1965	840.36	557.602	282.758
1966	744.32	599.603	144.717
1967	905.11	635.662	269.448
1968	943.75	687.687	256.063
1969	800.36	728.719	71.6411
1970	838.92	754.753	84.1667
1971	890.2	780.161	110.039
1972	1020.02	819.543	200.477
1973	850.86	861.013	10.1534
1974	616.24	870.433	254.193
1975	852.41	845.531	6.87891
1976	1004.65	857.541	147.109
1977	831.17	868.601	37.4311
1978	805.01	856.092	51.0822
1979	838.74	856.609	17.8688
1980	963.99	856.589	107.401
1981	875	864.788	10.2122
1982		848.675	

Fig. 14-14. Continued from page 195.

RESULTS

PERIOD	DJI CLOSE	FORECAST	ABS. VALUE OF ERROR
1951	238.99	0	238.99
1952	256.35	0	256.35
1953	255.49	0	255.49
1954	279.87	0	279.87
1955	388.2	0	388.2
1956	462.35	0	462.35
1957	419.79	0	419.79
1958	436.89	0	436.89
1959	574.46	0	574.46
1960	566.05	0	566.05
1961	610.25	0	610.25
1962	535.76	0	535.76
1963	646.79	0	646.79
1964	766.08	0	766.08
1965	840.59	0	840.59
1966	744.32	485.194	259.126
1967	905.11	518 883	386.227
1968	943.75	562.133	381.617
1969	800.36	608.017	192.343
1970	838.92	642.717	196.203

Fig. 14-15. Moving average for Dow Jones Industrial for 15 periods (continued on page 197).

RESULTS

PERIOD	DJI CLOSE	FORECAST	ABS. VALUE OF ERROR
1971	890.2	672.765	217.435
1972	1020.02	701.288	318.732
1973	850.86	741.303	109.557
1974	616.24	768.901	152.661
1975	852.41	771.687	80.7233
1976	1004.65	790.777	213.873
1977	831.17	817.071	14.0994
1978	805.01	836.765	31.7547
1979	838.74	847.313	8.57263
1980	963.99	852.157	111.833
1981	875	860.384	14.6165
1982		869.096	

Fig. 14-15. Continued from page 196.

RESULTS

PERIOD	DJI YEAR END CLOSE	FORECAST	ABS. VALUE OF ERROR
1951	238.99	0	238.99
1952	256.35	238.99	17.36
1953	255.49	240.726	14.764
1954	279.87	242.202	37.6676
1955	388.2	245.969	142.231
1956	462.35	260.192	202.158
1957	419.79	280.408	139.382
1958	436.89	294.346	142.544
1959	574.46	308.601	265.859
1960	566.05	335.187	230.863
1961	610.25	358.273	251.977
1962	535.76	383.471	152.289
1963	646.79	398.7	248.09
1964	766.08	423.509	342.571
1965	840.59	457.766	382.824
1966	744.32	496.048	248.272
1967	905.11	520.875	384.235
1968	943.75	559.299	384.451
1969	800.36	597.744	202.616
1970	838.92	618.006	220.915
1971	890.2	640.097	250.103
1972	1020.02	665.107	354.913
1973	850.86	700.599	150.261
1974	616.24	715.625	99.3847
1975	852.41	705.686	146.724
1976	1004.65	720.359	284.291

Fig. 14-16. Exponential smoothing results using .1 smoothing coefficient (continued on page 198).

RESULTS

PERIOD	DJI YEAR END CLOSE	FORECAST	ABS. VALUE OF ERROR
1977	831.17	748.788	82.3823
1978	805.01	757.026	47.9841
1979	838.74	761.824	76.9157
1980	963.99	769.516	194.474
1981	875	788.963	86.0367
1982		797.567	

Fig. 14-16. Continued from page 197.

RESULTS

PERIOD	DJI YEAR END CLOSE	FORECAST	ABS. VALUE OF ERROR
1951	238.99	0	238.99
1952	256.35	238.99	17.36
1953	255.49	247.67	7.81999
1954	279.87	251.58	28.29
1955	388.2	265.725	122.475
1956	462.35	326.963	135.387
1957	419.79	394.656	25.1337
1958	436.89	407.223	29.6668
1959	574.46	422.057	152.403
1960	566.05	498.258	67.7917
1961	610.25	532.154	78.0958
1962	535.76	571.202	35.4421
1963	646.79	553.481	93.3089
1964	766.08	600.136	165.944
1965	840.59	683.108	157.482
1966	744.32	761.849	17.5289
1967	905.11	753.084	152.026
1968	943.75	829.097	114.653
1969	800.36	886.424	86.0637
1970	838.92	843.392	4.4718
1971	890.2	841.156	49.0441
1972	1020.02	865.678	154.342
1973	850.86	942.849	91.989
1974	616.24	896.855	280.615
1975	852.41	756.547	95.8627
1976	1004.65	804.479	200.171
1977	831.17	904.564	73.3943
1978	805.01	867.867	62.8572
1979	838.74	836.439	2.30145
1980	963.99	837.589	126.401
1981	875	900.79	25.7897
1982		887.895	

Fig. 14-17. Exponential smoothing results using .5 smoothing coefficient.

RESULTS

PERIOD	DJI YEAR END CLOSE	FORECAST	ABS. VALUE OF ERROR
1951	238.99	0	238.99
1952	256.35	238.99	17.36
1953	255.49	254.614	875992
1954	279.87	255.402	24.4676
1955	388.2	277.423	110.777
1956	462.35	377.122	85.2277
1957	419.79	453.827	34.0373
1958	436.89	423.194	13.6963
1959	574.46	435.52	138.94
1960	566.05	560.566	5.48395
1961	610.25	565.502	44.7484
1962	535.76	605.775	70.0151
1963	646.79	542.762	104.028
1964	766.08	636.387	129.693
1965	840.59	753.111	87.4794
1966	744.32	831.842	87.5221
1967	905.11	753.072	152.038
1968	943.75	889.906	53.8438
1969	800.36	938.366	138.006
1970	838.92	814.161	24.7595
1971	890.2	836.444	53.7559
1972	1020.02	884.824	135.196
1973	850.86	1006.5	155.641
1974	616.24	866.424	250.184
1975	852.41	641.258	211.152
1976	1004.65	831.295	173.355
1977	831.17	987.315	156.144
1978	805.01	846.784	41.7745
1979	838.74	809.187	29.5526
1980	963.99	835.785	128.205
1981	875	951.17	76.1696
1982		882.617	

Fig. 14-18. Exponential smoothing results using .9 smoothing coefficient.

The arithmetic involved in calculating the moving averages and the correction factor is rather tedious and is well suited for computer calculation.

DOUBMOV/BAS PROGRAM

A BASIC program for double moving average forecasting is DOUBMOV/BAS on page 201.

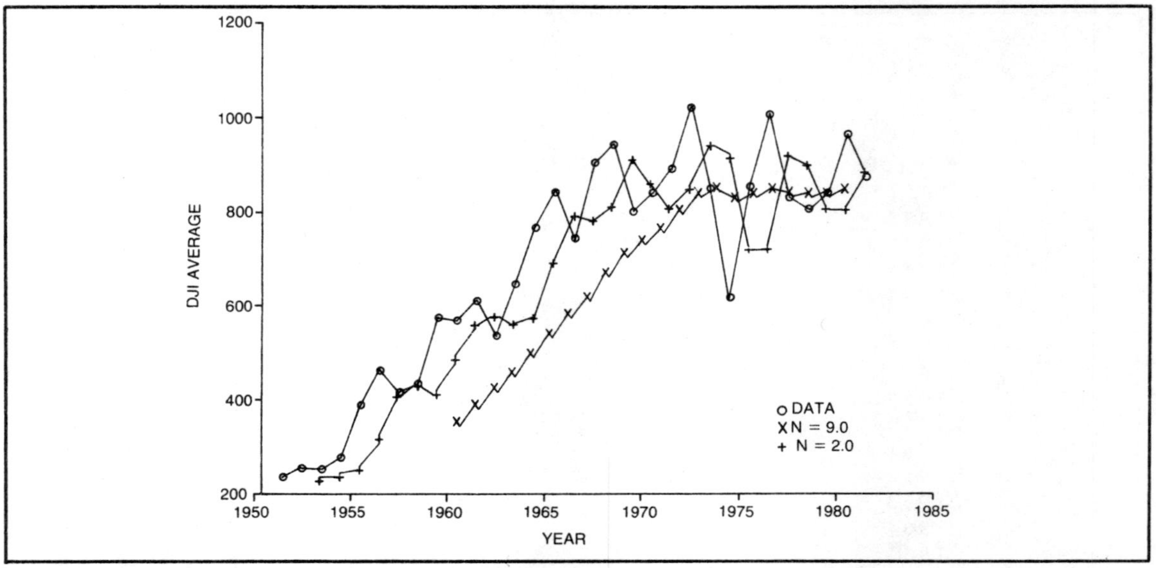

Fig. 14-19. Plot of moving average results for Dow Jones Industrial example.

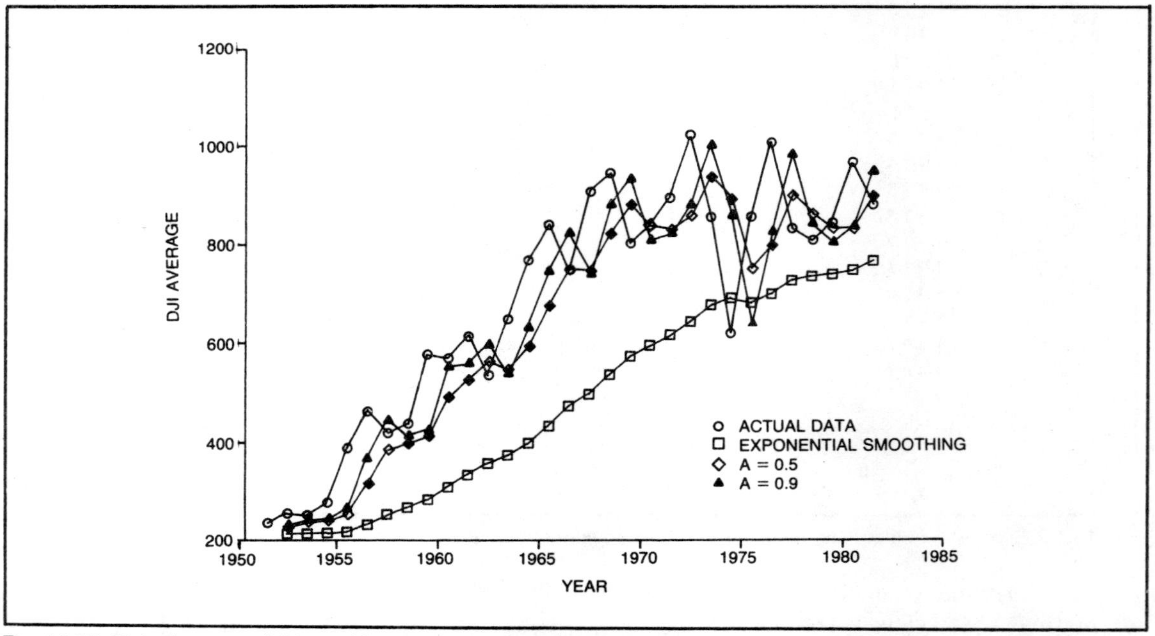

Fig. 14-20. Plot of exponential smoothing results for Dow Jones Industrial example.

DOUBMOV/BAS Listing

```
10 REM ***********************************
20 REM DOUBLE MOVING AVERAGE PROGRAM
30 REM FILENAME DOUBMOV/BAS
40 REM WRITTEN IN MICROSOFT BASIC
50 REM VERSION 1.0 BY LES 07/04/82
60 REM TESTED ON TRS-80 MODEL I WITH DISK
70 REM ***********************************
80 REM VARIABLES P = PERIOD, Y= FORECAST VARIABLE
90 REM S1 = FIRST MOVING AVERAGE
100 REM S2 = SECOND MOVING AVERAGE
110 REM N NUMBER OF DATA POINTS
120 REM NA NUMBER OF POINTS IN AVERAGE
130 REM F IS THE FORECAST
140 REM R IS FOR REMARKS
150 CLEAR 100 : REM CLEAR STRING SPACE MAY HAVE TO BE
160 REM CHANGED DEPENDING ON VERSION OF BASIC
170 CLS:REM CLEAR SCREEN CHANGE AS NECESSARY
180 DEFINT I,J,K,N : REM DEFINE I,J,K,AND N AS INTEGERS
190 DEFSTR R
200 DIM R(3),P(100),Y(100),S1(100),S2(100),F(100)
210 DIM A(100), B(100)
220 PRINT "PRESS D TO READ DATA FROM DISK K TO ENTER DATA FROM KEY BOARD"
230 Y$ = INKEY$ : IF Y$ ="" THEN 230
240 IF Y$ = "K" THEN 280
250 IF Y$ = "D" THEN GOSUB 1390 : GOTO 290
260 PRINT "PLEASE PRESS K OR D"
270 GOTO 230
280 GOSUB 830 : REM GO TO DATA ENTRY SUBROUTINE
290 GOSUB 970 :REM DATA CHECK SUBROUTINE
300 CLS
310 INPUT "ENTER NUMBER OF PERIOD TO BE INCLUDED IN AVERAGE ":NA
320 FOR J = NA TO N
330     S1(J) = 0
340     FOR J1 = J TO J - NA +1 STEP -1
350             S1(J) = S1(J) +Y(J1)
360     NEXT J1
370     S1(J) = S1(J)/NA
380 NEXT J
390 REM NOW DO SECOND MOVING AVERAGE
400 FOR J = NA*2-1 TO N
410     S2(J)=0
420     FOR J1 = J TO J-NA+1 STEP -1
430             S2(J) = S2(J) + S1(J1)
```

```
440      NEXT J1
450      S2(J) = S2(J)/NA
460 NEXT J
470 REM NOW CALCULATE A AND B
480 FOR J = NA*2 -1  TO N
490      A(J) = 2*S1(J) - S2(J)
500      B(J) = 2/(NA-1)*(S1(J)-S2(J))
510 NEXT J
520 CLS
530 INPUT "ENTER NUMBER OF PERIODS TO BE FORECAST";M
540 FOR J = 2*NA TO N
550      F(J+M) = A(J) + B(J) * M
560 NEXT J
570 CLS
580 PRINT "RESULTS "
590 FOR J=NA*2-1 TO N
600      PRINT P(J),Y(J),F(J)
610 NEXT J
620 FOR J = N+1 TO N + M
630      PRINT P(N)+J-N,F(J)
640 NEXT J
650 PRINT "PRESS H FOR HARD COPY "
660 Y$ = INKEY$: IF Y$= "" THEN 660
670 IF Y$ = "H" THEN GOSUB 1180
680 PRINT "DO YOU WANT TO CHANGE AVERAGING TIME "
690 GOSUB 1120
700 IF Y$ = "Y" THEN INPUT "ENTER NEW AVERAGING TIME ";NA ELSE 720
710 GOTO 320
720 PRINT "DO YOU WANT TO CHANGE NUMBER OF PERIODS TO FORECAST "
730 GOSUB 1120
740 IF Y$ = "N" THEN 770
750 INPUT "ENTER NEW VALUE OF M ";M
760 GOTO 540
770 PRINT "DO YOU WANT TO DO ANOTHER ONE"
780 GOSUB 1120
790 IF Y$ = "N" THEN END
800 GOTO 220
810 STOP
820 STOP
830 CLS
840 INPUT "ENTER NAME FOR FORECAST ";R(1)
850 INPUT "ENTER COMMENTS ";R(2)
860 INPUT "ENTER NAME OF FORECAST VARIABLE ";R(2)
870 I=1
```

```
880 PRINT "ENTER PERIOD -99 TO END PRESENT VALUE IN ()
    (" P(I);")";
890 INPUT P(I)
900 IF P(I) = -99 THEN 950
910 PRINT "ENTER VALUE OF FORECAST VARIABLE (";Y(I);")";
920 INPUT Y(I)
930 I=I+1
940 GOTO 880
950 N = I - 1
960 RETURN
970 CLS
980 PRINT "PLEASE REVIEW DATA TO BE SURE THEY ARE CORRECT."
990 FOR J = 1 TO N
1000      PRINT P(J),Y(J)
1010     IF J = N THEN PRINT "ARE THESE CORRECT Y OR N?":GOTO1030
1020      IF INT(J/12) -J/12 = 0 THEN PRINT "ARE THESE CORRECT"
          ELSE 1110
1030      GOSUB 1120 : IF Y$="Y" THEN 1090
1040      INPUT "ENTER INDEX NUMBER TO BE CORRECTED ";J1
1050      INPUT "ENTER CORRECT VALUE OF PERIOD ";P(J1)
1060      INPUT "ENTER CORRECT VALUE OF FORECAST VARIABLE ";Y(J1)
1070      CLS
1080      GOTO 970
1090     CLS
1100 NEXT J
1110 RETURN
1120 REM SUBROUTINE TO GET Y OR N
1130 Y$ = INKEY$: IF Y$ ="" THEN 1130
1140 IF Y$="N" THEN RETURN
1150 IF Y$="Y" THEN RETURN
1160 PRINT "PLEASE ANSWER Y OR N"
1170 GOTO 1120
1180 REM HARDCOPY SUBROUTINE
1190 CLS
1200 PRINT "PRESS ANY KEY WHEN PRINTER IS READY "
1210 Y$ = INKEY$ : IF Y$ = "" THEN 1210
1220 LPRINT
1230 LPRINT TAB(10);"RESULTS OF DOUBLE MOVING AVERAGE "
1240 FOR J = 1 TO 3
1250    LPRINT TAB(10);R(J)
1260 NEXT J
1270 LPRINT TAB(10);"NUMBER OF AVERAGING PERIODS = ";NA
1280 LPRINT
1290 LPRINT TAB(10);"PERIOD
```

```
";TAB(25);"VARIABLE";TAB(35);"FORECAST";TAB(45)"ERROR"
1300 FOR J = 1 TO N
1310    LPRINT TAB(10);P(J);TAB(25);Y(J);TAB(35);
        F(J);TAB(45);F(J)-Y(J
1320 NEXT J
1330 FOR J = N+1 TO N +M
1340     LPRINT TAB(10);P(N)+J-N;TAB(35);F(J)
1350 NEXT J
1360 LPRINT
1370 RETURN
1380 END
1390 INPUT "ENTER NAME OF FORECAST ";R(1)
1400 INPUT "ENTER REMARKS ";R(2)
1410 INPUT "ENTER NAME OF VARIABLE ";R(3)
1420 OPEN "I",1,"DATA/DAT"
1430 INPUT#1,N
1440 FOR J= N TO 1 STEP -1
1450     INPUT#1 P(J),Y(J)
1460 NEXT J
1470 I = J
1480 CLOSE
1490 RETURN
```

Example: Double Moving Average

Use double moving average to forecast the behavior of the stock market using the Dow Jones Industrial Average data in Fig. 14-10. Data entry for the program can be done either by reading a disk file or by entering data from a keyboard. The disk file must be in the format of the number of data points, N, followed by pairs of (X, Y) data. If data is entered from the keyboard, answer the questions. To conclude the data entry, enter −99 for X. The program provides a method for checking and correcting the data. Full instructions are provided in the program. After all data has been entered and corrected, you are asked to enter the number of periods to include in the moving average, and then how many periods you want to forecast. After all questions are answered, the computer calculates the moving averages, the correction factors, and the forecast. Forecasts and historical data are displayed on the crt. You are asked if you want hard copy. The line printer output includes all data shown on the crt and the value of the forecast errors for the historical data. These values are useful for defining the amount of smoothing that is best for a given set of data.

The hard copy for the example for several values of the number of averaging periods is presented in Fig. 14-21 through 14-23. All results are for a one-period forecast.

The results of the calculations are plotted in Fig. 14-24. The plot shows the behavior of the forecast and the degree of smoothing obtained for various values of the number of averaging periods. The plot shows that double moving average does remove the noise from the data and does follow the trend fairly well.

A major problem with the double moving average technique is that the method requires 2N (N is the number of averaging periods) data points before the method can be used. For a new business, this

PERIOD	VARIABLE	FORECAST	ERROR
1951	238.99	0	-238.99
1952	256.35	0	-256.35
1953	255.49	0	-255.49
1954	279.87	0	-279.87
1955	388.2	285.32	-102.88
1956	462.35	433.568	-28.7825
1957	419.79	562.135	142.345
1958	436.89	464.763	27.8725
1959	574.46	409.245	-165.215
1960	566.05	621.678	55.6276
1961	610.25	667.125	56.8749
1962	535.76	614.993	79.2326
1963	646.79	550.288	-96.5025
1964	766.08	618.68	-147.4
1965	840.59	879.175	38.5848
1966	744.32	948.685	204.365
1967	905.11	776.135	-128.975
1968	943.75	873.105	-70.645
1969	800.36	1074	273.642
1970	838.92	793.493	-45.4276
1971	890.2	741.018	-149.183
1972	1020.02	931.94	-88.0799
1973	850.86	1090.94	240.075
1974	616.24	905.935	289.695
1975	852.41	430.715	-421.695
1976	1004.65	735.488	-269.162
1977	831.17	1219.84	388.668
1978	805.01	901.98	96.97
1979	838.74	668.36	-170.38
1980	963.99	827.553	-136.437
1981	875	1020.6	145.6
1982		946.69	

Fig. 14-21. Double moving average for results for 2 periods of Dow Jones Industrial.

PERIOD	VARIABLE	FORECAST	ERROR
1951	238.99	0	-238.99
1952	256.35	0	-256.35
1953	255.49	0	-255.49
1954	279.87	0	-279.87
1955	388.2	0	-388.2
1956	462.35	0	-462.35
1957	419.79	0	-419.79
1958	436.89	0	-436.89
1959	574.46	531.564	-42.8962
1960	566.05	581.406	15.3558
1961	610.25	586.864	-23.3858
1962	535.76	647.438	111.678
1963	646.79	653.008	6.21808
1964	766.08	652.753	-113.327
1965	840.59	727.597	-112.993
1966	744.32	818.493	74.1735
1967	905.11	883.444	-21.6661
1968	943.75	962.194	18.4438
1969	800.36	989.506	189.146
1970	838.92	899.736	60.816
1971	890.2	911.724	21.5236
1972	1020.02	879.166	-140.854
1973	850.86	917.957	67.0974
1974	616.24	930.118	313.878
1975	852.41	793.208	-59.2019
1976	1004.65	781.942	-222.708
1977	831.17	795.168	-36.0019
1978	805.01	812 826	7.81574
1979	838.74	926.598	87.8574
1980	963.99	902.897	-61.0932
1981	875	863.837	-11.1629
1982		874.487	

Fig. 14-22. Double moving average results for 4 periods of Dow Jones Industrial.

PERIOD	VARIABLE	FORECAST	ERROR
1951	238.99	0	-238 99
1952	256.35	0	-256 35
1953	255.49	0	-255.49
1954	279.87	0	-279.87
1955	388.2	0	-388.2
1956	462.35	0	-462.35
1957	419.79	0	-419.79
1958	436.89	0	-436.89
1959	574.46	0	-574.46
1960	566.05	0	-566.05
1961	610.25	0	-610.25
1962	535.76	0	-535.76
1963	646.79	0	-646.79
1964	766.08	0	-766.08
1965	840.59	0	-840.59
1966	744.32	0	-744.32
1967	905.11	0	-905.11
1968	943.75	0	-943.75
1969	800.36	938.574	138.214
1970	838.92	948.486	109.566
1971	890.2	958.92	68.7196
1972	1020.02	999.651	-20.3687
1973	850.86	1044.98	194.123
1974	616.24	1022.73	406.486
1975	852.41	932.486	80.0755
1976	1004.65	928.695	-75.955
1977	831.17	928.457	97.2867
1978	805.01	882.625	77.6145
1979	838.74	869.644	30.9038
1980	963.99	858.988	-105 002
1981	875	871.155	-3.84534
1982		836.617	

Fig. 14-23. Double moving average for 9 periods of Dow Jones Industrial.

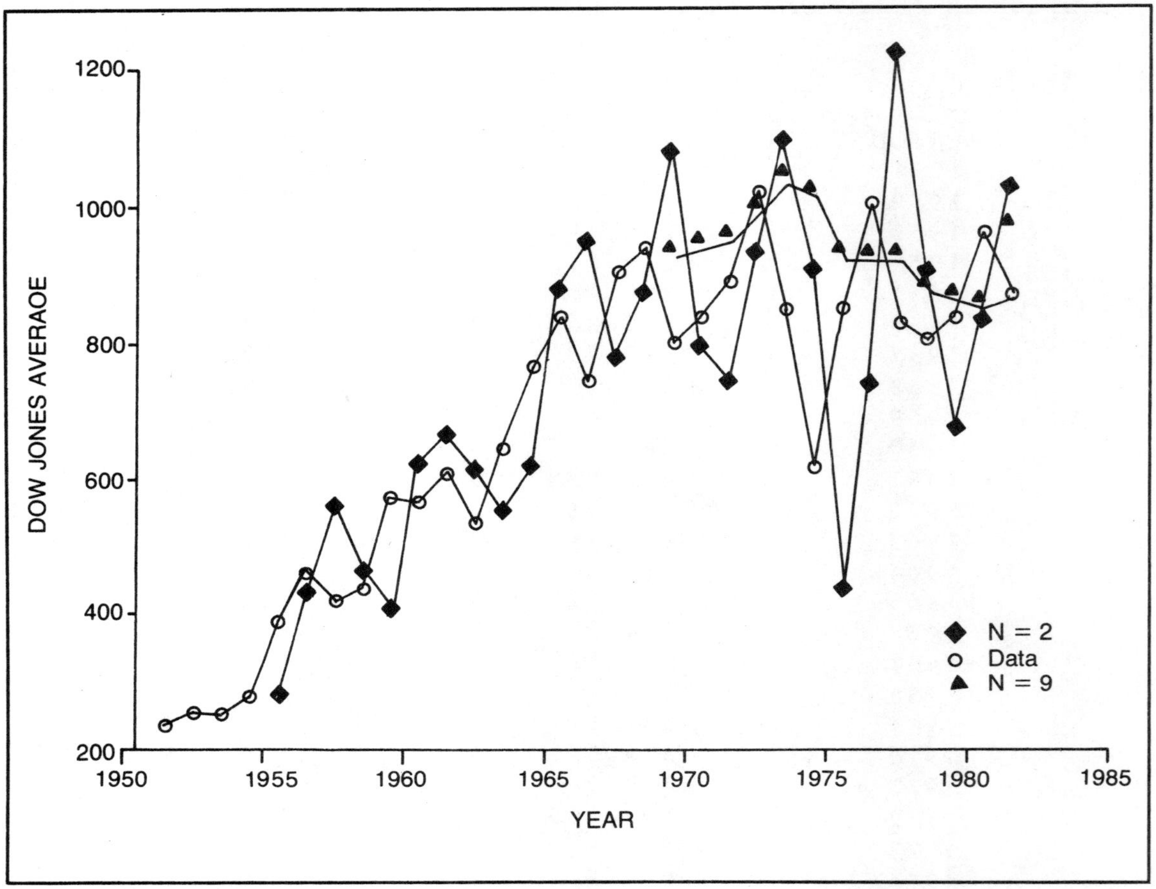

Fig. 14-24. Plot of double moving average results for Dow Jones Industrial.

requirement means that several quarters, months, or even years of data must be obtained before the technique can be used.

DOUBLE EXPONENTIAL SMOOTHING

As noted above, the double moving average technique is limited by the amount of data required. Double moving average technique also has the same limitation as single moving average in that it gives weight to all data. Double exponential smoothing provides the same basic tool as double moving average, with the advantage that less data is required (only three points) and recent data is weighted the most. Thus in most cases double exponential smoothing is a better technique than double moving average.

The concept of double exponential smoothing is the same as exponential smoothing. First the data is smoothed with exponential smoothing, then the smoothed data is smoothed again. The difference between the two smoothings is used to adjust the original smoothing to give a forecast. The adjustment step is basically the same as that used in double moving average.

Double exponential smoothing applies to data sets with a trend. The method can also be used in the case where the data pattern is horizontal. Finally, the method can adjust rapidly to a jump change in the pattern. All in all this is a very good technique.

DOUBEXP/BAS PROGRAM

A BASIC program for double exponential smoothing, DOUBEXP/BAS, follows.

DOUBEXP/BAS Listing

```
10 REM **********************************
20 REM DOUBLE EXPONENTIAL SMOOTHING PROGRAM
30 REM FILENAME DOUBEXP/BAS
40 REM WRITTEN IN MICROSOFT BASIC
50 REM VERSION 1.0 BY LES 07/04/82
60 REM TESTED ON TRS-80 MODEL I WITH DISK
70 REM **********************************
80 REM VARIABLES P = PERIOD, Y= FORECAST VARIABLE
90 REM S1 = FIRST EXPONENTIAL SMOOTHING
100 REM S2 = SECOND EXPONENTIAL SMOOTHING
110 REM N NUMBER OF DATA POINTS
120 REM NA NUMBER OF POINTS IN AVERAGE
130 REM F IS THE FORECAST
140 REM R IS FOR REMARKS
150 CLEAR 100 : REM CLEAR STRING SPACE MAY HAVE TO BE
160 REM CHANGED DEPENDING ON VERSION OF BASIC
170 CLS:REM CLEAR SCREEN CHANGE AS NECESSARY
180 DEFINT I,J,K,N : REM DEFINE I,J,K,AND N AS INTEGERS
190 DEFSTR R
200 DIM R(3),P(100),Y(100),S1(100),S2(100),F(100)
210 DIM A(100), B(100)
220 PRINT "PRESS D  TO READ DATA FROM DISK  K TO ENTER  DATA
FROM KEY BOARD"
230 Y$ = INKEY$ : IF Y$ ="" THEN 230
240 IF Y$ = "K" THEN 280
250 IF Y$ = "D" THEN GOSUB 1270 : GOTO 290
260 PRINT "PLEASE PRESS K OR D"
270 GOTO 230
280 GOSUB 710 : REM GO TO DATA ENTRY SUBROUTINE
290 GOSUB 850 :REM DATA CHECK SUBROUTINE
300 CLS
310 INPUT "ENTER SMOOTHING FACTOR "; AL
320 S1(1) = Y(1)
330 S2(1) = Y(1)
340 FOR J = 2 TO N
```

```
350    S1(J) = AL * Y(J) + (1-AL)*S1(J-1)
360    S2(J) = AL * S1(J) + (1-AL)*S2(J-1)
370    A(J) = 2 * S1(J) - S2(J)
380    B(J) = AL/(1-AL)*(S1(J)-S2(J))
390 NEXT J
400 CLS
410 INPUT "ENTER NUMBER OF PERIODS TO BE FORECAST";M
420 FOR J = 2 TO N
430     F(J+M) = A(J) + B(J) * M
440 NEXT J
450 CLS
460 PRINT "RESULTS "
470 FOR J=1 TO N
480     PRINT P(J),Y(J),F(J)
490 NEXT J
500 FOR J = N+1 TO N + M
510     PRINT P(N)+J-N,F(J)
520 NEXT J
530 PRINT "PRESS H FOR HARD COPY "
540 Y$ = INKEY$: IF Y$= "" THEN 540
550 IF Y$ = "H" THEN GOSUB 1060
560 PRINT "DO YOU WANT TO CHANGE SMOOTHING FACTOR"
570 GOSUB 1000
580 IF Y$ = "Y"  THEN  INPUT "ENTER NEW SMOOTHING FACTOR";AL
ELSE 600
590 GOTO 340
600 PRINT  "DO YOU  WANT  TO  CHANGE NUMBER  OF  PERIODS  TO
FORECAST "
610 GOSUB 1000
620 IF Y$ = "N" THEN 650
630 INPUT "ENTER NEW VALUE OF M ";M
640 GOTO 420
650 PRINT "DO YOU WANT TO DO ANOTHER ONE"
660 GOSUB 1000
670 IF Y$ = "N" THEN END
680 GOTO 220
690 STOP
700 STOP
710 CLS
720 INPUT "ENTER NAME FOR FORECAST ";R(1)
730 INPUT "ENTER COMMENTS ";R(2)
740 INPUT "ENTER NAME OF FORECAST VARIABLE ";R(2)
750 I=1
760  PRINT  "ENTER  PERIOD  -99 TO END  PRESENT VALUE  IN ()
```

```
(";P(I);")";
770 INPUT P(I)
780 IF P(I) = -99 THEN 830
790 PRINT "ENTER VALUE OF FORECAST VARIABLE (";Y(I);")";
800 INPUT Y(I)
810 I=I+1
820 GOTO 760
830 N = I - 1
840 RETURN
850 CLS
860 PRINT "PLEASE REVIEW DATA TO BE SURE THEY ARE CORRECT."
870 FOR J = 1 TO N
880     PRINT P(J),Y(J)
890    IF J  =  N THEN  PRINT "ARE THESE CORRECT Y OR  N?"  :
GOTO910
900      IF  INT(J/12)  -J/12  =  0  THEN  PRINT  "ARE  THESE
CORRECT" ELSE 980
910     GOSUB 1000 : IF Y$="Y" THEN 970
920     INPUT "ENTER INDEX NUMBER TO BE CORRECTED ";J1
930     INPUT "ENTER CORRECT VALUE OF PERIOD ";P(J1)
940      INPUT  "ENTER  CORRECT  VALUE OF  FORECAST  VARIABLE
";Y(J1)
950     CLS
960     GOTO 850
970    CLS
980 NEXT J
990 RETURN
1000 REM SUBROUTINE TO GET Y OR N
1010 Y$ = INKEY$: IF Y$ ="" THEN 1010
1020 IF Y$="N" THEN RETURN
1030 IF Y$="Y" THEN RETURN
1040 PRINT "PLEASE ANSWER Y OR N"
1050 GOTO 1000
1060 REM HARDCOPY SUBROUTINE
1070 CLS
1080 PRINT "PRESS ANY KEY WHEN PRINTER IS READY "
1090 Y$ = INKEY$ : IF Y$ = "" THEN 1090
1100 LPRINT
1110   LPRINT   TAB(10);"RESULTS   OF   DOUBLE   EXPONENTIAL
SMOOTHING"
1120 FOR J = 1 TO 3
1130   LPRINT TAB(10);R(J)
1140 NEXT J
1150 LPRINT TAB(10);"SMOOTHING FACTOR ";AL
```

```
1160 LPRINT
1170 LPRINT TAB(10);"PERIOD ";TAB(25);"VARIABLE";TAB(35);"FORECAST";TAB(45)"ERROR"
1180 FOR J = 1 TO N
1190 LPRINT TAB(10) P(J);TAB(25);Y(J);TAB(35);F(J);TAB(45);F(J)-Y(J)
1200 NEXT J
1210 FOR J = N+1 TO N +M
1220    LPRINT TAB(10);P(N)+J-N;TAB(35);F(J)
1230 NEXT J
1240 LPRINT
1250 RETURN
1260 END
1270 INPUT "NAME OF FORECAST ";R(1)
1280 INPUT "REMARKS ";R(2)
1290 INPUT "NAME OF Y VARIABLE ";R(2)
1300 OPEN "I",1,"DATA/DAT"
1310 INPUT#1 N
1320 FOR J= N TO 1 STEP -1
1330    INPUT#1,P(J),Y(J)
1340 NEXT J
1350 I = J
1360 CLOSE
1370 RETURN
```

Example

Use the double exponential smoothing program to analyze the Dow Jones data given in Fig. 14-10. Data input for the program is the same as for the double moving average program. Data can be read from disk or entered from the keyboard. The disk data must be in the format: number of data points N, followed by pairs of (X, Y) data. If the data is entered from the keyboard, data entry is terminated by entering −99 for X. A routine for checking and correcting data is provided. After all data is entered, you are asked to enter the value of the smoothing coefficient and the number of periods to be forecast.

The results of using the program for several values of the smoothing parameter (A) are given in Figs. 14-25 through 14-27 and plotted in Fig. 14-28 to give you an idea of how the method smooths the data and follows the trend.

A major problem with double exponential smoothing is selection of the smoothing parameter. There is no general guidance for selecting the best value. As pointed out above, small values of the smoothing parameter follow the trend fairly well but miss most of the fluctuations; large values of the parameter follow the fluctuations but can miss the trends. The selection of the best value for the smoothing parameter is basically a trial and error procedure.

ADAPTIVE FILTERING

Adaptive filtering is another forecasting technique based on time series analysis. The idea of adaptive filtering is to use historical data to train the

PERIOD	VARIABLE	FORECAST	ERROR
1951	238.99	0	-238.99
1952	256.35	0	-256.35
1953	255.49	245.934	-9.55598
1954	279.87	250.451	-29.4192
1955	388.2	263.295	-124.905
1956	462.35	315.511	-146.84
1957	419.79	381.496	-38.294
1958	436.89	409.937	-26.9532
1959	574.46	435.373	-139.087
1960	566.05	506.741	-59.3092
1961	610.25	551.761	-58.4889
1962	535.76	598.826	63.0656
1963	646.79	599.608	-47.1821
1964	766.08	641.967	-124.113
1965	840.59	716.985	-123.605
1966	744.32	796.765	52.4448
1967	905.11	811.069	-94.0413
1968	943.75	881.869	-61.8806
1969	800.36	943.568	143.207
1970	838.92	925.706	86.7855
1971	890.2	924.684	34.484
1972	1020.02	941.112	-78.9083
1973	850.86	1001.52	150.657
1974	616.24	973.252	357.012
1975	852.41	856.419	4.00934
1976	1004.65	866.507	-138.143
1977	831.17	933.295	102.125
1978	805.01	909.502	104.492
1979	838.74	880.677	41.937
1980	963.99	872.694	-91.2957
1981	875	916.327	41.3273
1982		910.563	

Fig. 14-25. Double exponential smoothing results using .2 smoothing coefficient.

PERIOD	VARIABLE	FORECAST	ERROR
1951	238.99	0	-238.99
1952	256.35	0	-256.35
1953	255.49	256.35	.860016
1954	279.87	259.83	-20.04
1955	388.2	283.995	-104.205
1956	462.35	397.335	-65.015
1957	419.79	497.536	77.7463
1958	436.89	471.23	34.34
1959	574.46	468.893	-105.567
1960	566.05	597.878	31.8284
1961	610.25	615.86	5.61011
1962	535.76	652.103	116.343
1963	646.79	576.211	-70.5795
1964	766.08	658.155	-107.925
1965	840.59	795.09	-45.5004
1966	744.32	896.581	152.261
1967	905.11	811.686	-93.424
1968	943.75	934.411	-9.3393
1969	800.36	996.407	196.047
1970	838.92	855.352	16.4315
1971	890.2	844.9	-45.3002
1972	1020.02	892.072	-127.948
1973	850.86	1033.22	182.357
1974	616.24	896.044	279.804
1975	852.41	615.835	-236.575
1976	1004.65	782.054	-222.596
1977	831.17	993.438	162.267
1978	805.01	875.607	70.5966
1979	838.74	808.88	-29.8604
1980	963.99	824.961	-139.029
1981	875	957.676	82.6757
1982		903.443	

Fig. 14-26. Double exponential smoothing results using .5 smoothing coefficient.

PERIOD	VARIABLE	FORECAST	ERROR
1951	238.99	0	-238.99
1952	256.35	0	-256.35
1953	255.49	266.766	11.276
1954	279.87	259.835	-20.0352
1955	388.2	295.785	-92.4151
1956	462.35	460.365	-1.98465
1957	419.79	539.403	119.613
1958	436.89	425.154	-11.7355
1959	574.46	444.511	-129.949
1960	566.05	660.52	94.4699
1961	610.25	600.626	-9.62409
1962	535.76	646.822	111.062
1963	646.79	506.079	-140.711
1964	766.08	697.094	-68.9865
1965	840.59	863.403	22.8134
1966	744.32	926.985	182.665
1967	905.11	720.204	-184.907
1968	943.75	984.631	40.8807
1969	800.36	1006.14	205.778
1970	838.92	737.646	-101.274
1971	890.2	828.739	-61.4608
1972	1020.02	920.947	-99.0733
1973	850.86	1112.67	261.809
1974	616.24	790.386	174.146
1975	852.41	440.806	-411.604
1976	1004.65	916.973	-87.6776
1977	831.17	1138.28	307.113
1978	805.01	784.043	-20.9675
1979	838.74	758.178	-80.5617
1980	963.99	841.084	-122.906
1981	875	1043.3	168.3
1982		858.246	

Fig. 14-27. Double exponential smoothing results using .8 smoothing coefficient.

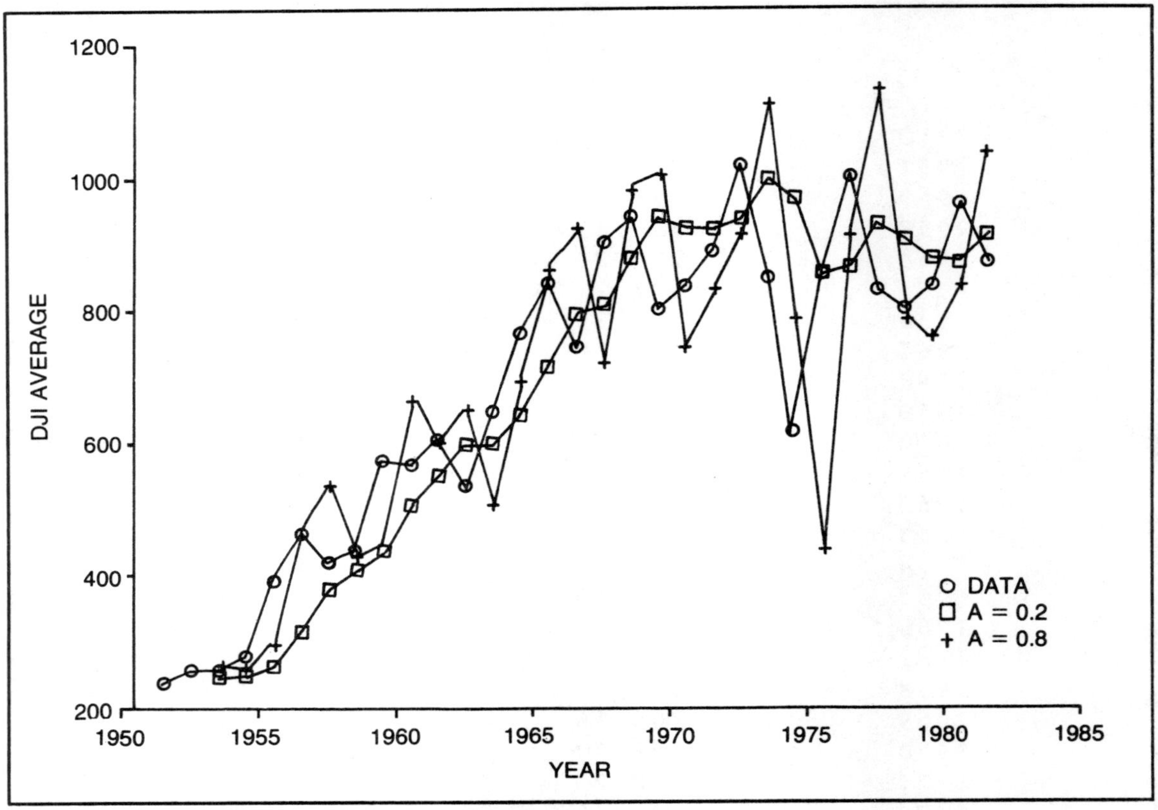

Fig. 14-28. Plot of double exponential smoothing results.

forecasting model to produce forecasts with minimum error. The model is then used to forecast the future. When future data is available it is added to the data pool and the model is retrained. Thus in principal, if sufficient data is available, the model should produce an accurate forecast and should produce a better forecast than some of the other techniques.

The basic steps in adaptive filtering are:

1. Collect historical data.

2. Determine the number of periods, N, to be used to smooth the data.

3. Use the first N data points to prepare a forecast for the N+1 period.

4. Calculate the error in the forecast.

5. Adjust the weights based on the error.

6. Repeat three, four, and five for all N historical data points.

7. Repeat all above steps until the error is zero or until a given number of iterations have been completed.

8. Make the forecast.

9. Continue to add data to the data base and continue to adjust the weights.

The adaptive filtering technique is more difficult to apply than previously discussed techniques, mainly because the computations are more detailed. However, since computers are capable of carrying out the calculations with little difficulty, the adaptive filtering technique can be a valuable tool.

ADAPT/BAS PROGRAM

A Microsoft BASIC program ADAPT/BAS is used for adaptive filtering. The program requires that data be read from a previously prepared disk file (a simple sequential file structure is used so tape files could easily be substituted for disk files). The program asks you for the number of periods to be used in the smoothing, then carries out the calculations and prepares the forecast for the next period. The listing follows.

ADAPT/BAS Listing

```
10 REM ********************************************
20 REM ADAPTIVE FILTERING FORECASTING
30 REM VERSION 1.0
40 REM WRITTEN IN MICROSOFT BASIC TESTED ON TRS-80 MODEL I
50 REM AND TRS-80 MODEL III DISK BASED SYSTEM
60 REM 07/22/82
70 REM BY L. F. SPARKS
80 REM REF INVESTMENT ANALYSIS WITH YOUR MICROCOMPUTER
90 REM PUBLISHED BY TAB BOOKS
100 REM NOTE THAT DATA ENTRY IS VIA A SEQUENTIAL DISK FILE
110 REM FILE STRUCTURE IS A$ AND B$ (TWO STRINGS)
120 REM N. NUMBER OF DATA POINTS
130 REM AND PAIRS OF X, Y DATA
140 REM ********************************************
150 CLEAR 1000 : REM CLEAR STRING SPACE
160 DEFINT I J,L N M
170 DIM X(100), Y(100), W(50), YN(100). F(100). E(100)
180 CLS  REM REPLACE WITH WHAT EVER IT TAKES TO CLEAR YOUR
SCREEN
190 PRINT
"=========================================================="
200 PRINT
210 PRINT "ADAPTIVE FILTERING FORECASTING PROGRAM
220 PRINT "VERSIONS 1.0 BY LES
230 PRINT
240 PRINT
"=========================================================="
250 LINEINPUT "ENTER THE NAME OF THE DISK FILE INCLUDING DRIVE
";F$
260 OPEN "I",1,F$
270 INPUT #1, A$, B$ :REM GET THE TWO STRINGS
280 INPUT #1, N
290 FOR I = 1 TO N
```

```
300      INPUT #1, X(I), Y(I)
310 NEXT I
320 GOSUB 1190 : REM CHECK DATA
330 CLS
340 INPUT "ENTER NUMBER OF PERIODS TO BE USED TO SMOOTH " P
350 REM NOW START THE CALCULATIONS
360 K = 1/P
370 FOR J=1 TO N
380     W(J) = 1/P
390 NEXT J
400 L = 100 : REM NUMBER OF INTERATIONS FOR TRAINING
410 CLS
420 PRINT "WORKING ON TRAINING
430 Z = 1E37
440 FOR L1 = 1 TO L
450      S = 0
460      H1 = 0
470      FOR I = P +1 TO  N
480              F = 0
490              FOR J1 = 1 TO P
500                      F = F + W(J1)*YN(I-J1)
510                      H1 = H1 + YN(I-J1)*YN(I-J1)
520              NEXT J1
530      H1 = SQR(H1)
540      E(I) = YN(I) - F
550      FOR J = 1 TO P
560              W(J) = W(J) + 2*K*E(I)/H1*YN(I-J)/H1
570      NEXT J
580      S = S + E(I)*E(I)
590 NEXT I
600 PRINT L1,S/(N-P+1),
610 FOR J = 1 TO P
620      PRINT W(J),
630 NEXT J
640 PRINT
650 IF S + .00001>Z THEN 680
660 Z = S
670 NEXT L1
680 CLS
690 INPUT "ENTER NUMBER OF FORECASTS "; M
700 CLS
710 FOR I=N+1 TO N+M
720      F= 0
730      FOR J = 1 TO P
```

```
740               F = F+W(J)*YN(I-J)
750      NEXT J
760     F(I) = F*HI
770     YN(I)=F
780 NEXT I
790 REM NOW DO FORECAST
800 CLS
810 PRINT "RESULTS OF FORECAST "
820 FOR J = N+1 TO N+M
830      X(J) = X(N)+J
840      PRINT X(J);TAB(20);F(J)
850 NEXT J
860 PRINT "PRESS H FOR HARDCOPY ANY OTHER KEY TO CONTINUE"
870 Y$ = INKEY$:IFY$="" THEN 870
880 IF Y$ =  H" THEN 950
890 CLS
900 PRINT "DO YOU WANT ANOTHER ONE Y OR N?"
910 Y$ = INKEY$: IF Y$ = "" THEN 910
920 IF Y$ ="Y" THEN XXX
930 IF Y$ <>"N" THEN PRINT "PLEASE ANSWER Y OR N":GOTO 900
940 END
950 PRINT
960 PRINT "HARD COPY ROUTINE. PRESS ANY KEY TO CONTINUE "
970 Y$ = INKEY$:IF Y$ = "" THEN 970
980 LPRINT " ADAPTIVE FILTERING OUTPUT"
990 LPRINT
1000 LPRINT A$
1010 LPRINT B$
1020 LPRINT
1030 LPRINT "INPUT DATA "
1040 LPRINT"PERIOD        VALUE"
1050 FOR I= 1 TO N
1060     LPRINT X(I),Y(I)
1070 NEXT I
1080 PRINT "PRESS ANY KEY WHEN NEXT PAGE IS READY"
1090 Y$ = INKEY$:IF Y$ = "" THEN 1090
1100 LPRINT
1110 LPRINT "RESULTS"
1120 LPRINT " PERIOD":TAB(25)·"FORECAST"
1130 FOR I= N+1 TO M
1140     LPRINT USING "#####";X(I);
1150     LPRINT USING "#####.###" F(I)
1160 NEXT I
1170 LPRINT
1180 RETURN
```

```
1190 REM ROUTINE TO NORMALIZE DATA
1200 HI = Y(1)
1210 FOR I=2 TO N
1220     IF Y(I)> HI THEN HI = Y(I)
1230 NEXT I
1240 FOR I=1 TO N
1250     YN(I) = Y(I)/HI
1260 NEXT I
1270 RETURN
```

MENU/BAS AND WRDAT/BAS PROGRAMS

A companion program for writing the disk files, WRDAT/BAS, and a menu program to drive the package, MENU/BAS, are also provided. The write data program is for the TRS-80 Model I or Model III and provides one of the best methods for entering data for a computer program. The program changes the screen into a multipage form to be used for entering data. The first page is used to enter remarks and information needed to identify the data. The rest of the pages are used to enter the data. You can move from page to page with the < and > keys and can move from column to column on a page with the left and right arrows. Move up and down a page with the up and down arrows. When you have entered all data, press the * key and you will be asked for the file name to store the data. You will also be asked if you want hard copy. After the data is stored on disk, program control is returned to menu the program.

The adaptive filtering program is based on work reported by Wheelwright and Makridakis in *Forecasting Methods for Management*, third edition, published by Wiley Interscience. They reported that best results are achieved if the data is normalized so that the values fall between zero and one. The program does this by dividing all data by the largest data value. The program stops the training if the error reduction becomes very small or after 100 iterations, whichever happens first. If you have large amounts of data, the program will take a long time to complete the training. If the slowness of the program bothers you, use Microsoft's BASIC compiler, BASCOM, to compile the program. The compiled program runs considerably faster. The MENU listing follows. The WRDAT listing begins on page 221.

MENU Listing

```
10 REM MENU PROGRAM TO BE USED WITH ADAPTIVE FILTERING
20 REM PRORAM
30 REM VERSION 1.0
40 REM MICROSOFT BASIC TESTED ON TRS-80 MODEL I AND III
50 REM WITH DISK BASIC
60 REM WRITTEN BY LES AUG 1982
70 REM ***********************************************
80 CLS
90 CLEAR 1000
100 A$ = STRING$(63,"=")
110 PRINT A$
120 PRINT "MENU FOR ADAPTIVE FILTERING PROGRAM
130 PRINT
```

```
140 PRINT "VERSION 1.0
150 PRINT
160 PRINT "WRITTEN BY LES
170 PRINT "REFERENCE INVESTMENT ANALYSIS WITH YOUR MICROCOMPUTER TAB BOOKS"
180 PRINT A$
190 PRINT "PRESS THE LETTER THAT CORRESPONDS TO THE PROGRAM
200 PRINT  YOU WANT TO RUN"
210 PRINT "<E>NTER DATA"
220 PRINT "<R>UN ADAPTIVE FILTERING PROGRAM "
230 PRINT A$
240 Y$ = INKEY$:IF Y$ = "" THEN 240
250 IF Y$ =  E" THEN RUN "ENTER/BAS"
260 IF Y$ = "R" THEN RUN "ADAPT/BAS"
270 PRINT  PLEASE PRESS E OR R"
280 GOTO 240
290 END
```

WRDAT/BAS Listing

```
10 REM ************************************************
20 REM DATA ENTRY PROGRAM FOR ADAPT/BAS
30 REM WRITTEN BY LES VERSION 1.0
40 REM FOR THE TRS-80 MODEL I OR MODEL III WITH DISK
50 REM MODIFIED 2 DEC 1981
60 REM
70 REM MODIFIED 1 AUGUST 1982
80 REM REFERENCE DATA ENTRY FOR TRS-80 ACCESS VOL 1 NUMBER 4
1982
90 CLEAR 1000
100 CLS
110 DIM X$(2),X(60),Y(90),R$(3) B(90).C(90),D(90)
120 IL=3 MX=11:JS=1
130 IC =12
140 T$="%       %"
150 PRINT STRING$(63,"=")
160 PRINT"DATA ENTRY PROGRAM"
170 PRINT STRING$(63,"=")
180 PRINT "DO YOU WANT TO UPDATE A FILE ALREADY ON DISK Y OR N?"
190 GOSUB 1100
200 IF Y$ = "Y" THEN GOSUB 1670
210 INPUT"ENTER NAME OF X VARIABLE ";X$(1)
220 INPUT"ENTER NAME OF Y VARIABLE ";X$(2)
230 INPUT"ENTER DATE ";D$
240 PRINT"ENTER UP TO TWO LINES OF REMARKS PRESS ENTER IF NO
REMARKS"
```

```
250 FOR J=1 TO 2
260     INPUT R$(J)
270     IF R$(J)="" THEN 290
280 NEXT J
290 CLS
300 PRINT STRING$(63,"=")
310 PRINT"YOU WANT TO ENTER THE FOLLOWING "
320 PRINT "NAME OF X VARAIBLE = ";X$(1)
330 PRINT "NAME OF Y VARIABLE = ";X$(2)
340 PRINT "DATE = ";D$
350 PRINT"REMARKS  "
360 FOR J=1 TO 2
370      PRINT R$(J)
380 NEXT J
390 PRINT"ARE THESE CORRECT Y OR N "
400 Y$=INKEY$:IFY$="" THEN 400
410 IF Y$="Y" THEN 570 ELSE IF Y$<>"N" THEN 390
420 CLS
430 PRINT STRING$(63,"=")
440 PRINT"REENTER INCORRECT DATA ENTER C IF CORRECT "
450 PRINT "NAME OF X VARIABLE = ";X$(1);"  ";:INPUT X$
460 IF X$="C" THEN 470 ELSE X$(1)=X$
470 PRINT"NAME OF Y VARIABLE = ";X$(2);" ";:INPUT X$
480 IF X$="C" THEN 490 ELSE X$(2)=X$
490 PRINT"DATE";D$;:INPUT X$:IF X$="C" THEN 500 ELSE D$=X$
500 REM
510 PRINT "REMARKS"
520 FOR J=1 TO 2
530      PRINTR$(J);:INPUT R$
540      IF R$="C" THEN 550 ELSE R$(J)=R$
550 NEXT J
560 GOTO 290
570 IP=IL
580 CLS
590 PRINT CHR$(23)
600 PRINT STRING$(30,"=")
610 PRINT " #    ": PRINT USING T$:X$(1); PRINT"       " PRINT
USING T$:X$(2)
620 J=JS:JL=JS+8
630 IF NJ<JL THEN NJ=JL
640 FOR J=JS TO JL
650 PRINT   J;"    ":X(J):TAB(20);Y(J)
660 NEXT J
670 PRINT @768,STRING$(31,95);
```

```
680 PRINT@832, CHR$(91);CHR$(92) CHR$(93)·CHR$(94) " ARE ACTIVE
USE * TO STOP";
690 PRINT@896."USE > TO GO TO NEXT PAGE < TO GO TO PREVIOUS
PAGE";
700 GOSUB 970 :REM POINTER CONTROL
710 IF ID<> 0 THEN 930 ELSE ID=1
720 IF X=62 OR X=60 OR X$="*" THEN 820
730 JP=IP-IL+1
740 GOSUB 1140
750 IF IC=12 THEN X(JP+JS-1)=Y
760 IF JP+JS-1>N THEN N=JP+JS-1
770 IF IC=34 THEN Y(JP+JS-1)=Y
780 IF IC =12 THEN IC =34:GOTO580
790 IF IC=34 THEN IC=12
800 IP=IP+1
810 GOTO 580
820 IF X=62 THEN JS=JL+1:IC=12:GOTO570
830 IF X<>60 THEN 860 ELSE JS=JS-9
840 IF JS<1 THEN JS=1
850 IC=12:GOTO570
860 IF X$="*" THEN GOSUB 1280  ELSE 930
870 LPRINT CHR$(12)  TOP OF FORM
880 PRINT"DO YOU WANT TO DO ANOTHER ONE "
890 GOSUB 1100
900 IF X$="Y"THEN RUN
910 RUN MENU"
920 END
930 PRINT@IP*64+IC," ";
940 IF IP>MX THEN IP=IL
950 PRINT @IP*64+IC,CHR$(94);
960 GOTO700
970 REM *** POINTER CONTROL FOR MENUES ***
980 PRINT @IP*64+IC,CHR$(94);
990 GOSUB 1100
1000 PRINT @IP*64+IC," ";
1010 ID=0
1020 IF X=27 OR X=91 THEN ID=-1
1030 IF X=26 OR X=10 OR X=13 THEN ID=+1
1040 IP=IP+ID : IF IP<IL THEN IP=MX
1050 IF IP>MX THEN IP=IL
1060 IF X =8 THEN IC = 12
1070 IF X =9 THEN IC =34
1080 IF X=8 OR X=9 THEN ID=1
1090 RETURN
```

```
1100 REM *** GET AN UNSHIFTED CHARACTER FROM KEYBOARD ***
1110 X$=INKEY$ : IF X$="" THEN 1110 ELSE X=ASC(X$)
1120 IF X>95 THEN X=X-32 : X$=CHR$(X)
1130 RETURN
1140 REM *** NUMERIC PARAMETER INPUT USING SUBR @ 1900
1150 PRINT @IP*64+IC,STRING$(4," ");
1160 GOSUB 1180 : Y=VAL(Y$)
1170 RETURN
1180 REM *** STRING INPUT, ADDING TO Y$ STARTING WITH X$ ***
1190 CC=CC+1
1200 Y$=X$
1210 PRINT @IP*64+IC,Y$;CHR$(95) " ";
1220 GOSUB 1100
1230   IF X=13 THEN CC=CC-1 : RETURN
1240   IF X=8 THEN IF LEN(Y$)>0 THEN Y$=LEFT$(Y$,LEN(Y$)-1)
1250   IF X=24 THEN Y$=""
1260   IF X>31 THEN Y$=Y$+X$
1270 GOTO 1210
1280 CLS
1290 PRINT STRING$(63,"=")
1300 PRINT"DO YOU WANT HARDCOPY "
1310 GOSUB 1100
1320 IF X$="Y" THEN GOSUB 1470
1330 PRINT"DO YOU WANT TO STORE DATA ON DISK "
1340 GOSUB 1100
1350 IF X$="N" THEN RETURN
1360 PRINT "BE SURE THAT DISK IS IN DRIVE "
1370 LINEINPUT "ENTER FILE NAME INCLUDING DRIVE # == ";F$
1380 OPEN "O",1,F$
1390 PRINT #1,R$(1)
1400 PRINT #1,R$(2)
1410 PRINT#1,N
1420 FOR JJ=1 TO N
1430   PRINT#1,X(JJ);Y(JJ)
1440 NEXT JJ
1450 CLOSE
1460 RETURN
1470 CLS
1480 PRINT STRING$(63,"=")
1490 PRINT"HARDCOPY OPTION BE SURE PRINTER IS ON "
1500 LPRINT STRING$(63,"=")
1510 LPRINT TAB(10)"DATE = "; D$
1520 LPRINT TAB(5)"FILE NAME = ";F$.
1530 LPRINT TAB(10);"REMARKS :"
```

```
1540 LPRINT TAB(5)"NUMBER OF DATA POINTS = ";N
1550 FOR J=1 TO 2
1560   IF R$(J)="" THEN 1580
1570   LPRINT TAB(5)R$(J)
1580 NEXT J
1590 LPRINT" "
1600 LPRINT " "
1610 LPRINT STRING$(63,"=")
1620 LPRINTTAB(5)"ITEM # ";TAB(24);X$(1)·TAB(45);X$(2)
1630 FOR JJ=1 TO N
1640   LPRINT TAB(5)JJ·TAB(24);X(JJ):TAB(44):Y(JJ)
1650 NEXT JJ
1660 RETURN
1670 CLS: PRINT "FILE UPDATE "
1680 INPUT"ENTER FILE NAME FOR FILE THAT YOU WANT TO READ IN
";F$
1690 OPEN "I".1,F$
1700 INPUT #1.R$(1),R$(2)
1710 INPUT #1.N
1720 FOR JJ=1TO N:INPUT#1.X(JJ).Y(JJ):NEXT JJ:CLOSE:RETURN
```

Example: Using ADAPT/BAS

ADAPT/BAS will be used to forecast the Dow Jones Industrial Average. Use the data given in Fig. 14-10 so you can compare the results achieved with all available techniques. You can also compare the predicted value of the Dow Jones Average for the end of 1982 with the actual value when the data is available. In this example you will use the entire package: MENU, ENTER/BAS, and ADAPT/BAS. The first step is to run MENU, which is displayed on the crt, as shown in Fig. 14-29.

The first step is to enter the data. Press E; ENTER/BAS is loaded and run. The crt display for the first page is given in Fig. 14-30A; the second page is given in Fig. 14-30B. Enter your remarks and press > to go to the next page. Since all other data entry pages are the same, only this one will be displayed.

Complete each page and press > to move to the next one. When you are done, review the data by pressing < to move back one page at a time. When you are convinced the data is correct, press * to file the data. Give the data the file name DJI/DAT. Answer N to the question "Do you want hard copy?"

Data is stored and control is returned to the menu. Press R to run ADAPT/BAS. The only questions that ADAPT/BAS asks are "FILE NAME?" which is answered by DJI/DAT, and "How many periods should be used for smoothing?" Since the stock market is supposed to follow a nine year cycle, enter 9. The computer begins its calculations and then displays the projection for 1982. Request hard copy, which is shown in Fig. 14-31.

Because graphs are easier to see and compare than tables, I have plotted this example (Fig. 14-32). There are three curves on the plot. The first is the plot of the actual Dow Jones Industrial Average year end close. The second is a plot of one period projections from 1971 to 1981. Note that the projections improve as time increases. The third curve is a plot of a nine year projection from 1977 to 1985. The nine year projection actually is better than the one year projections. A different set of

```
=======================================================
MENU FOR ADAPTIVE FILTERING PROGRAM

VERSION 1.0

WRITTEN BY LES

REF INVESTMENT ANALYSIS WITH YOUR MICROCOMPUTER  TAB BOOKS
=======================================================
PRINT PRESS THE LETTER CORRESPONDING TO THE PROGRAM

YOU WANT TO RUN

<E>NTER DATA

<R>UN ADAPTIVE FILTERING PROGRAM
=======================================================
PRESS THE KEY NOW
```

Fig. 14-29. Menu for adaptive filtering program.

```
A   = = = = = = = = = = = = = = = = = =
    DATA ENTRY PROGRAM
    = = = = = = = = = = = = = = = = = =
    DO YOU WANT TO UPDATE A FILE ALREADY ON DISK Y OR N?
    ENTER NAME OF X VARIABLE ? YEAR
    ENTER NAME OF Y VARIABLE ? DJ I AVERAGE
    ENTER DATE ? 10/09/82
    ENTER UP TO TWO LINES OF REMARKS PRESS ENTER OF NO REMARKS
B  ========================================
    #
    1        → 0            0
    2          0            0
    3          0            0
    4          0            0
    5          0            0
    6          0            0
    7          0            0
    8          0            0
    9          0            0
   ------------------------------------
   ↑↑→← ARE  ACTIVE  USE*TO  STOP
   USE> TO  GO  TO  NEXT  PAGE  <TO  GO
   TO  PREVIOUS  PAGE
```

Fig. 14-30. (A) Screen format, page 1, for data entry program; (B) screen format, page 2, for data entry program.

INPUT DATA		RESULTS	
PERIOD	VALUE	PERIOD	FORECAST
1951	238.99	1972	1020.02
1952	256.35	1973	850.86
1953	255.49	1974	616.24
1954	279.87	1975	852.41
1955	388.2	1976	1004.65
1956	462.35	1977	905.615
1957	419.79	1978	809.662
1958	436.89	1979	839.131
1959	574.46	1980	957.354
1960	566.05	1981	955.615
1961	610.25	1982	888.284
1962	535 76	1983	908.287
1963	646 79	1984	962 948
1964	766 08	1985	980.365
1965	840.36		
1966	744.32		
1967	905.11		
1968	943.75		
1969	800.36		
1970	838.92		
1971	890.2		

Fig. 14-31. Adaptive filtering output.

curves could be developed using a different number of periods. You should try to see whether you can find a better number of periods for smoothing. You should also compare this plot with similar plots for the other smoothing methods.

Adaptive filtering as presented here is a version of moving average smoothing. The main disadvantage of the method is the large amount of data required before a forecast can be prepared. In general the more data available for training the model, the better it will forecast.

Adaptive filtering can be made more complex than is shown here. The program presented works well and should be a valuable addition to your programming library.

LEADING INDICATORS

Because the future of any investment is closely tied to the future of the economy, investors should be interested in forecasting the future of the economy. One of the most often used techniques is based on analysis of leading indicators.

Because of the need to forecast the future of the economy, much study by government and industry has gone into developing methods for such forecasting. Most studies have shown that certain economic activities go up or down before the whole economy does. These activities are called leading indicators.

Leading indicators are used to forecast the future of the economy. For example, if the leading

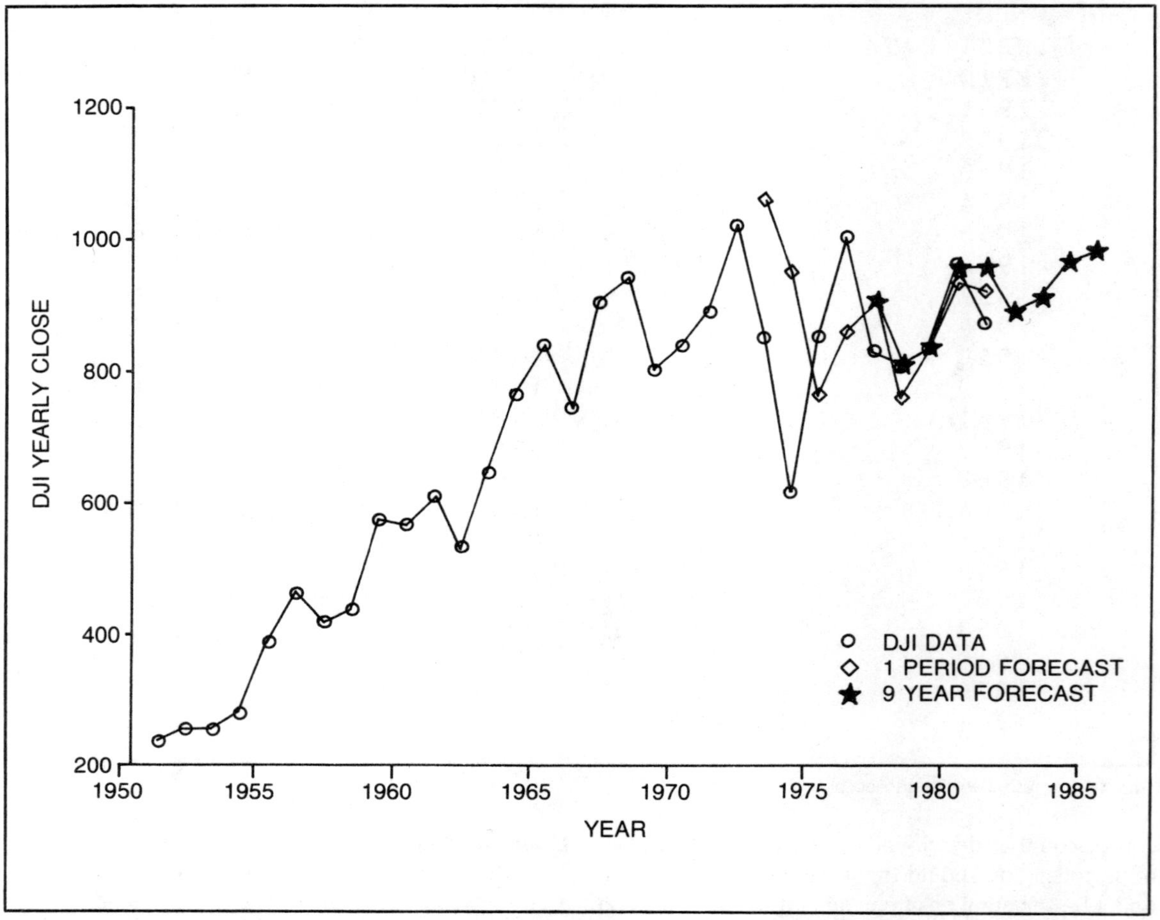

Fig. 14-32. Plot of adaptive filtering example results for 9-period smoothing using 9-year forecast from 1977.

indicators go up, the general economy can be expected to improve in the future. If the leading indicators go down, the general economy can be expected to fall. If all leading indicators agreed all the time, and if the time lag between the leading indicators and the economy were always the same, forecasting would be easy.

Unfortunately, neither of these conditions holds. The leading indicators often point in different directions. Even when they all point in the same direction, the time lag between them and the economy varies.

The first problem is a disagreement between leading indicators. This is treated by developing a composite index of selected leading indicators. The trend of this index is generally a better indication of the future than any single leading indicator. The government publishes data on the leading indicator index on a regular basis. This data is a valuable tool for forecasting.

There doesn't seem to be any good way to overcome the variation in the lag between leading indicators and the general economy. The average value of the lag can be used, at least for preliminary estimates. The average lag is 10.6 months. That is, the general economy lags behind the leading indicators by 10.6 months. However, the range is from 22 months to three months. Some of the leading indicators are shown in Fig. 14-33.

One of the things investors are most interested in, the stock market, is a leading indicator. Thus leading indicators are not of much use in forecasting the stock market.

The best way to use leading indicators is to keep a record of the government published index. The longer a given trend in the index lasts, the more certain it is that the economy will follow.

USES OF SMOOTHING AND FORECASTING TECHNIQUES

The forecasting techniques discussed above can be used to provide information needed for a complete investment analysis. For example, the techniques can be used to forecast interest rates, sales, stock prices, and appreciation of property.

Indicator	Average Lead Time (in months)
Profits	18.3
Housing starts	12.8
Housing permits	12.8
Consumer confidence	12.7
Business loans	11
Unemployment claims	11.3
Stock market	11
Help wanted advertising	10
New consumer orders	7.8
Automobile sales	5.0
Number unemployed	4.8
Unemployment rate	3.5

Fig. 14-33. Some leading indicators used to forecast the future of the economy.

The forecast values can then be entered into the major investment analysis programs. An example is provided in the next chapter.

The forecasting techniques are also valuable for managing the investment once it has been made. They are especially useful for making short term forecasts, which are most needed for the week to week management of your investment.

There are two good books on the application of the personal computer to forecasting the behavior of the stock market. *New Uses for the Home Computer in the Stock Market* by Thomas V. Lentz provides several useful programs to forecast trends in the stock market. The programs are written for the TRS-80. The book is available from Mr. Lentz in Elko, Nevada.

Another useful book is *Playing the Stock and Bond Market with Your Personal Computer* by L. R. Schmeltz. The programs in this book are written for the Apple II but can be adapted to other computers without much difficulty. The book is available at your bookstore.

These two books use many of the forecasting techniques discussed above as well as many more complex techniques.

The forecasting techniques discussed above can be used to provide the information needed for a complete investment analysis. For example, the techniques can be used to forecast interest rates, sales, stock prices, and appreciation of property. The forecast values can then be entered into the major investment analysis programs. An example appears in the next chapter.

Forecasting also is an important tool for managing your investments once they have been made. You should be careful when selecting your forecasting techniques. Examine all available techniques; work with them; then select the one that best fits your particular situation. In mnay cases you will want to develop some casual models to help determine the impact of your decisions on investments.

Chapter 15

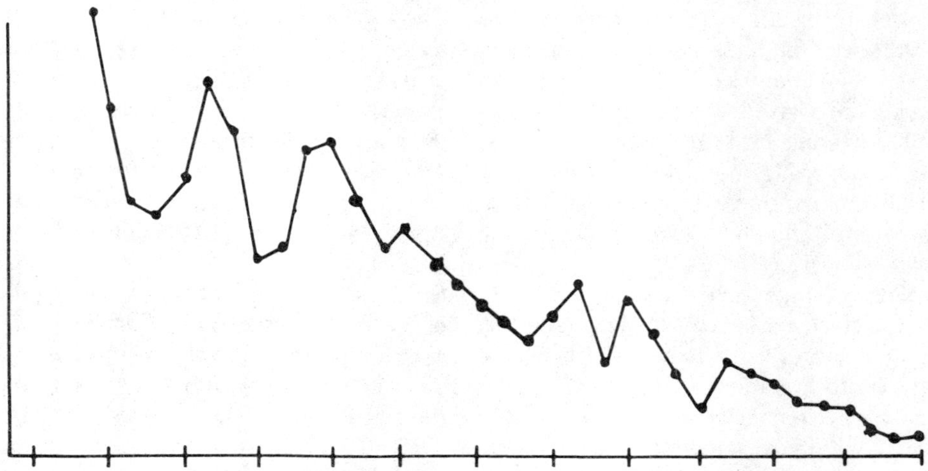

Putting It All Together

Combining forecasting techniques and present value techniques will give you a more complete investment analysis. The examples are intended to demonstrate the techniques and are not real problems, but they will show you how to use the techniques and how to interpret the calculated results.

STOCK MARKET EXAMPLE

The first example to be examined is a stock market problem. You want to select the best of several stocks for investment. Simple moving average smoothing will be used to forecast the future value of the stock price; then present value analysis will determine which of the stocks is the best investment.

The past price history for the stocks under consideration is given in Fig. 15-1. You want to forecast the prices one year into the future, that is, to 1982. The results of the moving average forecasts are given in Fig. 15-2.

In addition to the money earned (or lost) from the sale of the stock, you will earn the following dividends from each of the stocks:

Stock A $8.75 per share.
Stock B $9.00 per share.
Stock C $19.00 per share.

Looking at the forecast, you find that the projected selling price of each of the stocks is less than you paid, so the investment doesn't look too favorable. Let's continue the analysis. When you include the dividends, you receive the following cash flow at the end of the year.

Stock A $35 in dividends and $180 from the sale; total $215.
Stock B $36 in dividends and $190 from the sale; total $226.
Stock C $38 in dividends and $195 from the sale; total $233.

Perhaps the investment is not too unfavorable. You do get your money back. Or do you? The present value analysis will answer the question.

Year	Stock A	Stock B	Stock C
1970	$20	$30	$100
1971	$22	$40	$ 80
1972	$24	$35	$ 70
1973	$30	$45	$ 90
1974	$28	$46	$110
1975	$35	$50	$115
1976	$26	$40	$100
1977	$34	$45	$ 99
1978	$40	$40	$ 80
1979	$30	$35	$ 90
1980	$40	$45	$ 95
1981	$50	$50	$100
1982	?		

Fig. 15-1. Past price history for stocks.

The analysis is shown in Fig. 15-3. Investment A is a loser; the present value is less than your investment. This means that investment A would cost you money if it were chosen. This shows the real power of present value analysis.

This simple example is only a demonstration of the general technique, but it does show clearly the importance of both forecasting and present value analysis.

REAL ESTATE INVESTMENT EXAMPLE

Another example involving investment in rental real estate shows how to combine all the techniques discussed. We will use the real estate investment analysis program for the analysis.

The major data needed for the program are the projected income and expenses for the property.

Let's see what the investment opportunity is and what can be done to analyze it. You are offered the opportunity to purchase an apartment for $350,000. The data for the apartment is given in Fig. 15-4. In order to evaluate the investment, find out what other similar property is selling for. Apartments are selling for somewhat less than similar property in the same area, which could indicate a problem. Also see how other similar units are managed: the average vacancy rate is eight percent, which is much less than what your property experiences.

The high vacancy rate probably explains the low price, and may be a sign of some problem with the way the property is managed. You should make a note to look into the question later.

Next, find out how property has been appreciating in your area. Because a major new industry moved in five years ago, you feel that data for the last five years is the only data worth examining. This data is given in Fig. 15-5. Use the six data points in Fig. 15-5 to make the forecast. Because the data is limited, use a double exponential smoothing forecast. You need a five year forecast, which is within the capabilities of the double smoothing average technique. The results of the forecast for several values of the smoothing parameter are given in Fig. 15-6. There is considerable difference in the various forecasts; this is one of the problems with forecasting.

The various forecasts for different values of the smoothing parameter show quite a range in possible appreciation rates. Use a value of 16.5 percent per year as the appreciation rate. This seems conservative and within the range of the values predicted by the various forecasts.

You now have the information needed to run INVEST2/BAS. Assume an eight percent per year inflation rate.

The investment analysis shows that the net present value of the investment is positive, so the investment appears favorable. The inflation corrected net present value is −$6,051, which means profits from the investment did not keep up with inflation. Perhaps you should not make this investment.

But before you decide, look at the vacancy rate, which costs you $13,761 per year. You know that this vacancy rate is much too high (it's higher than the vacancy rate for similar apartments). Be-

RESULTS OF MOVING AVERAGE FOR 2 PERIODS IN AVERAGE

STOCK A

RESULTS

PERIOD	PRICE OF A	FORECAST	ABS. VALUE OF ERROR
1970	20	0	20
1971	22	0	22
1972	24	21	3
1973	30	23	7
1974	28	27	1
1975	35	29	6
1976	26	31.5	5.5
1977	34	30.5	3 5
1978	40	30	10
1979	30	37	7
1980	40	35	5
1981	50	35	15
1982		45	

RESULTS OF MOVING AVERAGE FOR 4 PERIODS IN AVERAGE

STOCK A

RESULTS

PERIOD	PRICE OF A	FORECAST	ABS. VALUE OF ERROR
1970	20	0	20
1971	22	0	22
1972	24	21	3
1973	30	23	7
1974	28	24	4
1975	35	26	9
1976	26	29.25	3.25
1977	34	29.75	4.25
1978	40	30.75	9.25
1979	30	33.75	3.75
1980	40	32.5	7.5
1981	50	36	14
1982		40	

Fig. 15-2. Results of moving average for two periods in average (continued on page 234).

RESULTS OF MOVING AVERAGE FOR 2 PERIODS IN AVERAGE

STOCK C

RESULTS

PERIOD	PRICE OF C	FORECAST	ABS. VALUE OF ERROR
1970	100	0	100
1971	80	0	80
1972	70	90	20
1973	90	75	15
1974	110	80	30
1975	115	100	15
1976	100	112.5	12.5
1977	99	107.5	8.5
1978	80	99.5	19.5
1979	90	89.5	.5
1980	95	85	10
1981	100	92.5	7.5
1982		97.5	

RESULTS OF MOVING AVERAGE FOR 5 PERIODS IN AVERAGE

STOCK C

RESULTS

PERIOD	PRICE OF C	FORECAST	ABS. VALUE OF ERROR
1970	100	0	100
1971	80	0	80
1972	70	90	20
1973	90	75	15
1974	110	80	30
1975	115	90	25
1976	100	93	7
1977	99	97	2
1978	80	102.8	22.8
1979	90	100.8	10.8
1980	95	96.8	1.8
1981	100	92.8	7.2
1982		92.8	

RESULTS OF MOVING AVERAGE FOR 2 PERIODS IN AVERAGE

STOCK B

RESULTS

PERIOD	PRICE OF B	FORECAST	ABS. VALUE OF ERROR
1970	30	0	30
1971	40	0	40
1972	35	35	0
1973	45	37.5	7.5
1974	46	40	6
1975	50	45.5	4.5
1976	40	48	8
1977	45	45	0
1978	40	42.5	2.5
1979	35	42.5	7.5
1980	45	37.5	7.5
1981	50	40	10
1982		47.5	

RESULTS OF MOVING AVERAGE FOR 5 PERIODS IN AVERAGE

STOCK B

RESULTS

PERIOD	PRICE OF B	FORECAST	ABS. VALUE OF ERROR
1970	30	0	30
1971	40	0	40
1972	35	35	0
1973	45	37.5	7.5
1974	46	40	6
1975	50	39.2	10.8
1976	40	43.2	3.2
1977	45	43.2	1.8
1978	40	45.2	5.2
1979	35	44.2	9.2
1980	45	42	3
1981	50	41	9
1982		43	

Fig. 15-2. Continued from page 233.

```
              PRESENT VALUE ANALYSIS OF STOCK A.

PRESENT VALUE OF ONE TIME CASH FLOW.
ENTER AMOUNT OF CASH FLOW ? 215
ENTER DISCOUNT RATE IN PERCENT ? 10
ENTER NUMBER OF YEARS TO DISCOUNT ? 1
THE PRESENT VALUE OF $    215.00 DISCOUNTED OVER  1 YEARS
AT A DISCOUNT RATE OF 10.00% IS $    195.45
DO YOU WANT TO DO ANOTHER ONE Y OR N?

              PRESENT VALUE ANALYSIS OF STOCK B

PRESENT VALUE OF ONE TIME CASH FLOW.
ENTER AMOUNT OF CASH FLOW ? 226
ENTER DISCOUNT RATE IN PERCENT ? 10
ENTER NUMBER OF YEARS TO DISCOUNT ? 1
THE PRESENT VALUE OF $    226.00 DISCOUNTED OVER  1 YEARS
AT A DISCOUNT RATE OF 10.00% IS $    205.45
DO YOU WANT TO DO ANOTHER ONE Y OR N?

              PRESENT VALUE ANALYSIS OF STOCK C

PRESENT VALUE OF ONE TIME CASH FLOW.
ENTER AMOUNT OF CASH FLOW ? 233
ENTER DISCOUNT RATE IN PERCENT ? 10
ENTER NUMBER OF YEARS TO DISCOUNT ? 1
THE PRESENT VALUE OF $    233.00 DISCOUNTED OVER  1 YEARS
AT A DISCOUNT RATE OF 10.00% IS $    211.82
DO YOU WANT TO DO ANOTHER ONE Y OR N?
```

Fig. 15-3. Present value analysis of stock A.

fore you reject the investment, analyze the vacancy rate issue to see why the rate is so high.

Talk with the seller and view other rental units. You find that the current owner of the apartment refuses to advertise. This may explain the high vacancy rate. Try to find a relationship between advertising and the vacancy rate. You obtain the data given in Fig. 15-7.

Although there is considerable scatter in the data, there does appear to be a relationship between advertising and vacancy rate. Run the linear regression program (see Chapter 14) to see what the relationship is. The results of the linear regression program for this problem are given in Fig. 15-8.

Based on the linear regression results, you feel that you have to spend $400 per month to

Type of unit	# Units	Rent
1 Bedroom	3	$465/mo
2 Bedroom	5	$550/mo
3 Bedroom	5	$700/mo

Vacancy rate is 15%
Expenses are $10,260 per year
We can borrow $200,000 for 30 year at 15.0% per year.
The discount rate is 12%

Fig. 15-4. Data for apartment.

Period	% Increase
1	9
2	12
3	10
4	16
5	15
6	16

Fig. 15-5. Period versus percent increase.

assure lowering the vacancy rate to eight percent. Let's see what the program reveals. Also assume that if you lower the vacancy rate to eight percent, the property will appreciate faster than it would with a 15 percent vacancy rate. This will raise the value of your property to the level of similar units.

The results from the investment analysis program are given in Figs. 15-9 and 15-10. Note that you earn money even considering inflation. This looks like a good investment. Assume that you buy it and start a major advertising campaign, keeping careful account of the results. After several months you notice that the vacancy rate has decreased to less than 8 percent. You could stop advertising,

```
RESULTS OF DOUBLE EXPONENTIAL SMOOTHING
APPRECIATION IN PROPERTY
% INCREASE

SMOOTHING FACTOR  .2

PERIOD          VARIABLE  FORECAST  ERROR
 1               9         0         -9
 2               12        0         -12
 3               10        0         -10
 4               16        0         -16
 5               15        0         -15
 6               16        0         -16
 7                         10.68
 8                         10.688
 9                         14.0256
 10                        15.6806
 11                        17.2726


RESULTS OF DOUBLE EXPONENTIAL SMOOTHING
APPRECIATION IN PROPERTY
% INCREASE

SMOOTHING FACTOR  .5

PERIOD          VARIABLE  FORECAST  ERROR
 1               9         0         -9
 2               12        0         -12
 3               10        0         -10
 4               16        0         -16
 5               15        0         -15
 6               16        0         -16
 7                         15
 8                         11.75
 9                         22.5
 10                        21.5625
 11                        21.6875


RESULTS OF DOUBLE EXPONENTIAL SMOOTHING
APPRECIATION IN PROPERTY
% INCREASE

SMOOTHING FACTOR  .1

PERIOD          VARIABLE  FORECAST  ERROR
 1               9         0         -9
 2               12        0         -12
 3               10        0         -10
 4               16        0         -16
 5               15        0         -15
 6               16        0         -16
 7                         9.72
 8                         9.846
 9                         11.3896
 10                        12.446
 11                        13.5673
```

Fig. 15-6. Results of double exponential smoothing.

Advertising $/month)	Vacancy rate (%)
10	17.6
30	19.4
50	16
80	14.4
100	16.6
120	17.8
140	13.4
180	9.8
200	11.0
250	7.0
300	6.0
400	4.0

Fig. 15-7. Advertising versus vacancy rate.

since you met your goal, but you don't, hoping to decrease the rate even further, since the lower the vacancy rate the higher your profit.

As part of management, you also are carefully informed of the value of similar property. Use this data to refine your forecasts and make sure the property is increasing in value as fast as it should.

Of course not all investments will turn out like the example above. Most will be marginal at best, and will be money "sinks" at worst. The whole idea of this book has been to present a useful tool that will help you analyze the problems with a given investment beforehand. You thus avoid bad investments and have more money for good ones.

The approach to investment presented in this book is basically conservative. It is not guaranteed to make you rich in 10 easy lessons (If I knew how to

```
RESULTS OF LINEAR LEAST SQUARES FIT

THE EQUATION IS Y =  19.6907  + -.0442588 * X

THE STANDARD DEVIATION IS  1.80451

DO YOU WISH TO MAKE A FORECAST Y OR N


CONT
ENTER VALUE OF ADVERTISING THAT FORECAST IS DESIRED FOR? 350
VALUE OF VACANCY % IS  4.20009
DO YOU WISH ANOTHER FORECAST


CONT
ENTER VALUE OF ADVERTISING THAT FORECAST IS DESIRED FOR? 350
VALUE OF VACANCY % IS  4.20009
DO YOU WISH ANOTHER FORECAST
ENTER VALUE OF ADVERTISING THAT FORECAST IS DESIRED FOR? 300
VALUE OF VACANCY % IS  6.41303
DO YOU WISH ANOTHER FORECAST
```

Fig. 15-8. Results of linear least squares fit (continued on page 238).

```
CONT
ENTER VALUE OF ADVERTISING THAT FORECAST IS DESIRED FOR? 350
VALUE OF VACANCY % IS  4.20009
DO YOU WISH ANOTHER FORECAST
ENTER VALUE OF ADVERTISING THAT FORECAST IS DESIRED FOR? 300
VALUE OF VACANCY % IS  6.41303
DO YOU WISH ANOTHER FORECAST
ENTER VALUE OF ADVERTISING THAT FORECAST IS DESIRED FOR? 200
VALUE OF VACANCY % IS  10.8389
DO YOU WISH ANOTHER FORECAST
```

Fig. 15-8. Continued from page 237.

```
                              INPUT DATA SUMMARY
TOTAL AMOUNT OF INVESTMENT                      $ 350,000.00
AMOUNT OF FIRST LOAN                            $ 200,000.00
YEARLY INTEREST RATE FOR 1ST LOAN                      15.00%
LIFE OF FIRST LOAN YEARS                               30.00   YRS
NUMBER OF LOAN PAYMENTS PER YEAR                       12
TIME AFTER INVESTING BEFORE REC. INCOME                 0.00 YRS
AMOUNT OF SECOND LOAN                           $  60,000.00
YEARLY INTEREST RATE FOR 2ND LOAN                      14.50%
LIFE OF SECOND LOAN YEARS                              10 YRS
NUMBER OF PAYMENTS PER YEAR  2ND LOAN                  12
ESCLATION FOR VALUE OF PROPERTY                        18.00%
COST OF SELLING AS % OF PRICE                           6.00%
ESCALATION FOR RENTS                                    8.00%
ESCALATION FOR EXPENSES                                10.00%
FEDERAL INCOME TAX RATE                                40.00%
FEDERAL CAPITAL GAINS TAX RATE                         20.00%
STATE CAPITAL GAINS TAX RATE                            0.00%
STATE INCOME TAX RATE                                  10.00%
DISCOUNT RATE                                          12.00 %
LIFE OF INVESTMENT                                      5 YRS
VALUE OF 3 YEAR PROPERTY                        $       0.00
VALUE OF 5 YEAR PROPERTY                        $       0.00
VALUE OF 10 YEAR PROPERTY                       $       0.00
VALUE OF 15 YEAR PU PROP                        $       0.00
VALUE OF ST LINE REAL ESTATE                    $ 280,000.00
YEAR PROPERY PLACED IN SVC                           1982
INFLATION RATE                                          8.00%
```

Fig. 15-9. Results of investment analysis program with 8 percent vacancy rate (continued on page 239).

```
========================================================
               INCOME ESTIMATES.
=========================================================

NUMBER OF 1 BEDROOM UNFUR    3 RENT $    465.00/MO    $    5,580.00/YR
NUMBER OF 1 BEDROOM FUR      0 RENT $      0.00/MO    $        0.00/YR
NUMBER OF 2 BEDROOM UNFUR    5 RENT $    550.00/MO    $    6,600.00/YR
NUMBER OF 2 BEDROOM FUR      0 RENT $      0.00/MO    $        0.00/YR
NUMBER OF 3 BEDROOM UNFUR    5 RENT $    700.00/MO    $    8,400.00/YR
NUMBER OF 3 BEDROOM FUR      0 RENT $      0.00/MO    $        0.00/YR
ALLOWANCE FOR VACANCIES  8.00% OR $   7,339.20/YR
TOTAL YEARLY INCOME $  84,400.80
================================================================
                    EXPENSES
INSURANCE  $   120.00/MO    $ 1,440.00/YR
LICENSES   $    10.00/MO    $   120.00/YR
PROP TAX   $      100/MO    $ 1,200.00/YR
UTILITIES  $    40.00/MO    $   480.00/YR
MANAGEMENT $   450.00/MO    $ 5,400.00/YR
JANITOR    $     0.00/MO    $     0.00/YR
ADVERTIS   $   400.00/MO    $ 4,800.00/YR
MAINT EXP  $   110.00/MO    $ 1,320.00/YR
MISC EXP   $    25.00/MO    $   300.00/YR
     TOTAL EXPENSES PER YEAR $  15,060.00



=========================================================================
                         *** SUMMARY RESULTS ***

  CURRENT YEAR DOLLARS PRESENT VALUE OF RENT PROFIT $ 108.967.00
  SELLING PRICE .......... $ 800.715.00
  COST OF SELLING ........ $  48 042.90
  BALANCE DUE ON LOANS ... $ 237 806.00
  BASIS FOR TAX PURPOSE .. $ 256,667.00
  TAXABLE PROCEEDS ....... $ 496 006.00
  TOTAL CAPITAL GAINS TAX  $  99,201.10
  NET PROFIT FROM SALE  .. $ 303,471.00
  PRESENT VALUE OF PROFIT FROM SALE - BALANCE DUE    $  37,260.10
  PRESENT VALUE OF TOTAL PROFITS - BALANCE DUE       $ 146,227.00
  ACCUMULATED EQUITY ...... $112,194.00
  PRESENT VALUE EQUITY .... $105,486.00
  CONSTANT YR DOLLAR   .... $102,307.00
  NET PRESENT VALUE (PROFIT  -EQUITY) =              $  40,740.90
  CONSTANT YEAR NET PRESENT VALUE ALL PROFIT-BALANCE $  10,097.00
=========================================================================
```

Fig. 15-9. Continued from page 238.

```
                    INPUT DATA SUMMARY
TOTAL AMOUNT OF INVESTMENT                    $ 350,000.00
AMOUNT OF FIRST LOAN                          $ 200,000.00
YEARLY INTEREST RATE FOR 1ST LOAN                    15.00%
LIFE OF FIRST LOAN YEARS                             30.00  YRS
NUMBER OF LOAN PAYMENTS PER YEAR                     12
TIME AFTER INVESTING BEFORE REC. INCOME               0.00 YRS
AMOUNT OF SECOND LOAN                         $  60.000.00
YEARLY INTEREST RATE FOR 2ND LOAN                    14.50%
LIFE OF SECOND LOAN YEARS                            10 YRS
NUMBER OF PAYMENTS PER YEAR  2ND LOAN                12
ESCLATION FOR VALUE OF PROPERTY                      16.50%
COST OF SELLING AS % OF PRICE                         6.00%
ESCALATION FOR RENTS                                  8.00%
ESCALATION FOR EXPENSES                              10.00%
FEDERAL INCOME TAX RATE                              40.00%
FEDERAL CAPITAL GAINS TAX RATE                       20.00%
STATE CAPITAL GAINS TAX RATE                          0.00%
STATE INCOME TAX RATE                                10.00%
DISCOUNT RATE                                        12.00 %
LIFE OF INVESTMENT                                    5 YRS
VALUE OF 3 YEAR PROPERTY                       $      0.00
VALUE OF 5 YEAR PROPERTY                       $      0.00
VALUE OF 10 YEAR PROPERTY                      $      0.00
VALUE OF 15 YEAR PU PROP                       $      0.00
VALUE OF ST LINE REAL ESTATE                   $ 280,000.00
YEAR PROPERY PLACED IN SVC                          1982
INFLATION RATE                                        8.00%

========================================================
              INCOME ESTIMATES.
=========================================================

NUMBER OF 1 BEDROOM UNFUR    3 RENT $   465.00/MO   $   5,580.00/YR
NUMBER OF 1 BEDROOM FUR      0 RENT $     0.00/MO   $       0.00/YR
NUMBER OF 2 BEDROOM UNFUR    5 RENT $   550.00/MO   $   6.600.00/YR
NUMBER OF 2 BEDROOM FUR      0 RENT $     0.00/MO   $       0.00/YR
NUMBER OF 3 BEDROOM UNFUR    5 RENT $   700.00/MO   $   8,400.00/YR
NUMBER OF 3 BEDROOM FUR      0 RENT $     0.00/MO   $       0.00/YR
ALLOWANCE FOR VACANCIES 15.00% OR $  13,761.00/YR
TOTAL YEARLY INCOME $  77,979.00
===================================================================
```

Fig. 15-10. Results of investment analysis program with 15 percent vacancy rate.

```
                              EXPENSES
          INSURANCE  $   120.00/MO    $ 1,440.00/YR
          LICENSES   $    10.00/MO    $   120.00/YR
          PROP TAX   $      100/MO    $ 1,200.00/YR
          UTILITIES  $    40.00/MO    $   480.00/YR
          MANAGEMENT $   450.00/MO    $ 5,400.00/YR
          JANITOR    $     0.00/MO    $     0.00/YR
          ADVERTIS   $     0.00/MO    $     0.00/YR
          MAINT EXP  $   110.00/MO    $ 1,320.00/YR
          MISC EXP   $    25.00/MO    $   300.00/YR
               TOTAL EXPENSES PER YEAR $  10.260.00

==================================================================
                        *** SUMMARY RESULTS ***

    CURRENT YEAR DOLLARS PRESENT VALUE OF RENT PROFIT $ 106,835.00
    SELLING PRICE .......... $ 751.100.00
    COST OF SELLING ........ $  45,066.00
    BALANCE DUE ON LOANS . . $ 237,806.00
    BASIS FOR TAX PURPOSE .  $ 256,667.00
    TAXABLE PROCEEDS ....... $ 449.367.00
    TOTAL CAPITAL GAINS TAX  $  89,873.50
    NET PROFIT FROM SALE . . $ 266,161.00
    PRESENT VALUE OF PROFIT FROM SALE - BALANCE DUE   $  16,089.10
    PRESENT VALUE OF TOTAL PROFITS - BALANCE DUE      $ 122,924.00
    ACCUMULATED EQUITY ...... $112,194.00
    PRESENT VALUE EQUITY .... $105,486.00
    CONSTANT YR DOLLAR   .... $102,307.00
    NET PRESENT VALUE (PROFIT  -EQUITY) =             $  17,437.70
    CONSTANT YEAR NET PRESENT VALUE ALL PROFIT-BALANCE $  -6,051.41
***YOU LOST $    6,051.41 IN PURCHASING POWER
==================================================================
```

do that, I'd be doing it, not writing this book.). The approach will eliminate more investments than it will find. It will keep you out of trouble, or at least flash danger signals to warn you of trouble. If you want to go ahead, that's up to you. I hope that you find the programs useful, as I have.

Appendix

PROGRAM TRANSLATION NOTES

The programs are written in standard Microsoft BASIC and should be transportable to most other BASICS with little trouble. The main commands that might cause problems are:

CLS This command clears the screen and places the cursor at the top of the display. Use whatever command your BASIC requires. The command HOME can be used with the Apple II.

INKEY$ This command checks the keyboard to see whether a key is depressed. It does not stop program execution until a key is pressed. As used in the programs, the command fetches a single character from the keyboard. The user does not have to press <ENTER> to get the character into the program. Thus the command is useful for cases where a single character input is required, such as in answer to questions.

Get (string) command of the Apple II is similar. However, GET(string) stops program flow until a key is pressed. This means that the TRS-80 code

```
10 Y $= INKEY$ : IF Y$ = "" THEN 10
```

can be replaced with 10 GET(X$)

If your BASIC does not have a similar function, use the normal INPUT command to get required information from the user.

INSTR(A$,B$) This command checks to see if B$ is contained in A$. It returns the position in A$ that B$ starts at. For example INSTR("YN","Y") is 1. If B$ is not contained in A$, then zero is returned. INSTR is used to verify that the proper data was entered with INKEY$. The most common use in the programs is to see if the user answered a yes or no question by pressing either Y or N. The code is:

```
10 Y$ = INKEY$ : IF Y$ = "" THEN 10 ELSE IF
INSTR("YN",Y$) = 0 THEN PRINT "PLEASE
        ANSWER Y OR N"
```

Multistatement lines Multistatement lines in Microsoft BASIC are separated by a colon (:). Some BASICs use the back slash. Multiline statements save memory and speed up BASIC.

LET Microsoft BASIC and most, if not all, other microcomputer BASICs do not require the word LET in statements such as LET X = 2. This is written as X=2.

REM There are several REM statements in the programs. These are remarks and are not executed. Most of them can be removed with no effect on the program. In fact, if you have less then 48K RAM, you will need to remove the REMark statements. Those at the beginning of the program are the best ones to remove.

PRINT USING This command makes it possible to format the output so it appears attractive. For example, PRINT USING "$####, #.##";A, prints the value of A in dollars and cents format with commas as required: $2,000.10. Several popular computers do not provide this command. It can be simulated with an appropriate subroutine. Perhaps the easiest for dollars and cents is to round the value of the variable to be printed to the nearest cent and then use the normal print statement. The rounding code is X = INT(X * 100)/100 where X is the variable that you want to print.

IF ... THEN ... ELSE Although all BASICs have the IF ... THEN ... construct, not all have the ELSE clause. If your BASIC does not have the ELSE statement, then the IF THEN ELSE must be replaced by several IF statements. For example:

```
100 IF X = 2 THEN 200 ELSE PRINT "ERROR"
110 STOP
```

becomes

```
100 IF X = 2 THEN 200
150 PRINT "ERROR"    160 STOP
```

Multistatement line following IF THEN If a multistatement line is used with IF THEN on the TRS-80, the statement is executed only if the IF THEN is executed. For example:

```
10 IF X = 2 THEN PRINT "X = 2": GOTO 100
```

The statement following the colon (GOTO 100) will be executed only if X = 2. In some versions of BASIC the statement GOTO 100 would be executed no matter what.

Negative powers CBASIC, for one, does not allow raising numbers to a negative power. The way around this is to rewrite the equation. For example:

10 X = 2*Y[−3 can be rewritten as 10 X = 2/(Y)[3

Defint J This statement defines all variables that begin with J as integers. Several BASICs do not allow defining statements. The easiest way out is to delete the statement. This will cause some loss of speed and increase memory requirements somewhat, but not enough to make much difference.

LPRINT This directs output to the printer. Use the appropriate statement for your BASIC. PR#1 for the Apple II.

PRESS <ENTER> Becomes PRESS RETURN on many computers.

These are the main statements and commands that might cause problems. Because most BASIC uses the same commands for numerical work, there shouldn't be much difficulty converting the programs to most microcomputer BASICS.

You have probably noticed that most of the programs have several multistatement lines where variables are set equal to zero. These lines serve two purposes. First, they make sure the variables are set to the values you want (this is not generally necessary with microcomputers where all variables are set to zero whenever you RUN a program). Second, these statements speed up the programs. By initializing all variables before any arrays are dimensioned, you make it possible for Microsoft BASIC to locate these variables rapidly. (ATARI BASIC does not store variables the same way; thus no speed gain is realized.)

MODIFYING THE PROGRAMS

I hope you find the programs as written useful and flexible enough to meet most of your needs. However, I'm sure you will reach a point where you want to modify one or more of the programs so they better meet your specific needs. How should you go about doing this?

The most likely place for modifications is the input data. You will probably find that you want to enter more or different data than used in the program. The data input module is fairly easy to modify; you can change the names of the data to meet your needs. Be careful that you don't err in the calculations. The list of variable names that is included in the remarks of each program should help you avoid problems. The tables that follow may also be useful.

Table of Dimensioned Input Variable Names for INVEST1

Note that all input data for INVEST1 is in the array V(I). The following list gives the name of the variable for each V(I). If, for example, you add expenses, be sure the total expense is stored in V(12).

I	Name of V(I)
1	Amount of investment
2	Amount of first loan
3	Interest rate first loan
4	Life of first loan
5	Number of loan payments per year
6	Time after investing before rec income
7	Amount of second loan
8	Interest rate second loan
9	Life of second loan
10	Number of payments per year
11	Estimate annual income
12	Estimate annual expenses
13	Escalation for income
14	Escalation for expenses
15	Federal income tax rate
16	State income tax rate
17	Discount rate
18	Life of investment
19	Value of three year property
20	Value of five year property
21	Value of 10 year property
22	Value of 15 year Public utility property
23	Value of straight line real estate
24	Year property placed in service
25	Inflation rate.

The easiest way to add expense and income detail is to add a subroutine to readin additional detail on expense and income; now total the new estimates and store the totals in V(11) for income and V(12) for expenses. This is basically what was done to convert INVEST1 to INVEST2.

Table of Input Variable Names for INVEST2

Data for INVEST2 are stored in six arrays: V(I) for general input data; NU(I) for number of rental units of each type; R1(I) for monthly rents and R2(I) for yearly rents; EM(I) for monthly expenses and EY(I) for yearly expenses. TI is used to store total yearly income and TX is used to store total yearly expenses.

I	Name of V(I)
1	Total amount of investment
2	Amount of first loan
3	Interest rate first loan
4	Life of first loan
5	Number of loan payments
6	Time before receive income
7	Amount of second loan
8	Interest rate second loan
9	Life of second loan
10	Number of payments per year second loan
11	Escalation for value of property
12	Cost of selling as percent of price

13	Escalation for rents
14	Escalation for expenses
15	Federal Income tax
16	Federal capital gains tax rate
17	State capital gains tax rate
18	State income tax rate
19	Discount rate
20	Life of investment
21	Value of three year property
22	Value of five year property
23	Value of 10 year property
24	Value of 15 year Public utility property
25	Value of straight line real estate
26	Year property placed in service
27	Inflation rate.

The loan module may be another place where changes are needed. You may need more than two loans, or you may need to include a different type of loan. Be sure you pass the required information on yearly principal and interest payments back to the cash flow program. The program looks for the interest payment for the first loan in the array IP(I) and the principal payment for the first loan in the array A1(I). The interest payment for the second loan is in array IZ(I) and the principal payment for the second loan is in array A2(I).

Bibliography

Investment analysis requires a considerable amount of work. Most of it is involved in collecting the information needed to make rational decisions. The more you know about the type of investments you are planning, the better your decisions are likely to be.

Much of the data needed for investment decision making is available from various on-line data bases that you can search with your microcomputer. You should look into these if you are serious about investing.

Another source of information and data are books. I realize that you won't want to read all of the books listed below, but you should look at the ones that cover the areas in which you are interested. Read a range of books in your area of interest. This way you will be exposed to a range of investment ideas and will not fall into a trap of following a single line of advice.

None of the books listed promise to make you a million dollars in 10 days with no work. What they all promise, as does this book, is to provide you with the tools that will help you make intelligent investments. The tools won't do the work for you, but they will make your work more productive.

Case, Fred E. *Investing in Real Estate*. Englewood Cliffs, New Jersey: Prentice Hall, 1978.

Dreman, David N. *Psychology & the Stock Market*. New York: American Management Associations, 1977.

Glahe, Fred. *Macroeconomics: Theory & Policy, 2nd Edition*. New York: Harcourt Brace Jovanovich, Inc., 1977.

Haley, Charles W. and Schall, Lawrence D. *Theory of Financial Decisions, 2nd Edition*. New York: McGraw Hill Book Co., 1979

Humphrey, Thomas J. *Basic Programming for the Financial Executive*. New York: Wiley, 1978.

Ladley, Barbara and Wilford, Jane. *Money and Finance: Sources of Print and Nonprint Materials*. New York: Neal-Schuman Sourcebook Series, 1980.

Lasry, George. *Valuing Common Stock: The Power of Prudence*. New York: American Management Associations, 1979.

Pindyck, R. S. and Rubinfield, D. L. *Econometric Models & Economic Forecasts*. New York: McGraw Hill Books, 1976.

Rachlin, Robert. *Return on Investment: Strategies for Profit*. New York: Prentice Hall, 1979.

Randle, Paul and Swensen, Philip P. *Making Your Money: An Investment Guide for Professionals & Entrepreneurs*. Belmont, California: Lifetime Learning Publications, 1979.

Ring, Alfred A. *Valuation of Real Estate*. Englewood Cliffs, New Jersey: Prentice Hall, 1970.

Robinson, Roland I. *Financial Markets: The Accumulation & Allocation of Wealth*. New York: McGraw Hill Books, 1974.

Rosen, Lawrence R. *Dow Jones-Irwin Guide to Interest*. Homewood, Illinois: Dow Jones-Irwin Books, 1974.

Seitz, Neil. *Financial Analysis: A Programmed Approach, 2nd Edition*. Reston, Virginia: Reston Publishing, 1979.

Smith, Jon M. *Financial Analysis & Business Decisions on the Pocket Calculator*. New York: John Wiley & Sons, 1976.

Stigum, Marcia. *Money Market Calculations: Yields, Swaps, & Break-Even Prices*. Homewood, Illinois: Dow Jones-Irwin Books, Date not set.

Szego, Giorgio P. *Portfolio Theory with Applications to Bank Asset*. New York: Academic Press, 1980.

Tuccille, Jerome. *Optimist's Guide to Making Money in the 1980's*. New York: Morrow, 1978.

Whitman, Martin J. and Shubik, Martin. *Aggressive Conservative Investor*. New York: Random House, 1979.

Index